museums of tomorrow: A Virtual Discussion

Issues in Cultural Theory 8
Georgia O'Keeffe Museum Research Center
Santa Fe
The Center for Art and Visual Culture
University of Maryland Baltimore County
2004

Distributed by D.A.P.
Distributed Art Publishers
New York
2004

Edited
with an Introduction
by Maurice Berger

Preface
by David Yager
by Barbara Buhler Lynes

With contributions from
Alexander Alberro
Bruce Altshuler
Maxwell L. Anderson
George Baker
Stefano Basilico
Maurice Berger
Jonathan P. Binstock
Dan Cameron
Karen Mary Davalos
Donna De Salvo
Carol Duncan
Mark Alice Durant
Jennifer González
Mary Kelly
George G. King
Barbara Kirshenblatt-Gimblett
Miwon Kwon
Raina A. Lampkins-Fielder
Simon Leung
Barbara Buhler Lynes
Olu Oguibe
Joan Rosenbaum
David A. Ross
Edward Rothstein
Irving Sandler
Michele Wallace
Alan Wallach
Sylvia Yount

Contents

6
Preface
David Yager
Barbara Buhler Lynes

10
Introduction
Maurice Berger

17
Symposium

19
Introduction
6–7 October

47
The "Corporate" Museum
8–9 October

81
The Politics of Collecting
10–11 October

113
Museums and Their Audiences
12–13 October

136
The Museum as Gatekeeper
14–15 October

156
Museum Education and Pedagogy
16–17 October

184
Conclusion
18–19 October

224
Selected Bibliography

228
About the Participants

234
Acknowledgments

235
CAVC Mission Statement

Preface

David Yager
Executive Director
Center for Art and Visual Culture
University of Maryland
Baltimore County
Baltimore

Museums of Tomorrow: A Virtual Discussion represents the second publication and collaboration between the Georgia O'Keeffe Museum Research Center and the Center for Art and Visual Culture (CAVC) at University of Maryland Baltimore County. This book is unique in its discussion of a vitally important topic: the future of the art museum. The innovative online format of the book's dialogue—its exchange of ideas across communities—has resulted in a remarkable publication.

Museums of Tomorrow: A Virtual Discussion affirms the ability of technology to facilitate important dialogues and exchanges over a relatively short period of time.

The role of CAVC is to publish, exhibit, and address the study of contemporary art, with an emphasis on issues of identity, race, technology, science, culture, and design. There is a commitment to highlighting art at CAVC, but like this publication, we are interested in challenging or realigning the structure, purpose, and sensibility of the art museum. CAVC also has retained its focus on issues of race, identity, and culture, despite the heat of controversy and debate, and regardless of popular trends.

The publications, exhibitions, and public programming projects of CAVC have generated national recognition—a testament to the collaborative spirit and innovative points of view of the curators, faculty, and staff of the University of Maryland Baltimore County. Equally important are partnerships that CAVC has fostered with cultural institutions such as the Georgia O'Keeffe Museum Research Center. *Museums of Tomorrow: A Virtual Discussion* represents the best of that collaborative spirit and innovative thinking across institutional settings. We are especially proud to be a part of it.

Barbara Buhler Lynes
Curator
Georgia O'Keeffe Museum
and The Emily Fisher Landau
Director Georgia O'Keeffe
Museum Research Center
Santa Fe

The Georgia O'Keeffe Museum Research Center is pleased to have sponsored the second in an innovative series of online symposia, *Museums of Tomorrow: A Virtual Discussion*. The event took place on the Museum's Website October 6–19, 2003, and attracted more than 15,000 visitors. It provided a much-needed, broadly based forum through which the art community, as well as the public at large, addressed the challenging and often complex problems confronted by museums in our ever-changing cultural climate.

While many museums are fortunate to continue to garner strong public and private support for their exhibition, education, and publications programs, others—especially those not located in major urban centers—are contending with decreased attendance and shrinking allocations. As museum directors, curators, and educators address these problems, along with those intrinsic to the demands of new technologies, and a culture that is increasingly media-conscious, they find they must often reassess institutional policies and priorities and seek new ways of defining the museum's function and purpose.

Because the activities museums organize relate in one way or another to all components of the art community—from those who make art to those who sell it; from those who conceptualize exhibitions to those who organize and promote public programs for them—the symposium was organized to elicit the opinions and ideas of participants from each of these various arenas. Twenty-eight well-known leaders—academics, artists, art critics, art historians, museum curators, directors, and educators—were invited to contribute to a discussion led and moderated by Maurice Berger, Senior Fellow, The Vera List Center for Art and Politics, New School University, and Curator, The Center for Art and Visual Culture, University of Maryland Baltimore County.

Invited participants included Alexander Alberro, Associate Professor, School of Art & Art History, University of Florida, Gainesville; Bruce Altshuler, Director, Program in Museum Studies, New York University; Maxwell L. Anderson, Leadership Fellow at the Yale School of Management; George Baker, Editor, *October* magazine, Assistant Professor of Art History, University of California, Los Angeles; Stefano Basilico, Curator, University Art Collection, New School University, New York; Jonathan P. Binstock, Curator of Contemporary Art, Corcoran Gallery of Art, Washington, D.C.; Dan Cameron, Senior Curator, The New Museum of Contemporary Art, New York; Karen Mary Davalos, Associate Professor, Chicana/o Studies Department, Loyola Marymount University, Los Angeles; Donna De Salvo, Senior Curator, Tate Modern, London; Carol Duncan, Professor of Art History, Ramapo College of New Jersey, Mahwah; Mark Alice Durant, Artist and Professor, Visual Arts Department, University of Maryland Baltimore County; Jennifer González, Assistant Professor, History of Art and Visual Culture, University of California, Santa Cruz; Mary Kelly, Artist and Professor of Art and Critical Theory, University of California, Los Angeles; George G. King, Director, Georgia O'Keeffe Museum, Santa Fe, New Mexico;

Barbara Kirshenblatt-Gimblett, University Professor and Professor of Performance Studies, Tisch School of the Arts, New York University; Miwon Kwon, Professor, Department of Art History, University of California, Los Angeles; Raina A. Lampkins-Fielder, Associate Director, Helena Rubinstein Chair of Education, Whitney Museum of American Art, New York; Simon Leung, Artist and Professor, Department of Studio Art, University of California, Irvine; Barbara Buhler Lynes, The Emily Fisher Landau Director, Georgia O'Keeffe Museum Research Center and Curator, Georgia O'Keeffe Museum, Santa Fe, New Mexico; Olu Oguibe, Artist and Associate Professor, Art and Art History, African-American Studies, University of Connecticut, Storrs; Joan Rosenbaum, Helen Goldsmith Menschel Director, The Jewish Museum, New York; David A. Ross, Director, Beacon Art Projects, Beacon, New York; Edward Rothstein, Cultural Critic at Large, *The New York Times;* Irving Sandler, Professor Emeritus, Art History, State University of New York, Purchase; Michele Wallace, Professor of English, Women's Studies, Film Studies, and Afro-American Poetics, City College of New York and CUNY Graduate Center; Alan Wallach, Ralph H. Wark Professor of Art and Art History and Professor of American Studies, The College of William and Mary, Williamsburg, Virginia; and Sylvia Yount, Margaret and Terry Stent Curator of American Art, High Museum of Art, Atlanta, Georgia.

We are indeed grateful to everyone who contributed to this lively, provocative discussion, and we are delighted to be able to publish this transcript of it, *Museums of Tomorrow: A Virtual Discussion,* in association with The Center for Art and Visual Culture, University of Maryland Baltimore County, as part of its outstanding series, Issues in Cultural Theory. We are grateful to Maurice Berger, editor both of that series and of this volume, for his sensitive moderation of the online symposium, for his inspiring commentary throughout this publication, and for his contribution of its introduction.

It is the hope of the Georgia O'Keeffe Museum Research Center that our sponsorship of this and other symposia will continue to provide stimulating discussions and important resources for the entire art community.

Maurice Berger
Curator
The Center for Art and
Visual Culture
University of Maryland
Baltimore County

Senior Fellow
The Vera List Center
for Art and Politics
New School University
New York

A museal sensibility seems to be occupying ever-larger chunks of everyday culture and experience. If you think of the . . . restoration of old urban centers, whole museum villages and landscapes, of the boom of flea markets, retro fashions, and nostalgic waves, the obsessive self-musealization per video recorder, [and] memoir writing and confessional literature . . . then the museum can indeed no longer be described as a single institution with stable and well-drawn boundaries. The museum in this broad, amorphous sense has become a key paradigm of contemporary cultural activities.
Andreas Huyssen
Twilight Memories: Marking Time in a Culture of Amnesia *(1994)*

What is the future of the art museum? Can the museum as we know it survive in an increasingly commercial, media-driven, and global culture? Vast societal changes—from the mainstreaming of multicultural politics to the rise of new technologies such as the Internet—have altered the cultural landscape, impelling many art museums to rethink policy and priorities. What then of the viability, relevance, effectiveness, responsibility, and role of the museum in an ever-changing world?

This was the central question examined by a national group of 28 renowned scholars, artists, museum directors, critics, and curators in *Museums of Tomorrow*, an Internet conference sponsored by the Georgia O'Keeffe Museum Research Center and held on the Georgia O'Keeffe Museum Website over a two-week period in October 2003. The conference offered its participants—and more than 15,000 visitors, including hundreds of museum professionals from around the country—an unprecedented chance to explore a range of important issues. The interchange of ideas never ceased during the two-week period of the conference because the dialogue remained active and available on the Internet 24 hours a day.

The conversation was both rich and productive. While it may have raised more questions than it answered, it revealed some of the most significant questions and problems facing art museums today, from the corporate culture of many museums to the ways these institutions see their role in society as repositories of culture, educators of the public, and forums for the study of art. Many participants, working within the culturally isolated environment of the museum, appreciated the opportunity to speak their minds, frankly and publicly, especially about the controversial or difficult issues that impact on their everyday lives. For others, it helped frame the terms of the debate—isolating important problems and questions—or allowed them to better understand the flash points and differences of opinions that charge these discussions. Most important, the conference's format allowed for a broad-based "interdisciplinary" dialogue that is all too rare in the world of the art museum, a conversation that allowed theorists to dialogue with practitioners, art historians with curators, artists with museum directors.

The discussion, divided into two-day sessions, each engaging a different topic, traversed many questions, some suggested by the participants themselves: How can museums reflect the needs of changing audiences and constituencies? What are the social and ethical responsibilities of curators and directors? Who is responsible for the content of exhibitions, and who decides which works befit a museum's permanent collection? What should be the role of new media and technologies in museums of the future? How do we deal with the increasing perception in society at large of the museum as culturally irrelevant or hopelessly elitist? How do we respond and adapt to the demographic and global shifts that are redefining national and international culture? Should art institutions be "marketed" in order to survive in an increasingly media-driven culture? To what degree do standards of "artistic quality" reflect cultural biases and ignorance? Is the central function of the museum that of educator, or should its mandate be limited to the archival and art-historical preservation of visual culture? And what is the museum's responsibility to its audience, both in terms of education and advocacy?

If the conference held one surprise, it was its contentious tone. Conferees argued about a number of things. They fought over the issue of standards and whether art museums were becoming irrelevant bastions of elitism or, conversely, vast "culture malls," driven by corporate interests. They disagreed about the nature and even the need for museum education. They squabbled over the question of whether museums have done enough to confront decades of institutional prejudice or to embrace formerly disenfranchised constituencies, such as people of color, women, and poor and working-class people. They even quarreled about the necessity of the conference itself.

This contentiousness speaks to an important, if not always understood, irony: the extent to which arguments about the museum, one of society's most hermetic and elitist institutions, are charged by some of the most basic and divisive social concerns. This is no more evident than in the discussion of the museum's past history of exclusionism, and the imperative, on the part of many institutions, to enfranchise diverse, heretofore ignored, communities. The conversation inevitably focused on the broader issues of race and racism, especially the ways white entitlement and prejudice have shaped attitudes and practices well beyond the museum world.

It is economic class that emerges as one of the most important, albeit implicit, social concerns, an issue that simmers just under the surface of the conference's penultimate session, "Museum Education and Pedagogy." The animosity expressed by several participants towards educational outreach, namely that it debases the experience of art, is forcefully countered by those who recall the power of museum education to enrich their own disadvantaged childhoods. These two positions ultimately hinge on a fundamental question that dates back to the earliest days of the modern museum: To whom does the museum belong?

While many art institutions of the 19th century limited their mission to the needs of a small coterie of wealthy and informed patrons, others—such as the Metropolitan Museum of Art, the Museum of Fine Arts, Boston, and the Smithsonian Institution—set out to explore the role of pedagogy as well as the potential of educational initiatives to attract culturally and economically diverse audiences. "The Museums of the future in this democratic land should be adapted to the needs of the mechanic, the factory operator, the day laborer, the salesman, and the clerk, as much as to those of the professional man and the man of leisure," wrote George Brown Goode, director of the Smithsonian's earliest national museum. For Goode, and scores of enlightened curators and directors to follow, the museum experience should appeal to more than the affluent or the cultural elite, reaching out to new and economically varied constituencies and inspiring widespread and informed interest in art and visual culture.

Reading between the lines of *Museums of Tomorrow*, one realizes both the necessity for this debate and the extraordinary degree to which the museum is caught up in a range of wide-reaching and consequential cultural and political matters—from the rise of new technologies of visual representation (from television to the Internet) to the culture wars of the past 25 years. Far beyond traditional educational programs, which invariably take place within the institution's walls and reach a relatively small and limited audience, this online conference, and its subsequent publication in book form, exemplify Goode's ideal of the "democratic" museum: a place where interested people from all over the nation and the world can explore, openly and freely, the future of one of society's most vital cultural institutions.

Introduction

Maurice Berger

I would like to welcome everyone to *Museums of Tomorrow*. Over the next two weeks, we will examine a range of questions concerning the art museum as an institution. This conference will be organized into two-day sessions, each of these devoted to a particular topic. I would like to dedicate the first session to the general question of the art museum's future in an ever-changing cultural environment. These changes—from the mainstreaming of multicultural politics to the rise of new technologies such as the Internet—have altered the cultural landscape and have impelled many art museums to rethink policy and priorities.

There is no doubt that many American art museums continue to flourish and grow. But most still confront multiple challenges. Funding opportunities, especially in the public sector, are drying up for many institutions. Art museums often find themselves in competition with other types of cultural institutions for audience and attendance. And curators and directors are often forced to choose between art-historically significant content and crowd-pleasing subject matter.

Beyond economic matters, museums are faced with a range of other issues and questions. I cite a few: the reality of changing audiences and constituencies; the social and ethical responsibility of the museum curator or director; the question of who is responsible for the content of exhibitions; the preservation and conservation of aging works of art; the role of new media and technologies; the "standards" of public taste and the threat of censorship; the pervasive understanding in society at large of the museum as culturally irrelevant or a bastion of elitism; the need to respond and adapt to the demographic and global shifts that are redefining national and international culture; the "marketing" of the museum in an increasingly media-driven culture; and the museum's need to redress its past history of prejudice and exclusion.

With these (and many other) issues in mind, I pose the following question to conference participants: What do you believe is the greatest challenge facing art museums today? I ask that you answer this question both conceptually and personally. Please talk about these challenges, but also let us know how your personal relationship to the art museum—as director, curator, scholar, artist, or critic—has shaped the way you understand these issues.

Barbara Buhler Lynes

George King and I would like to take this opportunity to welcome everyone to *Museums of Tomorrow*, which is being sponsored by the Georgia O'Keeffe Museum Research Center and moderated by Maurice Berger. We are delighted to host this exciting event and look forward to a lively and fascinating discussion.

George Baker

It seems to me that the history and the transformation of any institution cannot be separated from a reflection upon the public or the audience that the institution serves. So a relevant history of the art museum would attend to the public that a particular museum was configured to serve at different moments in history, as well as the ways in which, in return, the institution came to be used by a public beyond the institution's own self-understanding. In this light, the greatest challenge facing museums today stems from a crisis in the public the museum might be seen as desiring to address.

To generalize: With the increasing corporatization and privatization of culture in the United States, museums seem to pursue an increasingly corporate model of organization and address. This seems to have been embraced by many art institutions as a method of salvation in a transformed culture in which the public place of art has been questioned all along. In many ways, the Solomon R. Guggenheim Museum has become the standard bearer of this corporate model for museums, but it is an institutional organization that I think is also reflected in what we could call the "symbolic language" of museum architecture since the 1970s at least, beginning with the building of the Centre Georges Pompidou in Paris, France. A corporate model of the museum addresses its public as consumers of culture, as it increasingly enters into competition with the industries of leisure and entertainment. As an educator, I find it increasingly depressing that the museum has embraced its corporate backing, and its foundation in the realms of private wealth, for salvation—instead of looking to and emphasizing one of its other, older functions: pedagogy, research, and public education. There are exceptions of course, but never has the split between the museum and the university seemed stronger, a split echoed all the way down the line between the museum director and the art historian, the curator and the art critic, the museum public and the art student. Museums seem today in danger of abandoning their possible role as an institution for the education of a public. This "education of the public" might have been a class-oriented technique of symbolic domination in the past, but it can be rethought, reclaimed, and reconfigured today.

Maurice Berger

George, you wrote: "As an educator, I find it increasingly depressing that the museum has embraced its corporate backing, and its foundation in the realms of private wealth, for salvation—instead of looking to and emphasizing one of its other, older functions: pedagogy, research, and public education."

I think this sentence sums up the problem beautifully. Indeed, even smaller museums—such as those affiliated with universities, institutions one would automatically associate with pedagogy and intellectual risk taking—are being compromised by this problem.

Alexander Alberro

Prior to addressing directly the question that Maurice poses concerning "the greatest challenge facing art museums today," allow me to problematize the very nature of the way in which the question is conceived. For the question seems to carry with it the basic assumption that there is one homogeneous entity that falls under the rubric of an "art museum." Certainly, this is not the case. The danger is that such an across-the-board term glosses over the distinct practices, missions, goals, and challenges of different types of art museums. For example, the conditions faced by a private art museum supported by a substantial foundation are very different than those faced by a small university art museum, or by a museum located in a relatively small town, or by a large public metropolitan museum that relies on government support, or by museums that are specifically focused on a certain type of cultural production (that is, in historical terms, ethnic terms, national terms, and so forth). But since we need to begin somewhere, and since I am after all stating the obvious, let's take the question at face value bearing in mind its limitations.

From my perspective as a professor of art history, the most significant challenge faced by art museums today is that of how to remain viable without appealing to the lowest common denominator when conceptualizing shows. I am quite prepared to explain to the often very bright students at the large state institution at which I teach why exhibitions of motorcycles or *alta moda* are not covered in my undergraduate art history lecture courses. But coming up with the correct words to explain why these shows are so popular is another matter. At stake, of course, are much more than pedagogical issues. The very legitimacy of museums devoted to art is thrown into question by these exhibitions and, perhaps, by the very conditions that make the proliferation of such shows necessary.

Jonathan P. Binstock

How financial need and corporate influence affect the ways in which an institution construes its audience is a key part of the issue. A museum has a hard enough time figuring out who, in fact, is visiting the place—who it is serving—without the lens of corporate influence and, beyond that, financial desperation distorting the view. At the Corcoran Gallery of Art in Washington, where I am curator of contemporary art, we are just as likely to host a first-time visitor or tourist to the capital (it may be that more than 20 million of them walk past our doors each year) as we are a full-time artist or well-informed local museum-goer. Similarly, the full-time New York-based artist who visits N.Y. institutions may be circulating in a very different world from the full-time D.C.-based artist who is a regular member of our audience. The heavily federally funded National Gallery of Art, with its incredible Center for Advanced Studies in the Visual Arts, attracts yet another audience within the tourist-rich environment of the capital. The question of audience has unique ramifications for the given institution that poses it (to follow from Alexander's comments).

Given the open-ended variable of "audience," how might we define the "practical" and "academic" obligations of the museum as it seeks to serve its given audience? George suggests how the practical and the academic seem to be on divergent paths within the world of museums today. If I am correct in drawing this inference, then I would agree with him. It is often not clear to museums how an academically driven program might serve their practical needs over the long term, including their need for visitors and money. Suffice it to say, this is the business model I always have in mind when I define and realize exhibitions. Still, the question of what is practical and what is academic needs to be addressed. One case scenario is the dialogue that takes place within the museum institution: the "practical" needs of the administration and the "academic" needs of the curatorial staff often contribute to lengthy conversations about the nature of the museum's exhibition program. But this difference between seemingly oppositional forces extends well beyond the world of museum staff.

When I was a graduate student at the University of Michigan in Ann Arbor, the world of the art history department could not have been farther from the world of the studio arts department, both literally and figuratively speaking. That is, the division between the "academic" world of the historian and the "practical" world of the practicing artist was very wide. This gulf existed long before I matriculated in the university, and I don't know how it got to be that way. At the Corcoran, where we have a college and a museum, we work very hard to make the two sides of the equation work together productively. Because this is a common goal, I think we often succeed. But the world the instructors and students inhabit and the world the curators inhabit nonetheless seem to be very different. There are forces at play in the nature of our roles and ambitions that make it difficult for us to come together to identify a common goal. The situation was much worse at the Pennsylvania Academy of the Fine Arts, where I used to work, which also has a college and museum.

Maurice Berger

I want to add at this point that my use of the term "art museum" in no way implies a unified, normative institutional situation. Indeed, "art museums" constitute many things—from tiny alternative spaces to comprehensive monoliths like the Metropolitan Museum of Art. My emphasis here is really on the word "art," not "museum," since I want to narrow the focus of this conference to art museums, lest we ride all over the place—from history museums to science museums.

This is not to say that we should not question the disciplinary boundaries of the art museum—i.e., what constitutes art. For example, why is film very often part of the art museum's institutional mandate, but not television? We will explore this question later in the conference.

Jonathan, you wrote: "But the world the instructors and students inhabit and the world the curators inhabit nonetheless seem to be very different. There are forces at play in the nature of our roles and ambitions that make it difficult for us to come together to identify a common goal."

How does this discordance present itself as a challenge in the museum?

Another point you make—"But this difference between seemingly oppositional forces extends well beyond the world of museum staff"—is also important. The imperatives of pleasing the public v. producing art-historically rigorous exhibitions do not have to be mutually exclusive.

Dan Cameron

As curator at the New Museum of Contemporary Art, which specializes in contemporary art, I often find that I am observing how other museums function from an increasingly complex position, one that incorporates the privilege of a relatively narrow mission, but also the limitations of a fairly small audience base. Because our public expects us to continually explore what we mean by the simple term "contemporary art," a very positive institutional value is placed on being experimental, cutting edge, and open-ended. In a sense, we are being rewarded—relatively speaking, of course—for carrying on precisely the kind of research that many people would agree is rapidly disappearing from the missions of other art museums.

From this perspective, I would say that the greatest challenge facing art museums today is to define for a broad public what they mean when they use the term "art." Too many people, both within and outside our field, believe that they know what art is, and that this definition either excludes others or, in fact, themselves. With contemporary art, we are always faced with the task of trying to relate what artists do to what the rest of society is experiencing, but I have become increasingly comfortable with this challenge. As a consequence, any definition of art—regardless of the era—which does not incorporate the aspirations of the average citizen toward a better life just seems to be missing the point.

Irving Sandler

An important issue for this conference is who defines what "art" is, which "art" is of "significance" and "quality," and in general commands art-world attention. With regard to contemporary art, at least in my time, this was determined by a loose art-world consensus of certain artists, certain art publishers, art editors, and art critics, certain museum directors, curators, and trustees, a certain few art historians, and certain dealers and collectors. This, of course, is the "Establishment," What have the (shifting) power relations within this group been? Who has the power today? What is the role of the various constituents?

Donna De Salvo

By its very nature, I think the art museum is a mass of contradictions. It is a place in which artists and their works push boundaries and where accountants balance budgets, where a specialist and a once-a-year visitor are able to stand side by side in front of the same painting, where someone complains if you put [Auguste] Rodin's *Kiss* (a Tate favorite) on the fifth floor and another if you move it to the lobby. I don't think you can ever resolve these contradictions, nor would I want to, because that is part of the fundamental experience of a work of art. It cannot be easily pinned down, nor explained. If you rely upon marketing wizards to conduct focus groups, you are looking for consensus not contradiction. In this sense, I think we too often underestimate our audiences and their personal experience of a work of art.

So, perhaps we must accept, even exploit, contradiction?

Maurice Berger

Both posts raise a significant question for this conference: Who decides what "art" is appropriate for the museum? For decades, these decisions, governed as they have been by the art "Establishment," to quote Irving, have led to the abject exclusion of many cultural groups, especially women and people of color.

This issue also extends to disciplinary questions: What disciplines merit the definition of "art" for the purposes of the art museum? Are quilts works of art? (The recent Whitney Museum of American Art exhibition *The Quilts of Gee's Bend* notwithstanding, the answer would be no in many art museums.) Is *The Simpsons*—a brilliant and extraordinarily artful television program—any less a work of art than Mike Kelley & Paul McCarthy's *Heidi*? I will devote one of our two-day sessions to the issue of who determines what is art as well as the institutional bias, hierarchies, and traditions that underwrite these decisions.

Donna, you wrote: "If you rely upon marketing wizards to conduct focus groups, you are looking for consensus not contradiction. In this sense, I think we too often underestimate our audiences and their personal experience of a work of art. So, perhaps we must accept, even exploit, contradiction?"

Do you then see the imperative towards consensus and the inability to embrace contradiction as a significant challenge facing the museum?

Karen Mary Davalos

I would like to extend Alexander's comments about the heterogeneity of art museums and bring in George's comments about the corporate approach inside art museums. As a critic and ethnographer of art museums, I find that the biggest challenges facing the alternative art museum are the lack of options for equitable engagement with potential funders, the still-present perception that so-called ethnic art is not as universal as so-called Western art, and the misperception that alternative art museums address a limited audience (i.e., a Mexican museum only attracts Mexican-origin audiences and presents Mexican art, an African-American art museum only attracts African-American audiences, etc.). This list of challenges is related.

As George observes, the corporate model is successfully at-home in the art museum, and it is equally at-home in the university (but that is another conference). Given the success of the corporate model, alternative art museums have little room for negotiating with corporate, private, and public funders. The larger and typically metropolitan art museums set the terms of engagement so that alternative art museums must follow suit. For example, the corporate model is employed at Arte America in Fresno, California; El Museo del Barrio in New York City; and Centro Cultural de la Raza in San Diego. In these cases, the board of directors begins by hiring a new executive director to "professionalize" the institution. Recall when the Ford Foundation supported this type of development in the 1980s and 1990s? The drive to professionalize the institution also includes a redesign of the mission, displacement of artists, and a new stance toward the local and/or ethnic community that founded or supported the institution. For some institutions this has meant the abandonment of a group-specific focus, such as the original Puerto Rican art/culture mission of El Museo del Barrio, and the incorporation of a more generalized Latino mission, also witnessed at the Mexican Museum in San Francisco. Funders and museum administrators have promised that a Latino art mission will bring more funders and sponsors, but this remains to be seen. In fact, the Mexican Fine Arts Center Museum in Chicago has been successful while rejecting such a move, but no one holds it up as an example.

The history and origins of alternative art museums are grounded in the labor of artists, a relationship with local residents, and an oppositional stance to mainstream institutions and art history. Perhaps the real challenge is the neo-liberal model that makes the corporate model appear so natural.

Thus, the challenge facing art museums is to identify discursive, symbolic, and literal tools that displace the corporate model, and its root—neo-liberalism. The tricky part is reinvigorating the educational mission of the art museum without calling up the thoroughly classist and nativist discourse that drove education in art museums, ca. 1870–1930. As George correctly points out, the university and the art museum were more closely tied in the past, but some of those connections should not be repeated in the future, even if it is to dismantle the corporate hold on art museums. I am thinking of the eugenics movement, Americanization efforts, and the "city beautiful" movements.

I would anticipate that some readers would not consider alternative arts institutions in the same breath as art museums. (And I admit that the term "alternative art museum" does not do justice to the range and types of spaces to which I refer, but I am attempting to avoid the misnomer, "ethnic art museums.") Certainly, some *rasquache* (Spanish vernacular for making do with what is at hand, or art on a shoestring budget) art centers may not practice all of the functions of an art museum—exhibition, collection, preservation, and interpretation of art—but most practice at least two. Nevertheless, the continued presence of such institutions provides the public art museum with models for community outreach, new methods of representation, new approaches to so-called non-Western art, and of course, more dollars marked for "multicultural arts." In the 21st century, as populations change, the survival of alternative art museums will not be dependent on the public art museum, but the survival of the public museum will be dependent on the alternative art museum.

Maxwell L. Anderson

I've been an art museum director for 16 years, and just completed my presidency of the Association of Art Museum Directors. Perhaps a little throat clearing on the practical side of things might be useful at the outset. The choices of what to present in art museums are fewer than one might first assume. Putting to the side the contemporary art world (it's short on artists whose names spin turnstiles), there is an unspoken (and unhealthy) caste system in place. Major museum collections are in a position to barter artworks with one another and put together major shows. Midsize and smaller museums by and large are today only in a position to pay for access to major shows. (One major U.S. museum has lately taken to requiring seven-figure loan fees for some major shows.) So the choice for most museums—including university museums that are being pressured to mount popular shows, as is, apparently, Duke University's—comes down to whether one can "pay to play." It is a risky proposition since the assumption that earned and contributed income will more than make up the exorbitant costs of 1) the shared-cost budget (encompassing packing, shipping, and insurance), 2) the in-house costs of presenting the show (design, installation, education, merchandising, increased visitor services staff, and functions), and 3) the fee on top of that. Usually the results are less than hoped for. Only 5–8% of U.S. visitors buy catalogues—and besides, museums are notoriously loath to factor in the real in-kind labor costs associated with shows. If these were calculated, major exhibitions would rarely prove worthwhile on a financial footing.

But they do drive attendance and membership, which are more easily measurable than P&L. But what of it? Attendance may be comprised of as much as 50% non-paying or discounted (members, students, seniors, coupon-bearers, pay-what-you-wishers), and entry-level memberships make little or no money for museums, if one factors in (which few museums do) the costs of dedicated staff, direct marketing solicitation, events and receptions, design, printing, postage, and the like.

All of which adds up to an often lamentable business masquerading as big business. The press reports on exhibition stats the way local newscasters report on movie attendance—as if there is some direct corollary between audience response and the quality of what's presented.

Exhibitions are one of the things art museums do. But they rarely account for more than a fraction of the costs of running art museums—as opposed to the costs of collections care, research, publication, and education, which are bound up in the costs of labor, insurance, the physical plant, security, and so on. It would be healthy for the discussion on art museums to encompass, periodically, the core mandate of museums—to collect, preserve, and interpret, as well as to encompass issues of display. And it would be healthier still if the dependence on blockbusters could be reduced by devoting our energies to retaining or improving progressive tax incentives for individual donors, convincing foundations to return to direct support rather than create elaborate and costly project-focused passthroughs; incentivizing corporations to support philanthropically rather than purely from a return on investment; and obligating government on all levels to support arts institutions rather than to penalize them. The more art museums depend on the gate, the more they run the risk of losing their compass. What the public needs most from art museums is integrity in the fulfillment of an educational mandate, and curiosity about how diverse audiences can be served without pandering.

Stefano Basilico

I would have to agree with Donna when she says that museums are "a mass of contradictions." But I fear that the museum is less and less these days a place of risk.

The problem with blockbuster exhibitions, like the motorcycle show or the Armani tag sale held at the Guggenheim Museum, is not that they are not art, which they are not, but that the institution that promotes them is certain that no negative repercussions of any weight will result from them. Unfortunately, the almost certain condemnation of the art press does not count.

"Practical" and "academic" obligations are secondary to "safety," for the biggest fear of any museum functionary is the potential loss of audience. Unfortunately, as a curator for a university art collection, I fear that the University is not immune to this desire for universal acceptance. If you substitute "tuition-paying student" for "ticket-buying public," you get the same thing.

So, I think that the question of "audience" is a useful way to get to Maurice's first question. For myself, it is helpful to think of myself as a member of this "audience" when I ask what it wants from an exhibition. The two things I want most from anything and/or anybody who wants my attention is to be dealt with respectfully and intelligently, which is why *The Simpsons* Rule!

Barbara Kirshenblatt-Gimblett

I would agree, of course, that art museums—like all museums—are under enormous pressure. They have gotten bigger and more expensive. More is expected of them than ever before. Depending on the country, the ratio of public funds to private donors and earned income has also changed. Given their size and cost, it is inevitable that their institutional character has also transformed: business and management specialists hold top positions, additions to staff are in noncuratorial areas, and the work process may well be organized in the form of teams, following a business model, rather than driven by a curator, followed by a designer.

Reflecting on the matter internationally—to take New Zealand and France as examples—we can see what happens when misalignments of collections, institutional formations, and knowledge formations lead to the disbanding of institutions and redistribution of collections. In the cases I have in mind, the goal is to collapse the historical distinction between art and non-art. This may be intended to elevate ethnographic artifacts. Or, to seriously question the category of art as historically formed in colonial societies so as to level the playing field and keep treasures (Maori taonga, for example) from being absorbed into European categories, however honorific.

We can see how this works at the Museum of New Zealand, Te Papa Tongarewa, in Wellington, which was created by dismantling two national museums (the National Art Gallery and the National Museum, which was dedicated to natural history and ethnology) and forming one new museum. The new museum reorganized the collections (natural history, Maori taonga, social history, and art) and adopted a policy of integrating them in the exhibitions. In order to break out of what were thought to be entrenched attachments to the old order, teams led by concept leaders (not curators) developed the exhibitions. The place of "art" in the new institution continues to be contested, as does the role of "curator."

In Paris, several museums are being dismantled or reconfigured—the Musée national des Arts d'Afrique et d'Océanie, Musée de l'Homme, and Musée national des Arts et Traditions Populaires—and new ones created. The Musée du Quai Branly, which is scheduled to open in Paris in 2006, is dedicated to "the arts and civilizations of Africa, Asia, Oceania, and the Americas." The Museum of European and Mediterranean Civilizations will open in Marseilles in 2008. These reconfigurations are intended to accord the contemporaneous the status of the contemporary through such notions as arts premiers, an ambiguous term at best. Are these arts first in the sense of "before all others" or "first and foremost" or "most recent," if only by dint of being properly recognized as art only recently?

Another way to come at the question of the challenges facing art museums today might be to look at the museum itself as an art practice (all museums, not just the art museum), the blurring of the line between artist and curator (artists whose practice is curatorial and curators who work like artists), and the art (and curation) that takes up the museum itself as a form, institution, medium, and resource. Perhaps we can explore in future postings what such experiments might hold for a consideration of museums of tomorrow.

The challenges, as they emerge from these observations,

include the relationship of art museums to their histories, on the one hand, and to their publics on the other. The two are of course related.

Maurice Berger

The question of audience, I agree, is central to this conference. Yes, museums may be forced to show artists whose name recognition can turn turnstiles, to quote Max, but might it also be possible to draw in audiences on the basis of creative, smart, and hip programming. Can't an exhibition be art-historically and socially rigorous *and* appealing to the general public in some way? Yes, Stefano, *The Simpsons,* precisely because the show is really, really smart, and moving, and funny, and . . . deep. It doesn't talk down to its viewers. And it came out of nowhere, vis-à-vis the public's awareness of Matt Groening. It's also a blockbuster in terms of audience numbers.

Karen, I think your post suggests a two-day session all its own—on the increasing reliance on the "corporate" model in American museum culture.

A personal note: For the past decade, I've been working with an important "alternative" art institution—The Center for Art and Visual Culture at the University of Maryland Baltimore County. We're able to do unusual, controversial, and innovative programming—about race, gender, the art market, the museum, cultural theory, the politics of genetic engineering—in part because we function on a tiny budget and are not overly concerned with attendance. So, in keeping with Karen's remarks, we should not underestimate the importance of these institutions.

David A. Ross

The problems we are setting out to discuss seem to me rather tired. (Maybe I'm tired, as it's 2 A.M. here in Turin where I am writing this post.) But truly, it seems that another debate on the legitimacy of motorcycle shows, or the show-business aspects of the modern museum economy, is debated time and again in classrooms, in think-pieces by critics and cultural journalists, and (needless to say) in curatorial meetings and in museum boardrooms around the world.

At the risk of sounding like the recovering museum director I am, I'd like to suggest that we focus on the larger issues. We might explore the entire idea of the museum—not merely temporary exhibition policies (the tail that has replaced the dog). What about collection policies?

How are museums to redefine their roles in an era in

which the institution and living artists are active coconspirators?

Let's discuss agency. In an era in which the Internet supports a new set of direct relationships between artists and audiences, is the museum's agency of decreasing importance?

Let's address the global implications of the museum economy. Let's debate why cities will spend tens of millions of dollars to have a franchise of a New York museum in their country.

Let's seriously consider why we have created the museum economy that we now decry.

Can we discuss why we discourage respect for individual works of art, insisting on their recontextualization in either the museum's collection, or re-purposed in some thematic presentation? Does the museum presuppose the idea of an index?

Have we, as Gregory Bateson predicted, become a society that mistakes the menu for the food?

Of course museums of art have a future, but is it one we want to embrace? Is it one we can actually challenge in any meaningful way?

I'm looking forward to the discussion.

Barbara Kirshenblatt-Gimblett

Thanks, David, for the provocation! Let me start again.

1. How is the new media/technology environment in which we live, from which artists create, and with which museums operate altering the nature of the museum itself?

2. Do we come to value the historical and historicizing character of the museum more or less?

3. Is the museum compelled to follow, to become more like the media environment in which it sits, or is it freed to pursue an alternative path?

4. As others have already noted, much of the art that art museums show is complicit with (and often subversive of) the circumstances of its display, in contrast with museums of natural history and ethnography, for example. What then does contemporary art practice tell us about the museums of tomorrow?

5. How might attention to other types of museums and the kinds of exhibitions and installations they are doing inform our thinking about art museums—incidentally, our Internet conference is titled *Museums of Tomorrow,* not *Art Museums of Tomorrow.* Are we dealing with more than art museums? I hope so.

Take, for example, Quebec's Museum of Civilization

and such recent thematic exhibitions there as *Blue* and *Skin*. They use a patently theatrical approach, which indexes how the "museum experience" is being modeled on the "art experience" and more specifically the performing arts experience to produce what I like to call "museum theater."

6. I take this as an indication that something profound is changing in the sensory curriculum of the museum, which I like to think of as a school for the senses. That school has always deployed various technologies—Jonathan Crary's work comes to mind—or built on technologies that we associate with world's fairs and amusement parks. Technological innovation often happens first in the military and in the entertainment industry (and they learn from each other).

In thinking about museums of tomorrow, we might ask what kinds of bodies, what kinds of sensoriums, are artists and visitors going to bring to the museum, if they are not already doing so—distributed selves, multitasking, love of sensory derangement, high arousal thresholds. Young visitors who have cut their teeth on computer games, chat rooms, extreme rides, raves, and the like.

7. What are the implications of such developments for the very nature, the fabric, functioning, and experience of the museum? Will museums become one with what they exhibit? What might that look like?

Olu Oguibe

Ultimately our discussions will come in three forms: as reflection, as prediction, and as prolegomena. I would like to begin with the first two, especially as they relate to some of the opinions already laid out.

Over the past century the museum, in all its forms, has evolved from a charitable repository of culture to a commercial entertainment outlet that in many cases is hardly distinguishable from the movie house or the circus. There are exceptions to this generalization, one admits, but this trend is dominant.

There is a parallel trend which explains the foregoing, which is that capital, the mother of the museum, has also departed from its early bourgeois traditions of repository philanthropy—that old idea of giving back to the community—except where there is sufficient tax incentive. Yet again, in the era of off-shore banking and easy money laundering, even tax incentives are in fact hardly sufficient rationale for culture-designated philanthropy of the kind that founded the early museum.

Now, since it is unlikely that this trend will be reversed, it is quite obvious that the museum as a public service will eventually disappear and in its place will stand the museum as a culture mall, as indeed is increasingly the case. Regardless of how depressing or sacrilegious it may sound, everything about the museum from management to content and programming will be determined solely by market forces, and all that is presently held sacrosanct in museum traditions and culture will be subsumed under the exigencies of box office returns and shareholder dividends. Culture experts—the museum administration graduate and the bow-tied art historian/curator with his or her area specialist credentials—will be phased out from museum administration and replaced by finance, business, and public relations experts. And, popular culture will dominate museum content and programming.

I find this line of developments particularly engaging, even exciting, especially because those who shudder at the thought are obviously caught in a time-warp and seem not to have noticed how the most sacrosanct of all institutions, the Church, has undergone the same evolution as it reinvents itself to stay current, viable, and relevant. As noted earlier, there will be exceptions, of course, but the overall fate of the museum as an institution is not in doubt.

The foregoing is also far more interesting and fundamental than the effects of digital technology and culture on the museum. Five, seven years ago, there were anxious speculations that digital culture would drive certain forms of content and content delivery out of existence, and every imaginable form of culture would be streamed. Print was one such form, yet print has survived, and so has the already mourned bookshop. This goes to show that certain areas of culture will only be augmented by new technologies, but not fundamentally reconfigured or undermined. I believe that the museum falls in this category.

For one, the staple of the museum, the object, will survive. I believe that painting and sculpture and the multidimensional installation will all survive into the future of the museum, and that physical engagement with the work—whatever "the work" is or will be—will continue to be the mainstay of museum culture. I believe also that the physical structure of the museum will survive even as it undergoes changes to accommodate its emerging role as a culture mall. Digital content delivery will not replace the tactile or physical encounter with the work, and home content delivery will not replace the physical trip to the museum.

At present most of the virtual reality experiments that were tried in the mid-1990s have been abandoned. Some of those will no doubt be revived and refined as capital streamlines its strategies for profit making through museotertainment, and we may finally be able—for the right fee—to experience a near-lifelike virtual guided tour of a museum exhibit several thousand miles away, far beyond what present algorithms can accomplish. That, however, will depend solely on the profit viability of such technologies, but even so, they will not replace the tradition of the museum visit on which the museum gourmet restaurant, gift shop, and ancillary accessories outlets will continue to depend.

And the museum will survive as a structure because of its symbolism, because it will continue to represent evolving definitions of Taste, not regarding whatever difficulty we may have with those redefinitions. A good analogy is the theater which, despite the advent of cinema and the movie house, and home entertainment in the last half-century, has not changed fundamentally as a place since Christopher Marlowe and William Shakespeare. Like the theater, the museum as place, as location, will survive as we know it because capital needs for it to survive as a profit-making institution, and because capital will continue to harbor pretenses to an identification with Taste.

The preceding is prediction, not prolegomena, and there will be many who will differ on account of the exemplary exception. Yet, when the academy, the museum's last shield, completes its own transformation into a capital-driven institution, even the exemplary exception will find no respite. At best it will become a fossil, the museum of the past, and certainly not the museum of the future.

Maurice Berger

Olu, you wrote: "And the museum will survive as a structure because of its symbolism, because it will continue to represent evolving definitions of Taste, not regarding whatever difficulty we may have with those redefinitions."

A question: Do all cultures, communities, subcultures have the same need for institutional definitions of Taste? And does the museum serve the tastemaker role pan-socially and across cultural communities?

Miwon Kwon

Of the traditional functions of the museum, which include collecting, preserving, and displaying "great works" of creative human achievement, it is the last function, that of display, that seems to be the point around which assessments of the institution's future are measured most urgently. This is likely because it is the most visible aspect or product of the museums operation and because it is the most immediate interface between the institution and its public (barring the museum shop and restaurant). But what about collecting and preserving? It seems as if the display function is trumping all others, which is reflected in the museums getting caught up more intensely in entertainment and fashion. I imagine the future of the museum will concentrate even more energy and resources toward display, becoming ever more a showroom and less and less a sanctuary (for art, for us). Collecting and preserving, if maintained, will be in order to serve display imperatives. And I don't mean just the display of art; I mean the display of the museum itself (think of all the designer museums recently completed or under construction to serve as destination sites for cultural tourism).

I would like to request the following for the future of art museums:

—Get over the confusion between mass audience and general public. Appealing to a mass audience is not the same as serving or constituting a public.

—Instead of aspiring to showcase artists who will make the turnstiles rotate, that is, instead of thinking of the museum simply as a venue, aspire to truly support and nurture artists (and critics), financially, socially, and intellectually in order to facilitate a real public sphere.

—Don't be so susceptible to the "new." Commit to a historical consciousness—not in an antiquarian sense but in order to understand the present deeply, in relation to the forces and tides of humanity's past, which are beautiful and horrific, corrupt and honorable.

—Etc.

Alan Wallach

As a historian I think it important to distinguish between what we would like to see happen with museums and what is actually taking place—current trends that will determine the art museum's future. Of course, since the participants in this symposium influence art museums in various ways, what we would like may have some effect. Still, one sad fact of life right now is that museums are more and more adopting a corporate model, which means among other things increasing pressures on curatorial departments to come up with popular exhibitions. Accountants and chief operating officers may not have a direct say in curatorial decision making but their views will in the end be heard, and curators who are not team players may find themselves without employment.

Meanwhile, a number of familiar trends will continue or intensify:

1. Blockbusters will remain the fiscal heroin of the big museums—the Metropolitan Museum of Art, the Museum of Fine Arts, Boston, etc.
2. Museum managers will increasingly think of the museum in entertainment industry terms.
3. Rather than provoking or challenging their audiences, museums will be focused on keeping the turnstiles spinning, which these days often means putting on middlebrow entertainments (Norman Rockwell, [Giorgio] Armani, [Claude] Monet in 1903, etc.).
4. More and more, museums will exhibit popular art, but not in order to broaden critical understanding. Instead they will exploit its potential for nostalgia and commodity fetishism.

If we are concerned with the art museum's future we will have to think about museums politically. In other words, we will have to consider museums in relation to a politics of resistance.

Mark Alice Durant

I am in San Francisco this week, and on Saturday there was a two-block line outside the San Francisco Museum of Modern Art to see the [Marc] Chagall show. A few blocks away at New Langton Arts there is a Jeanne Finley and John Muse mini-retrospective; only three or four people visited the gallery the hour I was there. Over the years many "alternative spaces" have attempted to provide something other than the historically safe, pedigreed, and blockbusterish exhibitions of mainstream museums. Ideally, alternative spaces presented objects and processes that had yet to be classified and made safe by critical and historical distance. It appears as if this alternative model may have lost its urgency and/or relevance. What does this mean for museums, if anything? Is it kind of like the end of the cold war? Where and what are the alternative philosophies beyond just a knee-jerk opposition to anything corporate? Have the "alternative" art strategies been completely absorbed into museum culture? It seems that sometime in the 1980s the alternative gallery circuit became a kind of training ground for artists before they made the jump to big-time museums. What is the museum's role in "living culture"?

Maurice Berger

I didn't even have to leave SFMoMA to see this effect in action. I luxuriated in the Philip Guston show along with a handful of other visitors. Upstairs, the Chagall show was packed.

Keep the posts coming as we move into our second day.

Olu Oguibe

Thanks for your question, Maurice.

Though its details and perimeters may differ from culture to culture, the idea of Taste—that is, the delineation of tropes of distinction and refinement—is not culture-specific. Surely, in every culture and society there is a certain class that desires to define itself as distinct from the rest by inventing and defining Taste. In his writings about aesthetics, Hegel tried to reserve this desire or phenomenon for the so-called civilized cultures, but that distinction is as groundless as the idea of civilized cultures. Taste, ultimately, is a class matter, and all Taste is institutionally determined.

It ought to be noted, also, that the museum is not a pan-social institution, to use your term. In other words, the museum traditionally does not cater to all classes. In *Shooting Star*, Geoff Dunlop's great documentary on Jean-Michel Basquiat, the narrator begins with a statement that may seem mundane, but is relevant to our discussion because it does point to the general understanding of the place and role of the museum in culture. In the opening statement, he notes that the popular notion of Basquiat's background is that he was a child of the streets, "whereas, it turns out that his mother took him to museums and he attended public schools" (which in Britain means private schools). The invocation of museum visits instantly elevates the subject from the streets to a comfort class, and indicates that he was exposed to refined "culture" as a child. That is the historical role of the museum. In the future—as indeed we have begun to notice—the museum will broaden its reach as its traditional founding and target class distends, and as its mercantile propensities dictate, but in order to retain its appeal and market viability, it must also retain its class pretenses as a marker of refined sensibilities. It may become a mall, but it will be a mall of "culture"—a culture mall.

Ultimately, because the museum is a class invention and institution, its role and appeal within that class cuts across cultures in the same manner that its founding class has spread across cultures from continent to continent. My first one-person exhibition as an artist was held in the Didi Museum in Lagos. The Didi Museum was founded and endowed by the West Africa regional manager of the contracting firm of Taylor-Woodrow, a Nigerian entrepreneur who obviously belongs to the same class that founded the great museums in America and Europe or compelled the states and municipalities to establish those museums. Overall, the histories are similar, and so are the goals across societies and cultures.

Here is a quote from an email that I received recently from an Indian friend in Kingston, Jamaica:

...reading a fascinating book called The Great Indian Middle Class. *Trying to think about the middle class here. One of the things that hasn't been talked about much is the transcendental quality of middle-class culture. It's astonishing how utterly similar in belief systems, habits, taste, practices members of this class can be in places as far apart and different as Kingston and Delhi and Lagos I bet. There's a very funny book called* The Gin Drinkers *by Sagarika Ghose.*

So, yes indeed, inasmuch as we understand Taste to represent illusions of distinction, the museum does indeed serve that role from community to community, and from culture to culture, irrespective of where you find it, and sometimes even across cultures since "the great Indian middle-class" would certainly take pride in having visited exhibitions at the Tate or the Victoria and Albert while on vacation.

The question of what the museum ought to do is another matter, and one is doubtful as to whether the museum "ought to do" anything in particular beside pursuing whatever goal it sets for itself as an institution in a capitalist economy. One of the many points that I found interesting in Professor Alberro's brief, initial post is that on one hand he emphasizes the heterogeneity of museums, and on the other, by refusing to include museum exhibits of classic motorcycles in his class discussions, he almost insinuates that the art museum's legitimate area of concern ought to be synonymous with the "great art" history syllabus dedicated only to paintings, marble statues, and stolen ceramics. This may seem contradictory, but it is not because it does in fact buttress his point that different museums will serve different content expectations, even if he fails to observe that the art of the art history syllabus is, essentially, no different in class origins or status symbolism than the Harley-Davidson, and for that reason, the audience that goes to see a Monet show will most likely be the same one to go see a Harley-Davidson museum exhibition or travel to see the Rock and Roll Hall of Fame and Museum or collect Matthew Barney or Tracey Emin's brain-dead dismissibles—all of which fall within contemporary parameters of Taste. In other words, the motorcycle in the art museum is in fact not an aberration or a violation of the museum's calling.

One may have reservations about certain museum practices, and these are among the issues that I address in my book, *The Culture Game*. However, it does appear that the museum understands the challenges facing it as an institution, the most pressing of which is to survive and remain viable in changing cultures and economies. I have serious doubts that the museum fits in that classic question: Is there nothing sacred?

Raina A. Lampkins-Fielder

It's been said that museums develop in accordance with the general cultural climate and that shifts in public perceptions significantly influence a museum's understanding and projection of itself into the community. This can be to our detriment if we feel tethered to market-driven forces that compromise the integrity of our programming, permitting us only to be reactors to commercial trends. However, it's often suggested that external forces have challenged museums to rethink their missions, to re-envision themselves as educational, scholarly, and interpretive institutions as well as places of social interaction (not just as repositories of objects), and to respond to changing public expectations. After all, one of the strengths of museums lies in our ability to be responsive in ways that many other cultural or civic institutions cannot. As a museum educator, I am constantly thinking not only of how external forces determine what we do, but also of what our role is in influencing culture. Elaine Heumann Gurian asks if museums are just one of a number of "civic pillars" that keep society intact. Or are we (I hope!) constantly interpreting and reinterpreting, acknowledging accepted standards while striving to introduce new ones?

So, one of the biggest challenges that I see in museums lies within the museum walls themselves as we ask ourselves who we want to be in spite of everything, and for whom do we really feel responsible?

Maurice Berger

The dichotomy between the "museum" and the "street" may not be entirely codified. What of communities that turn storefronts into museums, into spaces for the expression of local visual culture? But I understand the distinction you are making.

Raina, you wrote: "As a museum educator, I am constantly thinking not only of how external forces determine what we do, but also of what our role is in influencing culture. Elaine Heumann Gurian asks if museums are just one of a number of 'civic pillars' that keep society intact. Or are we (I hope!) constantly interpreting and reinterpreting, acknowledging accepted standards while striving to introduce new ones?"

This is a very important point, which I think hinges on the pedagogical function of the museum. I will devote a two-day session to museum pedagogy and education. The tendency of art museums to marginalize or isolate their education departments (so that they have little input into the curatorial side of the museum) suggests (to me, at least) the makings of a serious problem: the museum's inability or unwillingness to teach its viewers rather than underestimate or overwhelm them.

Museums can undoubtedly teach us a lot—about art, about society, about ourselves. But do museums even acknowledge the broader implications of this possibility? As David Ross suggests, are directors and curators overlooking the bigger picture?

Jonathan P. Binstock

Following from Olu's contribution...the people who shop at J. Crew are not the same as those who shop at Club Monaco or Brooks Brothers. These stores, I think, offer clothing at a similar price point. I have yet to mention the Pradas of the world. Among the people who will visit Olu's culture mall (as they shop for culture, I presume), there will be different desires, driven by different senses of self. Some people, in turn, will go a long way to making their purchased product their own. Some people buy jeans at the Gap and wear them backwards. At The Lab at Belmar in Denver, Adam Lerner is trying to think of ways to help people see the contemporary art space as their own, to give them a sense of agency inside the institution.

Who will "shop" at the culture mall? Why? This brings me back to my original question: Who will the audience of the museum be? I think that this question depends heavily on where and what that museum is. Ultimately, a theory of capitalism or commerce will be outpaced by actual developments in museum practice, and, for that matter, actual developments in art. Indeed, art has a habit of consistently outpacing theory. This does not make theory useless, but I'd like to see the questions raised here linked to issues of place and geography. The museum will be a place to which people will go. That place, itself, will have a location. Museums serve distinct audiences. Understanding who a museum's public is, what the audience is (visitor surveys, etc.), does not have to be tantamount to pandering to it.

Alexander Alberro

There seems to be a general consensus that, following George Baker's observation, the museum has become increasingly commodified. And while I wholeheartedly agree with this point, I think that the process of cultural commodification is far more broad-reaching than museums, and in fact extends fully to the realm of universities (for more on this see the late Bill Readings's *University in Ruins*). Perhaps I'm more cynical than George, but I don't think that there is such a gap between curator and art critic, museum director and art historian (here I believe I'm agreeing with the comments of Stefano Basilico). It almost seems that a false ideal or principle of disinterest is being posited for the art critic and the art historian—a disinterest that is ideologically fraught.

However, if one is to take the view that the museum has been transformed along with other institutions into a commodified entity, the question of how and if it will continue to function—or perhaps following Olu Oguibe's line of argumentation, how it will function differently—still remains. For as Olu rightfully noted, the museum is not the only institution to find itself transformed (he points in particular to the similar fate of the Church). Surely, the museum will survive, and so will the university, albeit in altered ways. As Olu points out, similar discussions emerged in the past concerning the end of print culture, and more recently the end of film. Yet, in each of these cases (and there are many more), the crisis and anxiety of obsolescence brought about a critical reflection on the particular type of production in question, and pushed that type of production forward in new and often very interesting ways. Recall Walter Benjamin's famous dictum (or was it Hegel's?) that understanding occurs most pointedly at the moment when obsolescence draws close. What I mean to say is that although cultural institutions such as the museum might today be at a watershed point, instead of nostalgically yearning for the conditions of the good old days, we might do better to explore the productive possibilities of the bad new ones. What is today referred to as a museum is fundamentally different from what came under this term at the turn of the last century, and this is not necessarily a catastrophe. Just as (most recently) the culture wars of the '80s in my opinion, brought about significant changes in exhibition practices, so too the current period of crisis (is there a more apt way to define it?) might be seen as a moment of new possibilities—as a condition that if steered in the right direction might propel art museums in very different and productive ways. Indeed, I think that the very fact that this discussion is taking place today—that Maurice has brought together a broad array of individuals from many different backgrounds and disciplines to engage in a productive dialogue about the future of art museums—is at once symptomatic of this crisis and indicative of the possibilities that I mentioned above.

Maurice Berger

Alexander, you wrote: "What I mean to say is that although cultural institutions such as the museum might today be at a watershed point, instead of nostalgically yearning for the conditions of the good old days, we might do better to explore the productive possibilities of the bad new ones. What is today referred to as a museum is fundamentally different from what came under this term at the turn of the last century, and this is not necessarily a catastrophe. Just as (most recently) the culture wars of the '80s, in my opinion, brought about significant changes in exhibition practices, so too the current period of crisis (is there a more apt way to define it?) might be seen as a moment of new possibilities—as a condition that if steered in the right direction might propel art museums in very different and productive ways."

Absolutely. I do not see the purpose of this conference as an exercise in museum bashing, looking backward, or lamenting the museum as a moribund institution. Instead, I think we have a wonderful opportunity to theorize, think, muse—whatever we want to call it—about the *possibilities* for the museum. Yes, the commodification and corporate imperatives of some museums are real issues for us. And we'll deal with them in the next topic. But as the dialogue moves along, I want each of us to feel free to speculate about the future of the museum and its potential to change and flourish in relationship to the ever-changing cultural and social sphere around it. It would not be a terrible thing if museums learned from TV or the Internet or from other social and cultural forms.

Barbara Buhler Lynes

The biggest challenge museums face in the future is finding ways of keeping themselves viable financially while charting new paths that lead them away from the corporate models that increasingly threaten to transform the museum into nothing more than "a commercial entertainment outlet," as Olu so succinctly states. Much of what happens in the future will depend on the leadership abilities of museum personnel—directors, curators, the heads of education, development, and marketing departments—and how these individuals work together creatively to develop effective alternatives for the museum that complement its equally important need of raising revenues and balancing budgets. Of course, in doing so, all might indeed place themselves in positions of resistance, a subject Alan has raised, ultimately making all vulnerable to not having employment. But as those who are in positions that can influence the future of art museums respond to the challenges of understanding and coming to terms with the diverse needs of their specific audiences and constituencies, they also become involved in the process of self-examination, reflection, and redefinition from which new and inventive strategies can emerge.

Maurice Berger

Barbara, your post speaks directly to the issue of self-examination—personal (on the part of museum personnel) and collective (on the broader policies of display, didactic and educational context, collections and acquisition). I hope this conference helps facilitate just this kind of self-inquiry.

The "Corporate" Museum

8–9 October 2003

Maurice Berger

A number of the panelists in the introductory session have referred to the corporatization of the museum—the tendency on the part of many institutions to create programming (and erect destination buildings) geared towards enriching attendance and revenues. Obviously, the corporate model has much to do with the survival of museums in a highly competitive cultural environment. Most Americans would rather watch television or go to the movies than go to museums.

I agree with David Ross that the discussion of the subjugation of the museum by corporate interests is a bit old hat. After all, a range of artists, critics, and scholars have explored this issue with great depth and rigor. Yet the question of the museum's economic survival is not irrelevant to this discussion. Many institutions find themselves in serious economic trouble, forced to reduce programming and unable to organize controversial, challenging, or edgy exhibitions.

Over the next two days, I would like to talk about these issues. To what extent has the corporate model become the institutional model for the contemporary art museum? To what extent has content been compromised by the need to build audience? And what of the alternative institutions that have rejected this model in an attempt to celebrate the marginal, the edgy, the difficult?

And, lastly, what of the idea of "corporate" culture itself. Does the corporate model by definition stand in the way of museological progress? Or can it become incorporated into the progressive museum of the future? After all, corporations sometimes sanction, support, and distribute significant artistic content. Home Box Office's *The Sopranos,* Toni Morrison's *Bluest Eye,* Spike Lee's *Do The Right Thing,* and hundreds of recordings of [Arnold] Schoenberg or Philip Glass all function within a corporate environment.

A note to those participants who have not yet posted into the conference: Please feel free to incorporate your introductory remarks into your response to these questions.

David A. Ross

Well of course museums are like corporations. They *are* corporations, and need to be for many reasons. The problem isn't the corporate structure itself—they are, after all, not-for-profit corporations by definition serving an educational mission. The problem runs far deeper than the corporate structure itself.

The problem is one of governance—the same problem that underlies the problems facing many of our for-profit corporations. To use corporate-speak for a moment, in the for-profit world, it's a matter of balancing a responsible corporate ethos with the needs of shareholders to make a reasonable profit from their investment.

What is the analog in the not-for-profit world of art museums? Trustees, the putative shareholders, are supposed to hold the museum in trust to whom?

Just who are the shareholders? In other words, in whose interests are museums operated and maintained?

Are they run in the interests of casual visitors to museums (what museum marketing departments refer to as cultural tourists)? Surely artists are prime stakeholders. And of course students and scholars of art history have a great stake. Then of course there is the patron class. They can't (and won't) be ignored. What about an abstract stakeholder like history itself?

Clearly current governance covenants compel museum trustees to consider their fiduciary responsibilities above all others, yet there are restraints here as well. For instance, a museum can't (or shouldn't) sell its collection to pay its operating expenses. They shouldn't hold stolen or improperly acquired works in the collections. But beyond that, there is little that the profession (or government watchdogs) would frown upon.

So who watches the watchers? Who evaluates the actions (or inaction) of trustees? Recently I read a *Washington Post* review of an exhibition at the Corcoran Gallery that called for the removal of the board rather than the head of its director.

If one can recall a governor, can a community recall its museum board? And on what grounds?

And of course, if replaced, who will pay for the unmet (and perhaps unmeetable) costs associated with the essentially uneconomic museum enterprise—collecting, conserving, and educating?

I hate to appear simplistic, but perhaps we have a problem that needs to be understood in simple terms. It's still the economy, stupid. Its nature is reflected in our institutions and in the ways in which they behave. To expect otherwise is to be living in some idealized dreamland (or working in the Bush White House).

The corporate reformists are busy tending bigger problems, but at some point, museums (and universities) will become the rightful target of investigation and reform. Won't that be an interesting moment.

Let the show trials begin?

Irving Sandler

Problem. Has our use of the term "museum" become a glittering generality—what Tom Hess called "glidge"? When we say "museum," do we mean (with New York in mind) the likes of the Metropolitan Museum of Art, the Museum of Modern Art, the Whitney Museum of American Art, the New Museum of Contemporary Art, P.S.1 Contemporary Art Center—or my college museum, the Neuberger Museum of Art? Should we not be more specific?

Maurice Berger

Good question, Irving.

I think at this point we need to keep the idea of the "museum" intentionally open, since it can apply to a range of institutional situations. (We don't want to limit our discussion to one type of institution.) Yet, the priorities, demands, and sensibilities of these institutions can differ considerably. So, I think we should feel free to differentiate when appropriate.

After all, the corporate model may be far less applicable to a tiny alternative museum than to the Metropolitan Museum of Art.

George Baker

I want to expand upon and clarify a few things from my general post on the corporate museum from the beginning of the conference. I'm also responding obliquely to Alex's post questioning the terms that I set up. My polarization of museum and academic positions and personnel does not necessarily glorify one over the other; it was meant to register their current functional separation, when in the best of worlds, it seems to me, they would more often be working in concert. Also, I have no desire to celebrate the "good old days," but I don't see the need to love the "bad new ones" either. I don't think it is a regressive or backward-looking move to call for an intensification of the museum's pedagogical functions in the face of increasing corporatization.

I was struck by Maxwell Anderson's description of the museum as an "often lamentable business masquerading as big business." That description has made me want to test the following thoughts (I'm not convinced yet myself, I'm just testing).

What if it is the corporate model of the museum that is itself being overly attentive to the "good old days"? I'm not trying to retreat into David Ross's idealized "dreamland," but it occurs to me that the specific corporate model to which many world-class museums are now attracted is itself an obsolescent model. Yes, there are still corporations in the bad new days, but not like the ones in the good old days. I'm put in mind of my father and his generation—remember Frank Stella in his business suit? He personified the very type of the corporate cadre, an American dream of sorts, and now he and all his friends have been downsized into unemployment just before the old promise of corporate retirement.

I think there is a glamour to the corporate model that only comes from art and culture's seizing upon it as an already outmoded entity. So many young contemporary artists are reconfiguring their own practices around corporate models, around all the accoutrements of corporate culture—but it's a Surrealist device, an outmoded strategy, a postmodern nostalgia. So in the face of the Guggenheim model, one might want to argue: Franchises are so 1960s Americana. Sure they are still around, but the productive energies of the future don't flow from such a model anymore.

I mentioned the symbolic language of museum architecture in my initial post, and the design of most contemporary museums seems to bear out this musing. The post-'68 "culture factory" model of museum architecture embodied by a place like the Centre Georges Pompidou has surely shifted in the recent models of museums like the Tate Modern or Dia Beacon. The space being inhabited in the new museum architectures is presented as an already outmoded space—the old factory revamped as the new museum. I think Allan Sekula has shown how much the same can be said for the digital fantasia of the Guggenheim Bilbao—it is a fantasia built upon the obsolescent maritime industry of that city's recent past. Maybe others want to comment on museum architectures whose symbolism speaks of different referents, perhaps pointing us and the museum toward other organizational models.

What I am wondering: Is the corporate museum a postmodern ghost?

Miwon Kwon

The corporatization of the museum, a process in play since the 1960s but accelerated since the 1980s, is not only an issue of economics, although I'm fully aware that economics is what's leading the cultural transformations under discussion. I think the notion of the "corporatization" of the museum encompasses or stands in for a more far-reaching transformation in the basic institutional attitude toward art. (One might even question whether it is this attitude that makes the adoption of corporate ways of thinking and working more "logical" for art museums in the first place.) Because in the corporate mentality, the "public" to whom the boards of trustees, education programmers, curators, directors, marketing experts, etc., are beholden is understood to be the same thing as the "audience"—or more accurately the number of people going through the doors. As such, art is foremost thought of and treated as "content." And it doesn't really matter what this content is—motorcycles, Chagall paintings, designer dresses, latest "hot" stuff—as long as it does the job of luring in bodies. This is the phenomenon I'm thinking of when I think of the corporatization of the museum. The demoting of "art" in this process as a privileged category of cultural objects serving the elite may be described by some as an opening up of the previously exclusive and exclusionary operations of museums, making the institution more "democratic," but I think, in fact, this is totally misguided and wrong. (Here, I absolutely disagree with Olu. And call me an old-fashioned art historian, even though I don't wear a bow tie. There *is* a fundamental difference between art and design even if it's hard to tell the difference these days.) Populism is not radical politics! A society that elides differences and specificities in its cultural landscape is antithetical, in my view, to a democratic society. In a strange way, these two ends of the debate conjoin—the corporate motivation toward audience development for profit-oriented purposes and the left/liberal motivation toward expanding audiences and making the museums more "accessible" and "inclusive." In both instances, art is imagined to serve instrumental purposes that should have nothing to do with art.

I don't know that "alternative institutions" are exempt from this mentality. They have different content, perhaps, but I don't see that they operate with a profoundly different attitude. To single out certain cultural projects as Maurice does, like *The Sopranos* or *Do the Right Thing*, as "good" results of corporate sponsorship (that, hey, sometimes they can do the right thing), is a statement of taste preference, not a critique of structural conditions.

I'm not as hopeful as some of my colleagues that the museum can be rethought or redirected to be a site of vital public culture. I'm not even sure that it can be a site of aesthetic experience. I actually don't even expect it anymore, except when I visit really old museums. I think contemporary art museums are no longer interested in Art (yes, with a capital A), nor in poetic experiences that foster speculation, skepticism, and wonder. That one could describe art as providing "content" for a museum reveals an instrumental attitude about the function of art that makes me feel sick.

George Baker's rumination is very provocative. The pumping up of the sign value of museum architecture may further underscore my view that what's inside the museum doesn't really matter any more.

Maurice Berger

Miwon, you wrote: "George Baker's rumination is very provocative. The pumping up of the sign value of museum architecture may further underscore my view that what's inside the museum doesn't really matter any more."

I agree. And I certainly share some of your pessimism about the museum as a site of "artistic" practice and celebration. But I think George is correct in more ways than one. The very act of acknowledging the regressive, retro-mentality of "corporate" imperatives in the museum—the ghosts of the 1960s and '70s—could lead to structural and ideological changes that could ultimately recast what a museum is. Or are you convinced that such changes are impossible at this point, given the entrenchment of the regressive mindset you describe?

After all, distributing one's literary expressions on the net is a whole lot different from being published by Knopf. Can "institutions" once again devoted to Art (note, I didn't even use the word *museum* this time) reemerge from this kind of self-inquiry and evaluation?

Olu Oguibe

The question of the "corporatization" of the museum may be old hat, but it is an old hat that won't be thrown away soon since there are many still who have yet to come to terms with the truth of the museum's nature and future, which is that it is, after all, as David Ross rightly points out, an incorporated entity—a corporation; or, indeed, the fact that the museum is only not-for-profit in theory since it must keep those lines filing round the block if it is to survive its non-infinite public or charitable funding.

In fact, the museum of today may be not-for-profit, whatever that implies in real terms, but the museum of tomorrow will not, and its shareholders won't be the indeterminable "public" but real stockholders with expectations for concrete annual dividends in dollars and cents. The for-profit museum will include the neighborhood shop-front display room that Maurice referred to earlier, the brave new frontiers initiative.

As chair of the culture committee of the Glocal Forum, a think tank based in Rome, I recently invited Juan Ignacio Vidarte, Director-General of the Guggenheim Bilbao, to speak about the museum at the Forum's annual meeting. In his very concise presentation with charts, figures, and survey data, Dr. Vidarte outlined quite precisely how the Guggenheim project may be seen almost purely as a municipal capital venture or regional development scheme in which culture—that is, architecture, art, and other regional cultural resources—serve as the mainstay of a thriving tourist industry with maximum benefits in jobs, small businesses, municipal fiscal recovery, and political stability. None of that contemplation, consecration, Oh! Art, how holy thou art, stuff, which somewhat explains [Frank] Ghery's hideous yet crowd-pulling architecture for the museum.

David Ross states quite simply the ruthless fact of the matter, which is that the museum has overhead, and that overhead is always on the increase rather than decline. Beyond that, the museum is no longer a donation from the local boy who made good and leaves a healthy endowment for the museum's running and maintenance. It's the economy, stupid!

In the case of the Guggenheim Bilbao, the shareholders get their returns not so much in exposure to "great art" or education in the redeeming powers of art history, but in other concrete and increasingly more compelling terms: in continuously record-breaking tourist figures that translate into revenue, jobs, thriving local businesses, and the strategic undermining of nationalist anarchy. If art and near-fascist museum architecture should deliver these, then, long live both. The sublime encounter with a wall-bound piece of stained canvas or a remake of a Barcelona ham museum in vats of formaldehyde has less to do with it.

I mentioned the nature of the museum earlier. It ought to be noted that those who bemoan the imminent demise of the old museum—site of education, contemplation, and the sublime experience—are obviously either oblivious or deliberately negligent of the oft-repeated fact that the museum was never a site of innocence. From its very origins the museum, like the university, was always the product of ruthless capitalist profit making, built on the skulls of hundreds and thousands of poorly paid factory workers, coal miners, and oil-rig men who either died of tuberculosis or were buried alive in mining avalanches; or chattel slaves who worked generation after generation without due pay. From the proceeds and family fortunes, entrepreneurs built the hallowed monuments that have come down to us, and endowed them with means to acquire works of art. Museums are not some innocent natural resource like a game reserve or some ancient ruin inherited from the Aztecs. They began as money-laundering ventures where a fraction of the gains of ruthless profiteering was converted to a site for the "public good." Even so, the working families whose dead provided the labor and profits that endowed the museums were effectively barred from them by the very nature of the museum as a site. Donna De Salvo describes them as a mass of contradictions, and there is no greater, more inescapable contradiction than this fact of their origins.

In effect, the transparent architecture of the culture mall (or "corporatized" museum) is far more honest and more inviting and accommodating to the museum's expanding clientele than the sacrosanct sanctuary of old. It may be disagreeable to some, but it is true. At the opening of the new Tate Modern in London a few years ago, I mentioned to Tate director Nicholas Serota my surprise that the museum shop was not located more strategically, like the plan at Heathrow airport, where it is impossible to step in any direction without going through the shops. The Tate, as you probably know, relies heavily on the British National Lottery, and its box office and franchise proceeds for survival. The national lottery, like all such ventures, makes its money from the least-earning class of British society who remain the least likely to visit the Tate Modern.

The fully corporatized, nonpublicly subsidized museum will be a more honest institution because it will make its money directly from those that it serves, and not those who may not step through its doors because of its history, content, programming, airs and pretenses, or its architecture and ambience. And there is nothing to say that it will necessarily and routinely devolve to the "lowest common denominator" even as it keeps one eye on the ledgers and the other on the length of the line around the block.

When it becomes the dominant form of the museum, the corporate culture mall will also help reiterate another truth which art historians, museum professionals, critics, and so-called intellectuals know so well yet always ignore—which is that the museum is not the most important site of individual and communal encounter with art. It is an important site, no doubt, but art making and consumption go on and will continue to go on in spite of the museum.

Donna De Salvo

As much as we want to keep the terminology open, I do think it is worth noting that all arts institutions are not the same, some not even falling under the classification of "museum." The most obvious distinction is between those that collect and those that do not, and each has their own set of problems and challenges. Then there is scale. Undoubtedly, the larger the institution the more difficult it can be to navigate. Some are like ocean liners, whereas others have the maneuverability of a speedboat, rowboat, or even canoe. I value this diversity and feel it must be protected. Just as we decry the rise of the corporate over the family farm, we should also seek to preserve this multiplicity of perspectives.

Also, while it is true that museums are corporations (or, at least incorporated), I don't see how they can ever achieve what the corporation must do—realize *real* profit. I'm not being naive here; it just seems a fundamental difference. This is what makes stewardship, public or private, absolutely essential and goes back to David's comments as well as Miwon's remarks about the devaluing of the art experience.

Is the corporate model encouraging people to look at the package instead of what's inside? Has the institution become more dominant than the art it presents, or, where is the art in the art museum? What can we do differently?

Dan Cameron

There seems to be a schism opening up here in the discussion between the tough reality that David laid out, which is that museums must think and act like corporations in order to survive, and the question of the museum's program content, which Olu sees as being on the road of eventual transformation into a "culture mall."

I wonder if it's possible to maintain both realities at the same time. If the role of the museum board is supposed to be primarily one of governance and fiscal oversight, then it does not necessarily follow that corporatization is the only way to keep them happy. Yes, museums must continue to expand to meet increased overhead, and yes, we need both sponsorship and earned income to keep the doors open, but why does that seem to lead inevitably to the conclusion that brain-dead programs are the necessary result? Is there no faith anymore in the notion that corporate sponsors will back a program because it's smart and innovative and risk taking?

I think there is a historical explanation for the absence of crowds at "serious" art exhibitions that nobody seems to want to discuss, which is that for most of the 20th century, new art was made in opposition to public taste, and the less people grasped what artists were doing, the better the art world felt about itself. We are now reaping the questionable rewards of the avant-garde legacy of modernism. For a number of complex reasons, this historical imperative has recently reversed itself, and now we all seem to believe that we have a great product which nobody wants to buy—or, to put it more cynically, if we want to attract buyers, we have to cheapen ourselves.

I, for one, have no vested interest in needing to preserve the inherited cultural forms of museums, although I think we're stuck with them for the time being, at least as far as historical modes of art making are concerned. The most pressing issue for me is whether or not an institution like the Guggenheim Bilbao can only thrive by presenting mediocre programs in second-rate galleries, or will someone soon find a way to replace the current model of museum corporatization with one that rewards high-quality programming through public visibility and (shudder) profit?

George G. King

Depending on the corporate model an institution is formed after, all art museums today, in some way or another, have adopted or adapted to versions of some for-profit business practices that suit their respective institutions. The degree to which these practices are evident rest primarily, as David points out, with the board of directors. And we know that nothing as wicked as the Tyco scandal, which is now in its trial phase, as described in today's *New York Times*, can or will ever take place at an art museum.

I would hope that in the future a museum's art collection would never be relegated or reclassified as an asset in the hard-core business sense. All of us in this field understand the sacrosanct nature of the objects in each of our institutions, and one would hope that the hard-charging, asset-oriented business leaders who sit on a board would never compromise this issue.

Whether we like it or not, the marketing of museums and all they do is here to stay, and all of us as directors spend a good deal of time thinking about it, although many of us were not formally trained to do so. One term that is being used by some art institutions and creeping into their own corporate speak is the branding of our museums and how that brand can accurately promote all that a particular museum does. Personally, I find this way of thinking about institutional advancement as corrosive and not necessarily appropriate or applicable to art museums. We may have no choice in the future but to accept a certain version of branding, but I sincerely hope this won't be the case. I have been in this profession for 20 years, and 15 as a director, and I draw the line with using this kind of promotional language.

Stefano Basilico

As David said earlier, "They *are* corporations, and need to be for many reasons. The problem isn't the corporate structure itself—they are after all, not-for-profit corporations by definition serving an educational mission."

I agree with the first part of this statement, though I'm not so sure about the second, namely that the governors of the museum, the trustees, truly see their mission as an educational one. I believe that the majority of directors, curators, educators, etc., feel that their mission is, broadly speaking, education, but I'm not sure that trustees do.

The question of education may be why George [Baker] compared the museum and the university earlier. And it is why the same question of corporatization has been raised about the university that is now being discussed with regards to museums. If the business of business is making money, why can we imagine that any entity that sees itself as a business will not eventually want to be a better business and make more money? Not-for-profit status doesn't stop this from happening, since all it really does is uncouple the direct possible remuneration that the shareholders may receive, not the "imaginary" remuneration they hope to receive as the trustees of an institution whose *brand* is on the rise.

The sadness that Miwon feels, and I share, especially when I think about these issues—as opposed to going to look at, and think about art—is that the trustees who ultimately shape the direction of any and every institution, and thankfully not all trustees are created equally, do not necessarily share my value system and therefore don't have the same goals in mind for the museum that I have. F. Scott Fitzgerald's famous quote is apropos here.

Roberta Smith wrote a very interesting piece on the issue of trustee governance a few months ago in *The New York Times*, which raised similar points.

Before this generalization becomes totalizing I want to make it clear that different individuals will be differently disposed towards altruism. Thankfully, there must still exist some people—trustees—who do feel that not all interest is self-interest, and therefore they lead, or try and lead, their institutions down the proper path. Otherwise, we wouldn't be having this discussion.

Maurice Berger

Stefano, I find myself quite moved by what you said (and by the eloquent way you said it). Altruism is a very complex thing, indeed. What exactly is being given in the act of generosity and at what cost in return? But—alas—the educational imperative of the museum is not always high on the list of trustees (or even, sadly, of curators). Though I, too, am aware of remarkable exceptions.

Olu Oguibe

Dan Cameron makes a very important point I am mindful of, which is that the museum-going public, through their current preference for certain kinds of content, are obviously indicating a definition of Taste that some culture brokers have embraced because it is also profitable, and others are reluctant to accept because we believe that when it comes to matters of Taste, it is our duty to protect the untutored masses from themselves. I am not entirely insensitive to the point, and as I indicated earlier, the museum of tomorrow will not necessarily devolve to the lowest common denominator, whatever that is, in order to keep the cash registers churning. It simply will be true to itself.

When we speak of second-rate galleries, dismissible shows, and the "lowest common denominator," of course we are sticking to very familiar territory, namely the arena of hierarchies, which returns us to a question that Dr. Sandler posed on the first day of our discussions: What kind of art is it that meets our approval, and if we are realistic and true to ourselves, how are our criteria changing?

The audience that crowds out a Monet show but keeps its distance from a contemporary exhibit may not be saying much about the work in the contemporary exhibition itself, but rather a whole lot of other issues and factors that range from marketing and public relations to canonization, cumulative discourse, and veneration of the dead. The works that it files in to see today were also once rejected by an earlier public.

In other words, it does seem to me that there is no wrong party here; if history is anything to go by, the public will almost certainly ultimately file in to see works by the artists that it is ignoring today, and may in fact do so today if sensitized to it by an effective marketing machine; and those who advocate such work will be vindicated. Already one can see an Indie movement in the vein of a new age, Stonehenge cult eventually developing around the new Dia Beacon Project in upstate New York.

In the end, it may well have less to do with "the work itself," or the kind or hierarchy of art, than the ability of the museum to sell it to the public. Methinks that the Brooklyn Museum of Art provided one effective model when it used controversy as a marketing strategy in presenting the work of the YBA (to some, the Young British Assholes) in the exhibition *Sensation* a few years ago. The director publicly vowed to "have them lining up round the block," perhaps the first such official pronouncement in recent museum history, and deliberately played on the Mayor of New York and his well-known inhibitions, as well as publicly mouthing some rather silly, uninformed theories about dung veneration in Africa. With works by the likes of Ron Mueck and Mona Hatoum in it, the exhibition could not, overall, be dismissed as second-rate, even if the object of controversy, [Chris] Ofili's Madonna painting, hardly deserves a grade B– in an MFA painting class. Yet, with a little, very elementary public relations ploy, the museum was able to hoodwink the public like they have always loved to be hoodwinked since the London Crystal Palace Exposition of 1851, to line up round the block and see the exhibition.

That is, of course, only one model, but it worked quite predictably and is not to be dismissed, no matter what we think of it. It may have failed subsequently in Australia because the hosting museum caved in to pressure, but the Whitney Museum of American Art has used that ploy twice in a row since then; in the 2002 Whitney Biennial, and again this year in the exhibition *The American Effect*, in both instances displaying work that addressed the former Mayor of New York, and doing so rather remarkably in the same spot on the fourth-floor gallery! No doubt there will be other strategies, other devices and ploys, also.

In effect there is little or no dichotomy between my vision of the museum as a culture mall, and the points made by David Ross.

Karen Mary Davalos

I am fascinated by the progressive and conservative (as in status quo) narratives that weave in and out of the discussion about the corporate nature of the museum. Are we really as stuffy as we sound, defending Art—with a capital A—as if the thing really existed? Are we really that parochial? At least two of the scholars posting have made fine scholarly careers by deconstructing the notion of art, how it is experienced, etc. But in the context of the current topic, it appears that the notion of Art is the main line of defense against the corporate model in museums.

Okay, I can follow this logic, but if the attack on the corporate model in museums is actually an effort to shore up Western notions of art, well then you have lost me. It sounds like a backlash. This time the term "conservative" has another meaning, similar to the one we hear in California upon the gubernatorial election of an actor.

Miwon, I may be one of those leftists calling for the opening of the museum, but the trick, as has been suggested, is for the museum to stay one step ahead of the trend, and find marketing strategies that excite audiences and thus turn turnstiles. The good news: branding is too static and will not allow the museum to shift and dance with its audience, collection, exhibition, or interpretive methods. I refuse to believe that people are stupid; they know good spin when they hear it; that's why they elected Arnold.

(Easily swayed is not the same as dumb. Does that make me less of a Marxist/leftist? When one is spoken to, and if one is called by one's name, that sensation is profound. The nature of this experience does not depend upon or make one part of humanity's lowest-common denominator. It is humanity itself. It's more like watching the same commercial six times in one evening and laughing each time—the marketing department got it right. They were able to touch people. It's that structure of feeling that museum P.R. needs to have a handle on.)

I enjoyed Olu's reminder that museums were never the innocent sites we have imagined them to be—free of capitalist impulses and hierarchies. Given this history, can we then refocus our discussion on what museums can do in the future without reviving their origins?

In my simple mind, it's a critique of neo-liberalism, a rethinking of nationalism, and a clearer understanding of the complex webs of power and privilege—and yes, as a good radical feminist, I am referring to those social intersections that make Art really real to so many who are posting.

Maurice Berger

Karen, you wrote: "the trick, as has been suggested, is for the museum to stay one step ahead of the trend, and find marketing strategies that excite audiences and thus turn turnstiles. The good news: branding is too static and will not allow the museum to shift and dance with its audience, collection, exhibition, or interpretive methods. I refuse to believe that people are stupid; they know good spin when they hear it; that's why they elected Arnold."

Good point. Indeed, the arrogance of the left sometimes leads to the assumption that "ordinary" people are stupid. Yet, it's sometimes the smartest, most creative, and incisive forms of mass culture that capture the public imagination. (*The Simpsons*—a work of *very* progressive *art*, in every sense of the word—has been a hit for 14 years.)

My concern with the notion of Art, with a capital "A" is that we may be delimiting the definition of what visual art is. Again, I raise this point: Why the validation of "Film" (note the capital "F") and not television? Because [Jean-Luc] Godard talks over the heads of the masses and *The Mary Tyler Moore Show* talks directly to them (the sitcom's decidedly leftist ideology woven seamlessly into agile, gorgeously written scripts backed up by equally brilliant performances)? Is the idea of a major museum devoted to visual art and culture collecting television shows too far fetched? Not really. The Jewish Museum in New York has been doing it for 20 years, acquiring fine Art alongside thousands of TV programs in its National Jewish Archive of Broadcasting.

Maybe museums need to go beyond strategies of presentation and marketing to reconsider the question of what we mean by Art. Miwon, I would love it if you would chime in here.

Alexander Alberro

There seems to be a consensus (and I have to agree) that today museums are corporate entities. Thus far, so good. But I have to state quite frankly that I am utterly stunned by the suggestion, offered as a given (Maurice?), that television sitcoms such as *The Sopranos* and others, the epitome of monotony, feature significant artistic content. I can only say that this view is very distant (never distant enough?) from mine. By way of response, especially within the context of a discussion of the corporatization of the museum, allow me to advance the following premise.

The corporate model, like every other model developed by capitalism, can never be complete. Although this might very well be its goal, it will never be able to produce a totally seamless entity. Especially as that model grows, especially as neo-liberalism tries to achieve and claim its own end of history, the cracks, fissures, ruptures become increasingly evident and vulnerable. Whether it be called *umfunktionierung*, or *detournement*, or the politics of everyday life, the strategy of working critically within those spaces has been fundamental to much of the art of the modern period. And its vitality continues today: in the practices of many artists, scholars, curators, and seemingly as well in the programs of institutions such as the Museu d'Art Contemporani de Barcelona or the International Center of Photography in New York (to name only two), which have fairly consistently featured excellent exhibitions in the past few years.

One might counter that the notion of a critically engaged art and museum practice long ago went the way of the dinosaurs. But look what has happened to dinosaurs: children love them.

Bruce Altshuler

Although what Maurice has called the corporate museum—an institution creating programs and capital projects in order to maximize income and attendance—is increasingly a worldwide phenomenon, this development often occurs in very different circumstances outside the U.S. As David's mention of governance should remind us, most museums in the world are under the control of ministries of culture (whether on the national, regional, or municipal level), and independent boards of directors are unique to the U.S. (although there are a number of hybrid forms elsewhere).

I just have come from a meeting of Russian museum and arts professionals, self-described "cultural managers" who work in a very different kind of institutional world, negotiating with government bureaucrats for money while also coming under pressure to do things "the American way." In such new economies in-transition—from the former USSR and Eastern Europe to China and Vietnam—ministry officials are pushing museums to find nongovernmental funding and earned income to replace state support, though no one seriously believes that state funds will not be necessary to a significant degree in the future. Yet all of this occurs in a different environment than our own, one in which museum directors are often entrepreneurs able to take the institution in just any direction, no matter how distant from their museum's past activity.

Ironically, such an historical situation provides opportunities for radically new programming and the breaking of institutional inertia to a striking degree, sometimes to good and sometimes to ill effect. Often these new programs focus on contemporary art, which is popping up around the world in every sort of museum, from museums of history to natural history, as well as in traditional art museums. For contemporary art is seen by bureaucrats and cultural managers as a means of attracting new audiences and generating income. (In larger museums, in Asia especially, this involves importing name-brand artists from abroad.) And its use for these purposes certainly is a welcome development for local artists, and for young people eager to explore their new-found freedom. (I don't mean to idealize this, and I can be as cynical as the next person, but for anyone who has been to these countries the energy and excitement in this regard is palpable.)

So while pressure to increase revenue and attendance has brought much to criticize, leading museums to mount misguided exhibitions and to ignore collections and research, it has also generated space for new programs and projects, especially in the area of contemporary art. Of course this is not the whole story, but it is a development often unrecognized. (I ignore issues regarding exhibition and program quality, one critical issue being that mentioned by Donna—museums frequently condescending to their audiences. But that is a matter for another day.)

Maurice Berger

Alex, you wrote: "But I have to state quite frankly that I am utterly stunned by the suggestion, offered as a given (Maurice?), that television sitcoms such as *The Sopranos* and others, the epitome of monotony, feature significant artistic content."

I am stating my opinion, just as you are stating yours—an opinion that many of my colleagues agree with (and some, of course, do not). Obviously, not all TV programs contain artistically significant content. But neither does a good deal of what we call visual art, hence the role of critics, art historians, and curators to sort things out.

I don't think my view about TV as an Art form is a given at all within the art-historical or museum community. But it is also not a given that *The Sopranos* is a "sitcom." It is not. It is a drama.

I also want to make clear that I'm not implying that *all* art museums need to broaden the definition of art and that this definition should always include TV and film. Rather that this kind of rethinking about disciplinary boundaries may be necessary in the museum of tomorrow, whether it includes TV or not.

Irving Sandler

In dealing with museums, we must not overlook not-for-profit alternative "institutions," such as Exit Art and Artists Space in New York, the latter which I cofounded more than three decades ago and on whose board I still serve. Its purpose has been primarily (but not exclusively) to exhibit artists who are without galleries. Artists Space has a file of several thousand unaffiliated artists and tries to stay close to its constituency, which is also its major audience. The gallery has also mounted topical theme shows, a number of which have been controversial, e.g., *Witnesses Against Our Vanishing*, whose subject was the AIDS crisis. The NEA canceled a grant of $10,000, but with the help of the art world we fought for its reinstatement and won. Artists Space's staff is too small to fit the "corporate model." Most of the artists we have exhibited are unknown, and thus, we have not generated much P.R. No blockbusters here.

Yet, much of the gallery's funding comes from corporations. To my knowledge, none of them has attempted to influence its programs. My point again is, we should take into account the diverse role of museums—including alternative institutions. For example, the New Museum of Contemporary Art and P.S.1, Center for Contemporary Art, strike me as being less like the Museum of Modern Art or the Whitney Museum of American Art and more like Artists Space, but on a larger scale. That is, the New Museum of Contemporary Art and P.S.1 function as kunsthalles of contemporary art. Are their structures corporate? How do their structures affect what they do? Who decides what gets shown? Perhaps Dan Cameron can speak to this. Also Dan and Donna and other curators and David and Max, speak to the issue of whether curators who work in "corporate model" museums are free in deciding what gets shown. Who decides? Who approves? Who pressures you and why? Who makes up the audience for art? Since the early 1960s, there has emerged a sizeable, college-bred public whose members have taken at least one course in art history or a studio discipline and have become art conscious. They get their information from among the most knowledgeable art critics in the art world who write for the mass media: [Robert] Hughes in *Time* magazine, [Peter] Plagens in *Newsweek,* [Mark] Stevens in *New York Magazine,* [Peter] Schjeldahl in *The New Yorker*. The mass of sophisticated viewers (the new masses) numbering in the millions are turning the turnstiles of museums of every kind. They turn out in greater numbers for King Tut than for Richard Prince, but they turn out. How is Olu Oguibe's ad hominem and tasteless put-down of Ofili relevant to our discussion?

Dan Cameron

Irving's point about certain institutions being more like alternative spaces than "corporatized" museums is one I take to heart, especially at the present moment. The New Museum of Contemporary Art is currently embarking on a capital campaign to enable us to build a new facility on the Bowery, one that will double our size and significantly increase our overhead, programs, and staff. At every step in our process of consulting fund-raising experts, we keep hearing the same advice: Don't even think of becoming more institutional, keep maintaining your cutting-edge position, ignore the mainstream. The risk of losing our identity (and our constituency) seems so vividly real to our potential backers that one can almost detect a substantive anti-"corporatization" backlash in the philanthropic sphere.

Meanwhile, our programming policies remain somewhat unusual in that all program decisions are made by the staff and director, with absolutely no oversight by the board of trustees. This does not mean we have a rubber-stamp board: on the contrary, they are deeply engaged by virtually every aspect of the museum's governance, from fiscal management to the recent merger between the New Museum of Contemporary Art and Rhizome. But the exhibition program is, and has always been, a no-go area at the highest levels of oversight, and over time I've come to appreciate that the New Museum of Contemporary Art's ability to make an impact that is out of proportion to its size and budget has a lot to do with this policy, which is based on trusting the "experts" to do what they do best.

Will any of this change as we set out to build a facility that will push us into the forefront of New York art museums? Can we be edgy and welcoming at the same time? These and related questions have been part of our ongoing staff conversations and meeting agendas for more than a year now, making this symposium an extremely valuable forum for me to be a part of.

Karen Mary Davalos

Thank you, Maurice, for bravely and repeatedly asking us to consider what we mean by art. I wonder if the perspective voiced by Alexander is related to that once held about photography. Here I am careful not to isolate Alexander as the only one with such an interpretation of television, because I think he is naming a widely held position. But the phrase he used, "epitome of monotony," reminded me of the old debate about photography—it is reproducible, not original, etc., and in this repetition it is disqualified as Art.

I agree with the reply by Maurice. Not all of the stuff on television is quality, but we are missing something if we refuse to pay attention to this visual form. Eventually, the museums will recognize the transformation in the visual arts, just as they have with photography. I anticipate that cultural products "not of the hand," such as digital art, specific episodes of a television series, or even giclée prints, will enter the museum collections in the future. I am thinking that it will be difficult to draw audiences to exhibitions of television series, because they have already seen the items on display. I hope someone can correct me, but at this point I am more comfortable stating that the visual arts *collections* will be transformed.

I would also like to address Irving's questions to curators about who decides, who approves, and who pressures you, and why. I am not a curator, but I have served as a consultant to exhibitions of Chicana/o art and culture. In my day job, I am an ethnographer of the same. I have witnessed what I feared most in the museum world: money talks. Allow me to share the nightmare.

In the late 1990s, Cheech Marin (yes, one of the actors from the comic duo known as Cheech and Chong) decided to publicly promote Chicano art. He has acquired one of the largest (but not the largest, to correct the inaccurate claim circulated in all the press releases) private collections of art by people of Mexican descent living in the United States. This is a valid and historically familiar strategy—art patrons have been promoting or producing exhibitions of art for a long time. It is also a familiar method of acquisition. My concern is not with the private collector, but with the public relations firm selected to produce the national traveling duo exhibitions, *Chicano Now: An American Experience*, the cultural component, and *Chicano Visions*, the art component. He paired up with BBH, an events promoter out of San Antonio that has a track record in producing traveling exhibitions for science museums. You know the stuff: the human brain large enough to walk through. The company had a resident Ph.D. on the staff. I am certain he was a scientist.

Consultants included art historians, anthropologists, historians, independent curators, and artists, but this group did not make decisions. It appears that the scientist was the final authority on the exhibition labels and text. My investigation is preliminary, but I suspect that the curator of *Chicano Visions* was given specific instructions that went something like this: select large-scale paintings, avoid controversial content, and color is important. A young graduate student with museum experience and training in cultural anthropology (specifically tourism) was the coordinator for both exhibitions. He was the liaison to BBH. That is, I think he was hired as the filter.

Mr. Marin does own a fine collection of Chicano paintings, and the quality of the show is not my point. Or I should say, I am not willing to offer criticism of the art patron because of the historical significance of the private collector. It would make suspect too many of our institutions of art. I enjoy the contradiction, to revive a claim made earlier in the conference.

In general, the decision-makers were public relations and communications experts, and none had expertise in Chicano art or culture. In fact, in the same month in which the show opened at the San Antonio Museum of Art, the company was purchased by ClearChannel Entertainment. In the transition/merger, the resident scholar was let go.

Mr. Marin's cultural capital was enough to open a space within the museum world of exhibitions, but it has not been enough to stimulate the development of curators or collections. He did have enough influence to gain support for the production of five original digital videos by visual and performing artists: Culture Clash, Gustavo Vasquez, Lourdes Portillo, Robert Rodríguez, and Guillermo Gómez-Peña. The BBH-commissioned videos were displayed in the culture exhibit, *Chicano Now*. (I would again support Maurice's position on the visual arts, because these five works were the best part of the exhibition.)

The real nightmare is this: the audiences are voting with their feet (and pocketbooks in some places), and the show is receiving praise in each city. The exhibition catalogue contains very important art-historical essays. I wonder if curators and researchers will be out of jobs in the future? Or out of the museums of tomorrow? If they work for hire, will this allow them more authority or less? They were not necessary or essential to the example I have provided, so I am pessimistic about the answer to the last question.

Maurice Berger

Irving, I appreciate your historical insights into the notion of the "alternative" art space. They help put a number of things in perspective.

Karen, your points about audience and collecting are really smart and well-taken. I will devote two (two-day) sessions to each of these subjects.

Barbara Buhler Lynes

I want to chime in here to bring the single artist museum into the mix, namely the Georgia O'Keeffe Museum, for which I am curator as well as being the director of the Georgia O'Keeffe Museum Research Center. Obviously this museum was founded not only because O'Keeffe is one of America's best-known and most popular artists, but also because O'Keeffe and her art have long been a business—one dating from the 1920s, when Alfred Stieglitz, O'Keeffe's husband and agent, established a strong market for her work. This translated into her becoming financially independent by the end of that decade, and because she continued to orchestrate and control her market, while living very well for 98 years, she left an estate of $70 million at the time of her death in 1986.

Yet, O'Keeffe's art and life cannot be separated from their particular aesthetic—elegance, simplicity, and the modernist idea of less is more, and its importance to her as an artist. She consistently refused to cooperate with anyone who would not allow her to maintain her aesthetic integrity. For example, she always installed her exhibitions, and there is the famous example of the Whitney Museum of American Art laying out her work for its major retrospective of 1970. She immediately reorganized the pictures, while pointing out to the museum staff as well as to the press that chronological arrangements of her work compromised its visual integrity.

Of course, the O'Keeffe aesthetic paralleled that espoused by Stieglitz, but it's a mistake to think that he controlled her thinking on this issue (his verbal promotion of her work, with which she had fundamental disagreements, is another matter and the subject of a different discussion).

O'Keeffe understood her own power, and because her work has enjoyed tremendous selling power since the 1920s, she established rules for its reproduction, which are perpetuated by the Georgia O'Keeffe Foundation: her work cannot be cropped; reproduced as a detail; guttered; bled; reproduced with words superimposed on the image; and never reproduced in three-dimensional formats, such as on mouse pads, aprons, and hot pads, to name only a few.

Our mission is to perpetuate O'Keeffe's artistic legacy, and we do so through the usual business options—exhibitions, education programs, and publications. Many of our exhibitions present O'Keeffe's work with that of her contemporaries so that our visitors come to a new awareness of her place in the history of American Modernism, and any O'Keeffe exhibition we organize is based on new scholarly research and offers new perspectives on her achievement. Of course, we could mount more "popular" exhibitions, such as one similar to a display of the Jackie Onassis wardrobe that drew huge audiences at the Metropolitan Museum of Art, as we own all of O'Keeffe's clothes, but we feel compelled to resist this and similar kinds of commercialization because we don't think of it as art and prefer to hope that the O'Keeffe aesthetic can effectively guide our business sense.

Jonathan P. Binstock

Museums don't have to worry about going beyond received ideas of art. Artists already do this for them. It is up to contemporary curators (and their directors) to be receptive to what contemporary artists are making. As David Ross wrote on the previous topic, this is an "era in which the institution and living artists are active coconspirators." Art and entertainment are already all mixed up. Video, film, and computers in the galleries are readily linked to television, movies, the Internet, and other forms of mass entertainment. Museum-goers play games, fiddle with Palm Pilots, and so forth. If you think Bugs Bunny is brilliant, well, I'm here to tell you he's available for display in a variety of art forms, albeit manipulated in some way or another. I'm fine with this. Artists are pulling museums along, as they always have.

This is not to say that kunsthalles and general museums should show television shows and be done with it. Why should art museums show episodes of *Bugs Bunny*, *The Simpsons*, or *The Sopranos*, or, worse yet, archive these things when the functional, profitable corporate world is already doing this for us? I have my own "archive" of Soprano DVDs at home. It's not that I can't see exhibiting this material and collecting it when appropriate, for an exhibition or a given institution—The Jewish Museum is an excellent case in point. If The Jewish Museum has a Sopranos episode or two, I'm sure these episodes relate to that institution's mission. (As Irving Sandler and others have asked, what kind of museums are we talking about?) But for a kunsthalle or general art museum to go down this road would be disastrous.

Art is a relative term, but it cannot and will not be relativized out of existence—a line of thinking throughout this symposium. Capitalism and the preservation of class status via taste are predictors of this future. But people who make stuff—artists—whether it is preserved over time or not, will ensure that this future actually comes to pass. In addition to being a super great thing (when it is), art is a way of construing human expression and achievement. It is a tool for thinking in ways that other forms of material culture don't enable us to. If the Corcoran Gallery of Art decides to do a Simpsons retrospective (I hope I'm not giving anyone here at the mothership any bad ideas), what would be the ultimate consequence? I don't think we'd prove that Art with a capital "A" doesn't exist, but I do think that we'd relativize ourselves out of existence. For the best we could hope for from a successful Simpsons exhibition would be a transformative experience: we might actually become Olu's solvent culture mall (I love and hate this image and can't get it out of my head). But then we wouldn't be a museum. Instead of educating, we'd be giving people what they knew they already wanted.

Museums will succeed as non- or for-profit corporations when they have enough money to convince people, through marketing, that they need to experience something they've never experienced before, to have an experience that, perhaps, they can't even imagine. And for you cynics out there, I have particular examples of art in mind, such as Janet Cardiff and George Bures Miller's *Paradise Institute* (2001), one of the Corcoran's latest acquisitions. I won't try to explain the work here. Rather than lose a potentially captive audience I'll leave that task to the marketing executives.

Joan Rosenbaum

I apologize for joining the discussion so late. I've read through the various postings and see that The Jewish Museum, where I'm a director, has been mentioned a few times. While we are indeed a "specialty museum," we identify ourselves as an art museum presenting Jewish culture. Our goal is to reach a general museum-going public—one that is from all cultural backgrounds. Our collections are quite diverse and indeed do include, among the 25,000 works, as Maurice points out, a body of over 4,000 radio and television tapes. They serve as a piece of the puzzle that is The Jewish Museum, and I use that word seriously, as the history of the museum and its exhibitions and collections have embraced a 100-year debate of what should be best collected and shown in such an institution. It is a debate that frankly has helped the institution's survival, as it has kept up a certain dynamism as part of its identity. The mission and how it is best fulfilled is questioned all of the time, and I think that it's a useful model for maintaining an institution's vitality.

Regarding the corporate model and the various threats or opportunities as they have been explored in the various posts, there is no doubt that it is a very tough time in which to run a museum. The economy is very, very much the issue and one that can't be avoided for a minute. It determines whether people feel they can afford to visit, join, or give—whether they have the means or not. The work of a museum director in these times is far less the life of the mind and much more the cultivation and solicitation or development of donors, trustees, and audiences. Yet the whole matter of the institution's program, identity, and direction is a perpetual juggling act. Belt tightening means that curators have to think differently, that directors are more accountable, that there is far less means of making one's program known to potential visitors.

Yes, money matters hugely, but even if one considered the fantasy of a fully subsidized institution by an angel with no self-interest, that museum would still need imaginative and visionary curators or it would fail. It would need brilliant ways to mediate (display, interpret, present) art to a public filled with an extraordinary variety of expectations about what they will see, feel, learn once in this place—this museum. Even with all of that, what is shown, written about, collected may still not be terribly appealing to a huge number of people, and perhaps they would need something that takes them by the hand and brings them through the door so they feel comfortable, and so they might come back for something different.

For some museums this is indeed the Monet or Chagall exhibition. And for some it could be an exhibition about the Simpsons. Why not mount an exhibition about this clever TV show curated by a smart cultural commentator? The exhibition might provide a kind of analysis and perspective that a TV viewer may never have considered. It might turn out to give visitors some insight into all of the TV they watch and the endless barrage of popular culture that surrounds them.

Yes, in response to prior postings, the Guggenheim franchises, Dia Beacon, and the Tate Modern are tourist magnets that change a landscape and local economy yet are frightening in their kind of imperial vision. And yes, one should worry about the trend to make architectural wonders that are monuments to civic pride yet have second-rate galleries and have run out of money for an interesting exhibition program. But, in spite of these concerns, I have faith in the tremendous variety of human impulses that generate museums and their followings. Even when some of the trends are horrifying, at the same time there seem to be more jewel-like museums such as the International Center of Photography, the Center for Contemporary Culture in Barcelona, or fabulous exhibitions such as the recent show at the List Center at MIT, and an increasing number of new alternative spaces and university art museums. Finally there is always, as evidenced in this forum, a constant flow of new critical thinking to inform the imaginative curator and the brave director. Have courage!

Maurice Berger

I very much appreciate the personal tone of Barbara's and Joan's posts. They both suggest that theory can go so far before the reality of practice sets in.

And Jonathan: Once again, the point of my argument about television is *not* that its embrace would or should be appropriate to every art museum. Rather, I am concerned about what I suspect are disciplinary boundaries that are too narrow and tradition bound. Actually, I think Joan summed it up beautifully: a range of this kind of disciplinary tweaking is possible, but may well not be appropriate to most if not many art institutions.

Mary Kelly

I would like to jump into the fray with a few observations about the impact of the "corporate museum" on artists who exhibit in that context. As many have pointed out already, the corporate museum is neither new, nor hegemonic, but the way its transformations (and contradictions as Donna De Salvo insists) have been negotiated in practice is perhaps symptomatic of an ideological divide recurrent in the modern museum discourse since at least the 1850s. It was Olu Oguibe, I think, who mentioned the Crystal Palace as a precedent for the culture mall, but at the same time, the British Museum, for example, maintained a commitment to clutter and commentary, that is, to educating the "good citizen," and now, the Tate Modern offers a solution to the long-standing institutional predicament: entertainment on the one hand—the Great Hall engulfing the viewer in a spectacle of monumental (empty) space; pedagogy on the other—the galleries, small didactically ordered (claustrophobic) space. The architecture's symbolism, as George Baker suggested, speaks of different referents, in this case, all at once.

According to most of the panelists, the corporate aspirations of the museum are intimately linked to spectacle architecture and, I would add, to cinema, which is the dominant cultural form of our time. The museum's architecture, in the sense of its spatiotemporal disposition, modes of passage, codes of display, is the first, or at least most obvious, negotiation involved in exhibiting, and one strategy has been concerned with scale—larger objects (think of [Louise] Bourgeois's spider in the Great Hall) or complex systems ([Tim] Hawkinson, Mass MoCA), but even more importantly, the concern with "affect" (i.e., sock-it-to-'em impact) which has produced a diverse genre of immersive installations ([Bill] Viola at the J. Paul Getty Museum: art, architecture, and affect in perfect cinematic synch).

Alternatively, artists have engaged that negotiation critically, in fact, since the 1960s, initially focusing on the institution in its phenomenal forms; later, defining it in terms of discursive practices and specific sites; finally as the question of agency, blurring the line between artist and curator, as Barbara Kirshenblatt-Gimblett put it. I am not suggesting that one is a more appropriate response than the other, or that architects and curators, as well as artists, have not addressed this issue consistently and intelligently; rather, that these practices, seen in the wider scope of what we have been calling "corporate culture," reproduce the institutional dilemma at the level of reception. We are either entertainers (weird, shocking) or good citizens (dry, academic)—designations most artists would reject. Perhaps I am unusually pessimistic because the Terminator has prevailed over the good citizens of California in the recall election, but at this point, I would be more likely to opt for Miwon Kwon's "poetic experience fostering speculation," rather than the Simpsons, as an antidote.

Mark Alice Durant

Growing up in a working-class suburb of Boston in the mid-to-late 1960s, with barely a book in the house, I first discovered the public library. By the time I could negotiate public transportation alone, I had found the Museum of Fine Arts, Boston. No one in my family had ever visited this (or any other up to that point) museum. I certainly did not approach the Egyptian mummies,

Colonial furniture, or [James McNeil] Whistler paintings with anything that could be described as a critical eye. I was full of gratitude and awe and could not imagine that there would ever be enough time to uncover all of the wonders of those seemingly endless rooms. I am still grateful for those pleasures and opportunities to bask in the auras of fanciful things. The price of admission? Something less than $3, I believe.

The Museum of Fine Arts, Boston, was a crusty old place; as I got older and fancied myself an artist, my attitude grew adolescently hostile and my visits became less frequent: Where is the life? Where is the Art of Now! And how did they get their hands on all those mummies anyway?

I visited the Boston MFA again relatively recently, a nice Adam Fuss show (the art of now), a new wing with lots of light, a nice café, a big bookstore. There seemed to be more people there than I remember from my youth. The admission fee: $12 plus another $5 to see a special exhibition. Had I not been visiting like a tourist to my old hometown I would never have paid that admission price, and it goes without saying that my brothers and their children do not attend—it never even occurs to them.

My point is that first, let us not forget that museums, for all of their contradictions and even despite themselves, have served democratic or empowering impulses. Wondering/wandering boys and girls from provinces and ghettos do sometimes find their way into the larger world via the portals of museums. Yes, what gets presented and how it is presented is important, but access is more fundamental. And how to foster greater access? First, lower the price of admission. Second, take whatever money is left of the NEA and put it to fully funding art education in public schools, and in a generation you will have museum galleries full of high school students arguing the historical merits of Matthew Barney and Kara Walker.

Simon Leung

I enter the discussion late, but here are some observations: The first speaks to class and more importantly "capital" and what Stefano touched on—the interests of the trustees v. the other professionals who make art museums possible (curators, educators, historians, critics, artists).

I would like to focus on the issue of the corporatization of museums via a different route. One of the problems I see in focusing on museums as corporations and debating the perceived financial or even pedagogical success of museums based on criteria we use to discuss corporations is that we already know the results of the comparison: that there is no "real comparison"; that museums will only fail as profit-making corporations because there is no "real profit" to be made; that museums that succumb to the corporate motivation toward audience development for profit-oriented purposes will only fail as educational institutions because they don't care about "art"; that the museum's original function and historical mission is much more noble than the goal of the masters of capital, etc., and now that's changed because we are succumbing to the ubiquitous logic of global capitalism.

But we don't necessarily need to invoke Pierre Bourdieu to note that museums have always been the flip side to, the idealized and codependent banner of, the riches gained by the engine of capital, and modern art has always been tied to a patronage that comes from the ruling class—historically the new bourgeoisie. In other words, museums have always been corporate entities: they are the repositories of *Cultural Capital* guaranteed by real capital.

If we speak of the corporatization of the museum, aren't we really talking about the difference between various styles of the corporate already in place? That is, the difference between the Rockefellers (who had the sophistication and missionary zeal to transform the violence of capital into a discourse of cultural enlightenment) and a Charles Saatchi (whose sophistication lies precisely in the manipulation of public taste for the sign of '80s/'90s-style global capitalism—the commodification of '60s/'70s dissent into luxury goods)? And if we are talking about museums as "enlightened" institutions, we must remind ourselves of the many avant-garde traditions that have challenged the "proper" role of art as oppressively privileged sites of idealization. What we don't like is not the sign of the corporate in the museum, but the way in which museums no longer bother to disguise its violence.

If I hear Miwon correctly, what is at stake for her is the erosion of the ground that guaranteed the "speculation, skepticism, and wonder" that a complex art experience provides (and therefore Miwon's melancholic nostalgia for "Art" strikes a nerve with Alex, Stefano, and Mary). Some of us feel that there is truly no place left to withdraw from the constant attack of corporate culture from our lives, and yes, sadly—for I too live in California—the grip of the Terminator. But if this "erosion" indeed does take place, haven't we heard it, seen it before? That is, aren't those of us defending art with a capital "A," whether we admit it or not, partaking in an idealized notion of the enlightened public sphere? We "mourn" it because it retreats from us, because the societal mechanisms that make this public sphere possible in the first place—industrial capitalism—also contaminate, vulgarize, and yes, "corporatize" our contemporary aesthetic experiences: going to the museum isn't what it used to be.

But then the question is, what did it used to be? High modernists such as [Jürgen] Habermas, [Theodor] Adorno, [Clement] Greenberg all defended the post-enlightenment corollary to democracy, the public sphere. Michael Fried, writing in 1967, famously lamented the loss of a state of "grace" in the face of the incursion of minimalism. The list goes on. But if I stand on the side of "Art," and I do, certainly in my "taste" (forgive me but I've never been into the Simpsons), I still cannot abide a nostalgic model of "pre-corporate" enlightened viewership grounded in aesthetic withdrawal (I understand that's not what most of us are saying, but that argument gains ground in politically distressing times).

As Mary notes, artists have negotiated with this necessary institutional violence that founds the condition of the museological experience at least since the 1960s. These were, to put it simplistically, avant-garde practices that one can argue grew out of the historical criterion we place on serious cultural practices—be it abstract painting or more functionally directed revolutionary aesthetic forms. To my mind, the limits of the various site-specific or institutional critique enterprises do not necessarily mean that they fail in the face of the corporate refortification of capital. The best work in this historical vein has never been mere entertainment, nor the academic display of the passion of the good citizen.

I wonder if we can retool our understanding of the corporate this way: the corporatized museum is a site of *conflict*—a theater of war. Yes, exactly, Stefano—the trustees and you don't share the same values—and that, I would say, is not only a good thing, but a necessary condition of the private museum. I agree with Miwon that corporate-style populism is not only politically regressive, but convulses the body politic into a form of instrumentality that is ideologically coercive. However, I also believe that it is problematic to idealize a former cohesion that is at best illusory—however pessimistic we may feel.

As someone whose primary identification as a public person

has been tied to art for some 20-odd years, I have grown to think of the museum as this site of conflict because a museum has always been, and remains for me, a place to renegotiate subjectivity; and that may include dispelling the idealized versions of the self I hold most dear. With this in mind, I hope to further address the logical extension of this conflict zone—the corporatization of the artist.

Maurice Berger

Mark, you wrote: "My point is that first, let us not forget that museums, for all of their contradictions and even despite themselves, have served democratic or empowering impulses. Wondering/wandering boys and girls from provinces and ghettos do sometimes find their way into the larger world via the portals of museums. Yes, what gets presented and how it is presented is important, but access is more fundamental. And how to foster greater access? First, lower the price of admission. Second, take whatever money is left of the NEA and put it to fully funding art education in public schools, and in a generation you will have museum galleries full of high school students arguing the historical merits of Matthew Barney and Kara Walker."

Mark, this is a very important point to my mind. Museums do not just edify the old (like us, I'm afraid). They can also inspire, provoke, and influence young people. I, too, having grown up in a low-income housing project, know just how powerful this formative contact with art and its institutions can be. Later in the conference, I will devote two sessions—one on "audience," the other on museum "education"—that I hope will allow us to discuss the issue more fully.

Simon, you wrote: "I wonder if we can retool our understanding of the corporate this way: the corporatized museum is a site of *conflict*—a theater of war. Yes, exactly, Stefano—the trustees and you don't share the same values—and that, I would say, is not only a good thing, but a necessary condition of the private museum."

At some point in the conference I would love it if you could flesh out this notion of "conflict" and its structural and ideological implications for museological change.

Jennifer González

I have been reading the contributions of participants with much interest. Taken together, George Baker's initial post concerning the definition of the museum public and Olu Oguibe's observation that museums have always been tied to the history of the production of wealth allow us to consider how philanthropy and hegemony are inextricably linked in the production, dissemination, and repression of "public" knowledge.

As we are well aware, museums are frequently the site of epistemological battles precisely because they provide the institutional framework for the intersection of different, imaginary publics. They are far from disinterested in the way they allow these publics to interact with each other, with images and with objects. This is also true of systems of regulatory law.

One ongoing challenge for museums is how the concept of copyright will shape an ever-expanding field of visual discourse.

How will the "public" have access to archives, to images, and to objects in museums that are, or that are becoming, private corporations? Today's discussion addressed a number of concerns related to the corporate transformation of museums, such as the ways in which museums employ marketing tools for the purpose of economic survival, or reflect mechanisms of corporate style and branding.

How does the increasing identification of the museum with a corporation ensure that the institution will view its holdings as scarce assets that produce value, rather than as cultural treasures held in trust for an imagined community called "the public"? Even if the latter goal seems historically outdated and problematic, an ideological shift away from this essentially philanthropic if not disinterested position—a shift which has been developing over the last several decades—may have unexpected consequences.

Could the corporate museum of the future require, for example, that I pay different fees to see different works of art? Might my examination of a painting by [Francisco] Goya be limited to five minutes unless I can pay for more time? Will my digitally produced catalogues or postcards of favorite works of art have expiration dates? In short, when will the ideas of copyright be expanded into a new regime that regulates what might be called viewing rights (as is already happening on the Internet)? And to what degree is this logic already at work in museums that charge high admissions and membership fees and that issue special-event tickets?

A parallel concern is that the inevitability of capitalism, which seems to take hold in every avenue of human endeavor as Olu Oguibe suggests, has also had an increasingly tangible impact on the rights of artists. Last week I spoke on a panel with the artist Christian Marclay and copyright lawyer Lawrence Lessig at the San Francisco Museum of Modern Art. We were discussing the increasingly chilly corporate and legal climate within which sound art and forms of visual montage are becoming more difficult to produce and exhibit without expensive permissions of various kinds.

Lessig pointed out that U.S. law protects free enterprise, free markets, and even free speech (theoretically) but not free "culture." It became clear in our discussion that Marclay's installation piece *Video Quartet* (which stages a montage of video clips from popular Hollywood cinema) appeared to be immune from some of the aggressive tactics currently taken by corporations against copyright infringement because of its placement in the museum context as a work of art. Of course this tactic did not protect [Andy] Warhol's use of Mickey Mouse. Nevertheless, I think it is possible that museums may have a rather interesting and perhaps pivotal role to play in the future of what will probably be called the "copyright wars."

■ ■ ■

The Politics of Collecting

10 – 11 October 2003

Maurice Berger

Donna De Salvo in an earlier post yesterday reminded us that one difference between certain types of museums is that some collect and others do not. I would like to spend the next two days talking about the former. What does it mean to build a collection?

The issue of collection building raises many questions: Who makes the decisions to acquire works of art? Who decides which works befit a museum's collection—the director, curators, trustees, or collection committees composed of trustees and scholars? To what extent is it a conflict of interest for trustees (who may foot the bill for these purchases and who may own significant art collections) to decide what makes it into a museum's collection? Who, in the end, is best qualified to make this decision?

Indeed, one might ask what is the purpose of a permanent collection? To archive objects in an attempt to record art history? To establish standards of taste for the art world and the art historical community? To amass wealth (or as George King wrote yesterday, critically of course, to build "assets")?

These questions in turn lead to others about the role of collections and the public's and scholars' access to them. Who does the collection serve? To what extent is access to a permanent collection an important part of the museum's function to educate? And what of the collection's relationship to the museum's general audience—to what extent and how should it be made available to them?

Finally, what do you imagine to be the future of collection building? Can radical shifts in the policy of building a museum's permanent collection alter the very nature and ideology of the museum?

Michele Wallace

I do not teach art history. I am not an artist nor a museum administrator nor an art critic. Nor am I a member of any official employment category directly related to the constituent elements of an art museum. I think it only fair to mention, however, that I am the daughter of Faith Ringgold, one of the most highly recognized and accomplished black artists alive today. I am just coming back from having celebrated her 73rd birthday on October 8th at her lovely home and studio in Englewood, New Jersey. Despite her senior citizen status on public transportation and in movie theaters, Faith is far from retirement mode. In fact, she has never been more productive or worked harder. Part of that has to do with how much she loves to do her work, but the other part of it has to do with how long and how hard she has had to struggle to get to her present status in the art world, which is at the top.

What galls me, however, is that the top she currently occupies (and I think I can show how this is relevant and useful to our current discussion) is not the real top but an entirely different plateau from the real top, which is still reserved exclusively for white male painters (and some sculptors) generally of a Western European or North American background and education. Today, Faith's art (I believe) is reasonably well represented in most of the major museum collections in the United States and in a range of museums in other countries. But some of the most prominent collections have been depressingly sluggish and/or reluctant about publicly displaying the works they own. For instance, the *Street Story Quilt* (1985), which has been owned by the Metropolitan Museum of Art since 1990, was only just recently placed on public display for the first time in the Lila Acheson Wallace Wing of Modern Art in May of 2003, owing almost entirely to the pressures exerted by a newly formed multicultural committee as an action subgroup of the Board of Directors. This group is hard at work attempting to change, from the inside out, the unwritten exhibition practices of museums concerning works by artists of color. The Guggenheim Museum owns *Tar Beach* [1988], which I am told it sometimes quietly places on display without notice, partly as a consequence of the fact that children regularly appear there asking to see it. The painting is featured in a very popular children's book written by Faith, and children turn out to be the most loyal fans of all. Even once they grow up, they never forget the images and narratives that nurtured their emotional, spiritual, and intellectual development, thank god. Those who are interested in being supportive should make the halls of the Metropolitan Museum of Art and the cylindrical stratosphere of the Guggenheim Museum a regular part of their itinerary. I think we should make it our business to know what works by artists of color and (some) women and (some) gay artists are in these collections, and if we feel as though we aren't seeing as much of them as we might like, we should ask for these works by the name of the artist at the information desk, in order to let them know how we feel about this. I think the upper administration thinks it makes absolutely no difference to us who they show and don't show, and that they are equally willing to commend themselves on our behalf for their blockbuster successes. I know most of Faith's major paintings intimately, and yet when I saw *Street Story Quilt*, it surprised me. I had never seen it before because it was completed around the time I went to teach at the University of Oklahoma in Norman in 1985, and I didn't fully return to New York until 1989, soon after which the Metropolitan bought it and locked it away. Faith and I made a special trip into the city just to see it on Mother's Day. It was like the missing link, the one you needed to see in order to understand all the quilts that had come before, since she did the first one with the help of my grandmother, Mme. Willli Posey, to the most recent ones, which are part of her ongoing *Jazz* series.

I think art museums need desperately to know how deeply many of us care about the artists we study and love. They need to know that there is an informed public out here who would like to see more of the works by Romare Bearden, Horace Pippin, Wifredo Lam, William Johnson, Bob Blackburn, Jacob Lawrence (just to name six widely collected black artists, although all of them are dead) even when it isn't Black History Month, or when there isn't some corporation-sponsored multicultural alternative fest. For those museums with collections, the buying of certain works is one step (and we know that most of the buying and selling doesn't concern living artists at all)—a step they are ever so reluctant to take in the first place when it comes to artists of color, despite the fact that they can generally acquire a work of art by a "black" artist for anywhere (my guesstimate) from one-tenth to one-twentieth of the price of a commensurate work of art by a "white" artist, and that is assuming, of course, that the black artist is working in the more traditional media of painting or sculpture. If he or she is working in the more nouveau, more fashionable precincts of conceptual or installation art (of course there are the notable exceptions such as David Hammons), the price takes a nosedive once again (especially if the artist is also a woman and/or gay) and may not include much more than the cost of paying the artist to come to town for the weekend, install, and attend the opening. When the exhibition is over, unbelievably, the entire thing may be scraped from the walls and dumped in the garbage. Contrary to the misguided notion that more ephemeral artistic materials translate in our world into something with a more revolutionary or politically subversive aura (as opposed to the sanctity of the artistic object prior to the age of mechanical reproduction), what we are witnessing here is a replay of the folk wisdom I grew up with: nothing from nothing leaves nothing! I love art museums. I have never been in an art museum I didn't like. They are my favorite places to be, the places where I feel most comfortable, perhaps because I began to be a regular visitor of museums from such an early age with Faith who was then a student of art. For me, museums (I would have to include the Museum of Natural History in this formulation, since it has more than its fair share of art objects) are like temples and temples are like museums. As a black woman, it always seemed to me to be a door that stood open, and welcoming, compared to some of the other racial barriers in society.

In this culture (or at least the part of it I grew up in—I am 51 now!), we worship aesthetic mastery, particularly in art and music, and the older I get, the less of a problem I have with that. Of course, as I recently heard somebody say, all organized religion is for purposes of domination and imperialism. I guess, for that matter, the same is true of corporate markets. On the other hand, it seems to me the only thing to argue about when it comes to the future of museums is that they will profit precisely to the degree to which they can be made to reflect the very best and brightest of our accumulative aesthetic visions and our ethical standards for educating the young and providing the full grown with edifying and robust entertainment.

Donna De Salvo

The collection is a core part of institutional memory. Once an object has entered into it, it cannot be erased (unless the museum deaccessions or the work implodes due to inherent vice). This is why collections are so important. The temporary exhibition serves one purpose, and has one kind of impact; however, the collection is something else. Once a work has been acquired by a museum, it becomes a permanent part of a history as constructed by that particular institution.

Now, I agree with Michele that just because a work is in a collection, there is no guarantee that it will be exhibited. The Museum of Modern Art, for instance, has some extraordinary works by artists from Mexico and South America. Many of these were acquired during [Alfred] Barr's tenure, but not routinely shown. Such was the case with Frida Kahlo's paintings and drawings, which were more often exhibited as loans to other institutions.

However, this tide has begun to change, and along those lines, the Metropolitan Museum of Art committee sounds promising.

This is why the first step—the acquisition of a work—is the most critical. If the work is not there to begin with, you cannot move it to the next step—to put it on display. As we all are aware, there are many people who are part of this process, and the politics of these relationships is something I am sure we will explore over the next two days. More often than not, though, a curator or several working together are able to drive the process forward, or at least advocate on behalf of an acquisition. They must then convince many people, not least of which are the director and funding sources (committees, individuals, etc.), before the work can be submitted to the board of trustees for final approval. This entire process, at least in my experience, is rarely linear and can be a bit like a plate-spinning act.

It is very moving to read Michele's account of children requesting that a particular work of art be put on display. It reinforces the museum's role as a facilitator between artist and public. It also raises the fundamental question—who are we collecting for?

I often think about the early beginnings of museums, at least in the U.S. Many started life as an annex to a library or university, thus making clear their educational remit. Museums today have so many more challenges, not least of which are how they respond to artistic developments that include installation-based work. Is there anything useful to be recovered from these old models?

Many museums, Tate Modern being one of them, have moved away from a chronological hang to explore multiple stories and narratives. If the collection is the institutional memory of a museum, does it also function as one view of a cultural history? If so, what is the relationship between all these museums in constructing a "global" perspective?

Olu Oguibe

Maurice, let me pick up one or two things from the last topic that are relevant to the present discussion, and note first that we have had an artist's voice in the conference all along because I certainly speak as an artist irrespective of the other hats I wear as a theorist and art historian. I know the museum from the distance of what David Ross would call a stakeholder, as both part of the public and an interested party—someone who visits museums as a spectator, organizes exhibitions for museums as a collaborator, as well as exhibits in museums as an artist. This detail—I dare not say distinction—certainly informs my experience of and attitude to museums and museum practices.

I should mention, also, that I love *The Simpsons*, even *King of the Hill*, and that I find both far more profound than a great deal of contemporary art that I come across as a curator. This point is relevant to the extent that it would certainly indicate my stance on what to collect, preserve, or promote were I on a museum board. I do not mean to imply that profundity would necessarily be my sole or decisive criterion in such a position, but just to underline the fact that it does exist in forms often derided and avoided by orthodox arbiters of Taste.

One other point that ought to be obvious from my contributions so far is that I am reluctant to associate the museum—any museum—with the democratic ideal, except to the extent that we understand democracy only in its original, Greek inflexion, reserved, that is, for certain classes. This is not simply historically determined; it is also inherent in the essentially corporate nature of all museums, including the independent "alternative space." Ultimately, all decisions come from within the institution or space, rather than outside it, and institutions may tolerate only dispositions that are not inimical to their internal dynamics and survival.

That the museum is essentially not a democratic institution, neither in its constitution, administrative structure, nor regular disposition, is necessarily reflected in the choices and agenda made manifest in the museum collection. In other words, a museum will collect and promote what it chooses to collect and promote.

How power relations within the museum determine its collection, in other words who, specifically, has the final word, differs from museum to museum, obviously, as from one administrative regime to another. Instances of directors and curators let go or forced to resign because of "artistic differences" between them and the ultimate power brokers within a museum are quite commonplace. In some cases these "artistic" differences revolve around what to collect or display. However, in many cases curators, directors, and their hired consultants are just as influential in determining what to purchase or receive, and how to treat it once procured, and many have used their position to promote specific and sometimes not entirely rational interests. For a museum that collects, what to collect obviously strikes at the heart of its purpose and direction, and respective interests stake their claims on this. "Conflict of interest" is not a term that bears much weight in museum culture.

Any public expectations regarding the breadth and configuration of a museum's collection may only be a matter of right with regard to museums that receive public fiscal support. In such cases, accountability to the public is not only logical but indeed ought to be statutory, and that accountability extends to every aspect of the museum's operation including its collecting practices. With regard to museums that do not receive public, that is to say, state or municipal, fiscal support, such expectations are merely moral, and one need not dwell on them.

What is remarkable is that historically American and European museums that routinely receive public fiscal support have also doggedly failed to recognize and reflect in their collecting practices the cultural diversity in the source of that support. The result is that certain constituencies—as part of a tax-paying or gambling public—are perpetually and disingenuously robbed of the logical proceeds of their contributions to museums by seldom having artists from such constituencies, or work that speaks to or is of direct relevance to them, admitted into the museum collection. In America more than Europe, this has been cause for concern and public outcry since the early 1970s when Howardena Pindell and others took rather radical steps to bring this pattern to public attention and paid dearly for it with their careers. In France a public challenge of that magnitude would be as ground-shaking as the Revolution of '68.

It does no good to protest and say we have all heard this before; it is, indeed, irresponsible so to speak, because it matters little how often we have heard it as long as concrete and significant change is not evident. For those who have only modest knowledge of how museums operate, Michele Wallace's narrative of current struggles within museums to allow certain acquisitions display opportunity is rather quite revealing. The resilient resistance—or shall we say resentment—within our major collecting museums toward material from certain constituencies points to a shocking residue still lodged at the heart of our society and, perhaps more remarkably, our much beloved bastions of civility and Taste. The anecdotal schoolchild from the low-earning family in the Projects may have been allowed in the museum on group excursions, but did the schoolchild know what was withheld or hidden?

Museums that are located within and oriented toward

specific communities in our cities are no less implicated in such practices, and power tussles to make their collections more reflective of the complexity of the communities that they serve are no less frequent.

One speaks of the need for concrete and significant change. This would require a fundamental shift in thinking that comes not so much from a liberal change of heart as from a cold and calculating acceptance of the inherent logic of change. One need not be a bleeding-heart advocate of market forces to find compelling appeal in the power of the profit motive to instigate such shifts where liberal pretenses have routinely failed. While the management and advisory boards of orthodox museums constrict themselves to preserving and promoting the same narrow sliver of culture that they have historically procured and promoted, the museum of tomorrow—the culture mall—like cinema, publishing, network television, and the fashion industry will embrace and effect this shift not only because it is logical, but also because it makes economic sense.

May I add rather quickly that when one speaks of publicly funded museum collections reflecting the breadth and complexity of the public that partly funds them, this does not imply or demand a "Global Perspective," as Donna puts it, as much as a simple, honest reflection of the diversity of London's tax-paying public since the Slavery Abolition Act of 1833, for instance, which is asking no more than that they get the local perspective right.

Maurice Berger

Olu, you wrote: "It does no good to protest and say we have all heard this before; it is, indeed, irresponsible so to speak, because it matters little how often we have heard it as long as concrete and significant change is not evident. For those who have only modest knowledge of how museums operate, Michele Wallace's narrative of current struggles within museums to allow certain acquisitions display opportunity is rather quite revealing."

Beautifully said. With due respect to David Ross's first post, I do think there's plenty of room for further discussion and analysis of the politics *and* economics of the museum. This is so, I think, because things are remarkably slow to change. A psychoanalyst welcomes the graduation of a patient only *after* the cure has worked its way through the patient's psyche and is reflected in healthy changes in actions and behavior. The museum is not ready to be discharged from its inherent responsibility (at least to my mind) to "look at itself." The words in quotation are appropriated from a remarkable 1992 exhibition organized by Donna De Salvo at the Parrish Art Museum: *Past Imperfect: A Museum Looks at Itself.* (Later in the conference, I'll begin a two-day topic with discussion of the show.)

Alan Wallach

To respond to one of Maurice's questions about access to the permanent collection and the museum's "function to educate" one might begin by asking: Is education the museum's actual function?

In their formative years in the 19th century, American art museums drew upon the South Kensington model. Museums took education as their primary mission. They would educate, which is to say acculturate and Americanize, a largely immigrant and working-class public. However, beginning about 1900, with robber barons like J. P. Morgan increasingly in control, major U.S. art museums acquired the means to focus on collecting masterpieces. Although they never abandoned their pretensions to public education, education often became the least of the museum's concerns. Or rather, with the rise of official formalism—the belief that the work of art can speak for itself and therefore can be appreciated by anyone—American art museums could simply throw open their doors and claim that anyone could enjoy the works on display. They thus became in practice efficient engines of social and cultural exclusion even as they argued that the art was a public good.

In the latest phase of their history, which began in the 1960s, American art museums have made more noise about education. Granting agencies piously require an educational component in all grant proposals. Money is usually available for certain forms of education, e.g., to frog-march ghetto schoolchildren through the collections. Yet as Vera Zolberg has insisted, museum education remains a "devalued profession." Museum directors rarely boast about what they have done for public education. Instead, they remember above all the works acquired on their watch.

Education and acquisition for the permanent collection are thus valued very differently within the culture of the museum. New acquisitions can be shamelessly publicized and exploited. I recall the hullabaloo surrounding the Metropolitan Museum of Art's acquisition in 1961 of Rembrandt's *Aristotle Contemplating the Bust of Homer.* Attendance rose dramatically. People lined up to see a million-dollar painting while upstairs the Dutch galleries featuring dozens of Rembrandts remained virtually empty. Thus the Rembrandt was fetishized, an object that stood for the unfathomable mystery of art and money.

The incident was symptomatic of the status of museums' permanent collections. As at the Metropolitan, we encounter the usual treasure-house sort of display—Art as masterpiece, as proof of ineffable genius, removed from any sort of historical context and inaccessible to those without the necessary background or habitus.

I am aware of a few bright spots, at least when it comes to American art—the Luce Foundation funded galleries that take American works out of storage and put them on permanent display along with a good deal of didactic material; a growing interest in exhibiting the American collection in a way that evokes the works' relation to their historical contexts (Newark Museum of Art, Brooklyn Museum of Art, the Detroit Institute of Arts). Still, I could be wrong to be so pessimistic. Indeed, one might conclude that museum education flourishes as never before given the eagerness with which museums ply visitors with brochures, audioguides, videos, computer stations, etc.

And yet I do remain skeptical. Museum culture has not significantly changed during the last 30 or so years (although certain trends might be noted). Nor has the museum audience. The percentage of the population that voluntarily visits art museums in the U.S. and in Europe remains at 20%—and that 20% is not surprisingly the best educated, which is to say the most affluent portion of the population.

One might argue that a democratic society is obliged to democratize art. I agree. But art in our society has long been associated with hierarchy. Indeed Bourdieu's argument regarding "distinction," although now in need of serious modification, still applies. And a hierarchical society—a society based upon the structural division between classes—cannot also be a democratic society. Thus the struggle to democratize art can only be a feature of the overall struggle for democracy—a struggle which these days we seem to be losing.

Michele Wallace

There are many interesting things about Donna's line of inquiry relevant to my own. I think it is appropriate to the mandate of those of us who wish to make this country a better place to want to examine closely the systematics of museum collections, curators, and the corporate involvement in the process. I think she's right about the fact that everything begins with the purchase of the work of art and its placement in the collection, which can actually occur by a number of routes. Moreover, my understanding of the matter is that the likelihood of the purchase depends upon the extent to which collectors are already collecting this artist, the extent to which such collectors are willing to work with museums, and, finally—in regard to the potential for large, well-publicized exhibitions—the degree to which the artist's work can be rendered comfortable with corporate sponsorship and public relations.

I don't think I need to point out that even the most appealing of traditional Afro-American artists can suffer in all three categories, for both obvious and less obvious reasons. Not too many wealthy, high-profile international collectors collect Afro-American art. Every year I get the *Art News* issue on collectors, hoping that might change, but if it has, it is scarcely reflected in their pages. The second problem is the well-off people who do collect Afro-American art. They tend to be black, rich, and totally uninterested in making a contribution to expanding the exhibition presence of Afro-American artists in the major museums. Indeed, there are some really famous cases of high-profile black collectors who refuse not only to lend their works to exhibitions but who make it a policy in general to allow no one who isn't a close friend or family access to the work. From the point of view of the black artist in the collection, this is about as bad as it gets.

With respectful consideration to Olu's desire to see the world's museums become more "democratic" in their exhibition criteria, after years of observing the processes and machinations of museums, galleries, and what might loosely be referred to as the art world (including a wild-and-woolly period in which I accompanied my Mom in a series of street protests and actions against the major museums for their lack of artists of color and women artists in the late '60s and early '70s), I am not convinced that any of the various ways in which democracy works in the real world (which so far has always been far short of the utopian ideal) would contribute substantially to an improvement in museum practice.

I do think, however, that the children in the museums can be a powerful force for changes at all levels. As I understand it, most major museums have expanded their educational programs in particular to encompass school children, who are shown the collection and given art instruction in special facilities within the museum. So much so that Faith was mentioning to me that she is getting worried about the various children's museums, whose mandate it is to do much the same thing and who may be getting squeezed out by this competition for funds with the major adult museums. I think this process, however, can be the most powerful force for change because the thing that needs to happen is that children, particularly children of color, particularly poor children, need to be conversant in art history and the culture of museums, in order not only to become artists but also to become art educators, curators, museum administrators. The reason I advocate the world's children coming into the museums is because this is their cultural legacy. This is their chance to access in microcosm one of the most instructive narratives concerning the development of civilization and empire through the ages. They need to know it because the story hasn't stopped. It continues.

Jennifer González

Those participating in this symposium are well aware that the history of collecting in the United States and Europe cannot be separated from the history of colonization. Yet this rather obvious observation remains, like others that "we have all heard before," easily dismissed as a serious subject of study by theorists and museum institutions themselves. It is the silently acknowledged taboo subject that ruffles the feathers of the institutional elite because it is the material evidence of their own hegemony. For this reason collections are jealously guarded, but their origin stories remain largely unexamined.

Despite a flourishing body of scholarship that has appeared over the past two decades on early cabinets of curiosity, the origins of museums and princely collections, scant attention has been paid to the relation between the rise of these collections and the "age of discovery" with which they were coincident. It is well documented that objects from the Americas and other parts of the globe graced early cabinets and museums. And while some scholars are willing to concede that the age of "wonder" was linked to the age of "discovery," others want to insist that one cannot tie the politics of this epistemological transformation to the simultaneous violence of colonialism and cultural ransacking that followed.

We know that museums are often the repositories of spoils of war. This is true of museums of art as well as museums of anthropology. The Musée du Louvre and the British Museum are classic examples. In this country, the (sometimes bemoaned) Native American Graves

Protection and Repatriation Act was a watershed legal ruling that began an important, if belated, reversal of this long history of colonial acquisition.

Recently, I was lecturing on the theories of Louis Agassiz who hired the daguerreotypist Joseph Zealy to photograph the bodies of African slaves in order to better prove his theory of polygenesis. According to scholar Brian Wallis, Agassiz may have been inspired in this endeavor, at least in part, by the collection of physiologist Samuel Morton, who had amassed 600 human skulls, primarily of Native Americans, that he kept as a collection in Philadelphia. Agassiz found this collection to be a marvelous resource for scientific inquiry, but apparently did not concern himself with how Morton acquired the human skulls.

Although collecting is neither entirely driven nor shaped by pre-existing taxonomies, there is little doubt that the impulse to categorize objects (into movements, styles, types, hierarchies) underlies the institutional logic of collecting. This history is tightly linked with the history of the categorization of flora, fauna, and human species. Insofar as the museum has long been the site where the discourse of human difference has been a primary subject of display, can we be entirely surprised that it has been institutionally slow to change its conception of who counts as an artist and who counts as an anthropological specimen? I submit that scholars have barely scratched the surface of the history of collections and the impact of this history on the contemporary politics of acquisition, exhibition, and archiving.

Nevertheless, many contemporary artists have played a significant role in drawing public attention to the collecting and exhibition practices of museums—both in the past and the present. Fred Wilson's *Mining the Museum* is one key example.

While museum collections are often quite wonderful repositories that preserve and protect, they also serve the purposes of cultural amnesia when their protective function renders invisible both works of art—such as Faith Ringgold's work—and historical evidence. Collections are accretions of institutional identity built up slowly and steadily over time. It is only when the identity of the institution and the identity of its addressee begin to change that the collections and acquisition policies will also change. It is clear from the comments of others who have posted today that this change is tentatively underway.

Karen Mary Davalos

I want to begin by acknowledging the rich commentary and analysis by Michele and Jennifer. I would say, "Ditto."

One addition in three parts. First: The collection practices of the so-called alternative museums for and by Mexican Americans, or Chicanas/os, are not precisely as Olu has implied. Most significantly, the classificatory scheme of the collection is decidedly oppositional. The Mexican Fine Arts Center Museum in Chicago (with an emergent collection less than 15 years old) does not refer to art from ancient civilizations as pre-Hispanic or pre-Colombian, but uses a decolonial referent, pre-Cuauhatémoc, the last emperor of the Aztecs. The Mexican Museum in San Francisco has yet to settle on its classificatory scheme, changing and modifying precisely because the art historical system does not fit the vision they have of the objects in the permanent collection.

Second, the objects themselves are acquired as part of a larger patrimony and simultaneous erasure from the national body, memory, and citizenship. Not to shore up the nation's image of itself. Certainly, someone makes a decision what to collect, and the decision may reinforce hierarchies within the institution. But I would not equate those hierarchies with the ones that have driven public museums in the U.S., as Michele and Jennifer pointed out. They referred to the making of race, class, gender, to name a few hierarchies.

When viewing an object, a Mexican/Chicano visitor at a so-called alternative arts institution for and by Mexicans in the U.S. is not racialized the same way she or he is at the public museum—with all of its colonial and imperialist tendencies. It becomes a personal referent to history, belonging, and group identification. It is that relationship that changes collections in these institutions and makes them dramatically distinct from the ones at the Metropolitan Museum of Art, the Los Angeles County Museum of Art, and on and on. I believe that Michele's example about the children seeking out *Tar Beach* at the Guggenheim is very possibly a similar phenomenon.

Third, and last, the collections of which I speak are somewhat compensatory and transformative at the same time. They are making up for the missing record from the public museums that are not very public after all. And they are transforming how we envision the public, art, and the social position of Mexicans in the U.S. That is, in relation to the collections at public museums that either lock out artists of color or keep them hidden in storage, the collections at Mexican American/Chicano arts institutions are liberatory, democratic, and critical spaces. This can be said of other alternative spaces, but in this case it is the collections that enunciate a racialized critique of American collecting practices inside public museums.

Thanks again to Jennifer and Michele.

Maurice Berger

Jennifer, you wrote: "Those participating in this symposium are well aware that the history of collecting in the United States and Europe cannot be separated from the history of colonization. Yet this rather obvious observation remains, like others that 'we have all heard before' easily dismissed as a serious subject of study by theorists and museum institutions themselves. It is the silently acknowledged taboo subject that ruffles the feathers of the institutional elite because it is the material evidence of their own hegemony. For this reason collections are jealously guarded, but their origin stories remain largely unexamined."

This point, echoed in posts by Karen and Michele, seems crucial to me: power protects itself, always. I would add this: It is not just the fear of losing this hegemony that prevents self-inquiry; it's also the fear of coming face to face with one's own bigotry.

My understanding of the latter allows me to be a bit more sympathetic (but hardly optimistic) about this resistance. The "art world," per se, is probably a lot more liberal (or even socially progressive) than the population at large. Yet, when it comes to the question of race—and the abject exclusion or dismissal of other, "alien" cultures—the art world is not all that different.

The other day, I found myself "defending" Toni Morrison to a young writer friend of mine. What an absurd situation—one of our nation's greatest writers and critical thinkers, a Nobel laureate no less. After a while, I realized that it was not the question of Morrison's "artistic" merit per se that *was* driving our argument. (Though it was the subject of our debate.) Race, or rather the irrelevancy of the complex cultural and intellectual idioms inherent to Morrison's writings to a guy interested only in Michael Cunningham and Dale Peck, was at the root of our disagreement. The young man was white and middle class. When I asked him to name his favorite writers, not a single one deviated from the tribe (with respect to gender *and* race, I might add).

Yet, in some sense, this tribalism embarrasses and troubles many of us—especially in an art world that thrives on tweaking the norm, pushing the envelope, and blurring boundaries. To some extent, the art world has opened up to such cross-cultural possibilities, but these gestures still feel to me like multiculturalism without teeth. Crumbs thrown by the guilty to the formerly insulted and ignored. One more Kara Walker exhibition is not going to convince me that things have changed on a deeper, more formative level.

I think we need to get over our embarrassment, if simply to free ourselves from the straightjacket of bigotry, complacency, and smugness. Maybe then, we'll find out just how much we can learn from each other.

Michele Wallace

Maybe I don't know all I think I know, *but* I am getting a little concerned about how this category of "public museum" is being thrown about as though it really meant something that was on its way to being counter-hegemonic. In my observation, it rarely does. At least in the U.S., the degree to which a museum is dependent upon public monies is also the degree to which it doesn't have much curatorial clout. Public monies come with long involved governmental strings, and it is never ever sufficiently generous enough to sponsor the kind of grandeur that we associate with the well-received artist in the art world. The whole attack on the NEA of years ago killed off that trend indefinitely. Even in the so-called public museum, perhaps even more so, it is corporate funding that calls all the shots.

If there is any doubt about this, just remember the last time you saw what you thought was an edgy show in a "museum" and remember how you remarked upon the fact that it wasn't traveling, it didn't get a series of big fancy openings, it didn't have all kinds of off-shoot product associated with it, and it might not even have gotten a catalogue. These are the kinds of things that corporate sponsors gratefully spring for. And why are they grateful? Because they are getting more out of it than anybody else involved. So that's the way public museums work. The more a museum depends upon government money, the less it is able to do for its artists or for its public, the more dependent it is ultimately on the vagaries of the marketplace. I guess it is like a catch-22. Damned if you do, damned if you don't.

But I don't agree that there is nothing we can do to change things. We just need to get clear about what universe we are operating in and what it is we would like to achieve and for whom. Okay, so that really is hard, I know. But I don't think, for instance, that the problem of the museums is as bad as the problem of public education in general. And I do think that the big "international" museums, or the museums that customarily attract an international audience, seem much more symbolically problematic and troubling than local or university museums. But I have begun to see all museums as "history" museums, and as such, factories of historical narrative. To think of them as such is exciting to me because I believe that museums are subject to all kinds of changes and interventions that are simply unfathomable in most arenas of academic knowledge.

I learned that from the Art Strike, Art Workers Coalition, and Women Artists Coalition actions of years ago. It is hard to believe when New Yorkers seem so extraordinarily compliant in every aspect of their everyday lives these days, but I think it a fragile peace at best just waiting to be given a useful direction for resistance. I think it is entirely possible that any number of things could set it off. Perhaps it will be the Republican Convention. Who knows?

Not that I want to see people dodging police horses again and getting their heads bashed in as they were in the '60s and '70s, because I do think that the police force that would be arrayed against us would be terrifying, but let's face it, making dramatic changes in something as genteel as the "art world" isn't unfathomable. We who would like to see change have simply not come to any kind of agreement among ourselves about what form that change should take. This remains to be decided upon, or in other words, the residual tribalism is still getting in our way.

I think if people who work in the art world would just stop anticipating so much what rich people would prefer, we just might be able to get something useful done in terms of getting museums to reflect more adequately the histories of the arts of the world's diversity and struggles. Really, I am thinking about the museums that have been decimated by the war activity going on in the world. Museums and wars don't coexist well. Do we have to think of museums solely in terms of nationalist boundaries? That seems not particularly constructive or instructive to me.

Maxwell L. Anderson

Maurice asked us about permanent collections—the logic of their creation and the ways in which they have a life.

Naturally museums spend a lot of energy rationalizing the whole—the accumulation of individual choices of donors, trustees, collectors, and curators. The vast majority of acquisitions come through gifts and bequests—60–80% of museum's holdings, by some accounts, and purchases figure modestly in the equation. So the courting of extant collections is the primary business of most curators, while contemporary curators face fewer hurdles in making significant acquisitions simply because prices are lower for those who are prospecting for talent.

This all adds up to the fact that the majority of curators are really channeling the very individual taste of collectors and the dealers who supply them; the chain of command is quite defined.

This isn't all bad. A clever curator can make excellent use of whatever comes her/his way in service of teaching a lay public about moments or themes in art history. And she/he can suppress the less than compelling examples of creativity that creep into collections through undue pressure or indolence in filtering offers of gifts and bequests.

But there is something wonderful about the obligations of stewardship, quite apart from the market-driven mechanics of how works of art end up in collections. A stroll through the storerooms of the world's great museums is a very romantic opportunity to see the dreams of others—artists and accumulators both—in private splendor. Directors are always asked: How much of the permanent collection is on view? For a lot of major museums, the answer is no more than 5%. Metropolitan Museum of Art director Philippe de Montebello's memorable answer to the question was, allegedly, "about 90% of what you would want to see." This is likely true, but it doesn't change the fact that seeing these testaments of talent on shelves and racks, waiting for their closeup, is a poignant reminder that most of human creativity is destined to vanish, and that this is not such a bad thing. The digital chapter we've entered makes it possible to preserve so much more than deserves to be preserved, and we have accordingly never needed arbiters of quality more than now. Ultimately the students on our campuses will demand some compass of quality, even as the graying professoriate looks down on what is without question an exercise designed as much to prop up the art market as it is to educate an audience.

All of which is to say is that I am nostalgic about a time when rigorous learning about art-historical typologies was less suspect. Those of us who have remained committed to museums can say this without embarrassment, as can artists who look for their place in a continuous creative conversation. The collections of museums are the touchstones for curators, artists, and students in thinking about their place in the world, and need to be tenderly guarded.

David A. Ross

This may be the central topic of our conference. If the collection defines the art museum, a discussion of the politics of collecting should help us understand why it is that museums are such powerful forces in our society.

Collecting is the most profound (and direct) reflection of the notion of a museum's agency. As a result, an examination of a museum's collections (not just the 5% on view, but the entirety of a museum's permanent collection) reveals everything one needs to know about an institution, and creates an indelible permanent recording of its willingness and capacity to engage with its constituent communities.

This is why I was always so very reluctant to sell (deaccess) anything from a museum collection—even though in one case at the Whitney Museum of American Art, it was clearly the right thing to do. (Here I refer to the completion of the selling of the remaining few works of the museum's twice built and twice sold folk art collection.)

But in general, one should not confuse the works of art selected for display—generally reflecting a consensus of current curatorial opinion—with the collection itself. The collection as a whole reflects the multigenerational building effort to construct as complete a picture as possible of the museum's chosen (or designated) field. And it is precisely those generational layers that provide the richness and real diversity necessary to attempt what is actually humanly impossible: to complete a collection.

Collecting is an intellectual activity refined through the addition of better and better examples of what the collectors consider to be of both primary and indexical value. That can only be guessed at in real-time—especially in the collecting of contemporary art—so the meta-processes of display and publication provide ways in which those decisions are subject to public scrutiny.

The "politics" of collecting, then, is visible at several points, and should itself be the subject of critical scrutiny (if it can be read). For example, when specific collecting subjects or even an entire medium are ignored—as the

Whitney for 60 years would not collect photography. Or, when collecting is corrupted by conflicting interests (as it occasionally is), unless the entirety of a collection is subject to critical scrutiny, it can be possible (again, it occasionally has been the case) that decades may pass before that corruption is exposed.

This is not only the case of obvious corruption—the acquisition of works illegally brought to market—but also in more subtle ways (as part of questionable tax-avoidance schemes intended to benefit trustees, as direct conflicts of interest supporting a particular gallery or collector's marketable holdings, etc.).

Though recent tax scandals in New York have made several of these scams front-page news, the reality is that art collecting (for museums in particular) remains an unregulated investment category, and it is my sense that soon both state and federal governments will step in—most likely in a heavy-handed manner—in an attempt to establish some sense of fair play.

For instance, right now, the members of a museum's collection committee (which putatively serves as a watchdog protecting the public interest) get the direct equivalent of inside information about artists and works deemed worthy of entering the museum collection. They are fully free, and under no moral or ethical cloud, if they leave the meeting, go directly to the studio or gallery, and acquire similar works for their own (marketable) private collections. This tidy arrangement serves many interests in a convergent fashion, and presents no real conflict, unless you believe (as some do) that the public's interests are not being fully served. But is there a better way?

Yet could you get truly knowledgeable people, with the financial capacity to help the museum collect, to play this role if you forbid the collecting of work that they learned of as a result of their service and generosity? (In many private museums, members contribute $10,000 to $50,000 annually to serve on acquisition committees.)

And corruption of the collection is only the most spectacular (and saddening) aspect to examine. Other equally significant reflections of the social contract between the museum and its community are visible as a historical record of profound accuracy.

The exclusion of work that does not fit the culturally determined definition of art has already been discussed, and deserves and demands further consideration, for it continues to plague the idea of a museum collection.

Beyond the serious issues of cultural determinism, racism,

and various forms of class bias that underlie the ways in which we agree on what should be collected in our art museums there is one even larger issue.

Why distinguish art, and its history, from other forms of history? Why isolate art's history from the other ways of seeing and remembering? Why isolate one nation's art from another? To repeat my earlier "Big" question, whose interests are served by the maintenance of the categories of collecting to which we have grown so accustomed that we fail to even see them as blinders?

Let me end this overly long post with a story.

When Joseph Beuys was considering where to donate a major body of his work, he chose a small general museum in Darmstadt, Germany, as the recipient. As an artist, he liked the fact that it mixed natural history and art history, as for him the borderline between these two ways of knowing the world was a social construct he wished to ignore or subvert.

Maurice Berger

David, you wrote: "Why distinguish art, and its history, from other forms of history? Why isolate art's history from the other ways of seeing and remembering? Why isolate one nation's art from another? To repeat my earlier 'Big' question, whose interests are served by the maintenance of the categories of collecting to which we have grown so accustomed that we fail to even see them as blinders?"

I think this notion of boundaries and categories—national, disciplinary, technological, historical, and even attitudinal —is crucial. David, I will ask panelists in the final two-day session to "imagine" their version of the vital museum of the future. After your erudite, informative, and incisive comments on the "politics" of collection, the legacy and stability on which many museums are built, after all, I can't wait to hear your reply.

And, Max, you wrote: "This all adds up to the fact that the majority of curators are really channeling the very individual taste of collectors and the dealers who supply them; the chain of command is quite defined."

An important point. While you say this situation is not necessarily bad, I'm curious: Do you—or anyone else in the conference—envision a way of circumventing this fairly rigid chain of command?

Jonathan P. Binstock

Maurice, my experience at the Corcoran Gallery of Art may go part of the way to answering your last question. I think available financial resources greatly inform how rigid the structure, "the chain of command," is from dealers and collectors to museum collections. With a gift (from a donor, collector, dealer, or artist), the main way works enter museum collections, the "chain of command" is virtually unassailable.

For museum purchases—which often pool together funds from private donations, the museum's endowment, philanthropic groups associated with the museum family, such as the Women's Committee or Friends of Contemporary Art—the acquisition process can be very different. If there are a lot of these resources, then the chain of command is probably stronger because the flow of capital is more constant and the roles of arbiters more entrenched. At the Corcoran, this is not the case. The most difficult task in the process for me is identifying which among the many objects worth preserving will become my acquisition "cause." For it takes a lot of time and energy to actually get my various supporters and superiors on board, raise the money, etc. The task of patching together a financial package to pay for a given work can take as long as two years, especially given the priorities of other curators at the museum. For as long as the process is, I better be committed to the object in question. With little available money, individual agency is ever-more crucial, which makes circumventing the "chain of command" easier. More on this below.

The process is not as mysterious as it may seem from the outside. It is in essence a lot of hard work. As a contemporary curator, my decisions are informed mainly by looking (*a lot*) and, thereafter, by reading criticism and speaking with colleagues, who include, importantly, dealers and collectors whose tastes and ideas I admire. Such people, of course, also have a lot at stake when their preferences connect, or don't connect, with museum practice. It's a complex situation. I don't mean to undermine the importance of an institutional voice, but, in the end, individuals build museum collections. Individuals must negotiate the complexities and competing forces described by symposium participants, and individuals may, or may not, be able to circumvent the "chain of command," depending on the type of acquisition in question.

Contemporary art, with its large-scale installations, site-specific commissions, multi-video projections, and the like, are going a long way to circumvent the "chain of command" you speak of. The situation harks back to the radical conceptualists of the 1960s, but with a twist. Very few individuals can acquire a work as logistically demanding as *The Paradise Institute* by

Janet Cardiff and George Bures Miller. The piece comes in 33 crates and occupies about 1600 square feet when installed. The work requires a team of riggers whenever one wants to move it. Assembly is a two-week process. This is a task only for an institution capable of handling it. As it happens, Cardiff and Bures Miller make very few consumer art goods, that is to say, objects an individual might reasonably purchase for his or her private collection. In this case, the art has, I think, in many ways circumvented the "chain of command" because it's basically unavailable to the private-collector marketplace. In this instance, we might also consider the fact that Luhring Augustine, the artists' gallery, has probably not made with this particular piece the money they would normally expect, or hope for, from their business transactions. The costs associated with developing, fabricating, and exhibiting this work are exceedingly high.

Mark Alice Durant

I love that story about Joseph Beuys. I wish that more museums could show science and art together, not for purely pedagogical purposes but for the sheer delight of being able to contemplate aesthetic and scientific inquiry within the same frame, so to speak. I know it is highly impractical in the real world of museum politics, fund-raising, and territoriality. At Harvard University, nearby to where I grew up, within a few blocks one can stroll through the Fogg Art Museum, the Peabody Museum, the Busch-Reisinger, and the Carpenter Center. One's eyes can gleam in front of a magnificent Max Beckmann, and 20 minutes later you can roll those same eyes while scanning the decaying taxidermied South American anteaters at the Peabody. As much as I envied those preppy privileged students who seemed to own Harvard Yard (I was taught that the only way I was going to Harvard was to be a janitor), it did not prevent me from finding ways to utilize its close resources. Although in theory those small museums could be a kind of model (in the European sense), obviously they are funded by the enormous resources of their host institution and somewhat rare.

While I do not experience the nostalgia that Maxwell Anderson feels for a time when rigorous art historical exhibitions were less suspect, I agree that they should be part of what museums do and they should do so without apology. There is an ongoing oppositional tone through many of the posts, implicitly or explicitly suggesting that there is a conspiracy of privilege in the conduct of most art museums. Obviously. Nevertheless, through wealth art collections are built and often donated. Whatever the ulterior motives of the donor are, I don't care as long as the work becomes publicly available.

Also implicit in the discussion is that "edgy" shows are becoming more rare and safer shows the norm. I am not sure what an edgy exhibition is. Do you mean the shows that wear their politics on their sleeves like certain infamous Whitney Biennials? Many artists (and curators and collectors) cultivate a parasitic relationship to content, choosing their subject matter and/or materials in the attempt to "subvert," "undermine," "confront," "terrorize." Whatever. I believe that work that puts "effect" ahead of material rigor, intellectual openness, generosity, and respect for the intelligence of the audience is highly suspect. If the museum is a public space for private contemplation, then I think it's possible that exhibitions of some of the tired old masters can be every bit as edgy as anything in the contemporary art world.

A number of years ago I saw a show of late Degas drawings and paintings at the Art Institute of Chicago. I was not particularly interested in what I assumed would be a warmed-over review of yet another 19th-century French artist. I was at the time doing performance and installation work, as far as one could get, I suppose, from the concerns of a modernist master. To my great surprise, I was deeply moved by the drawings on newsprint, by his insistent search for the line to describe the bent knee or arching back of his dancer/models. He had nothing left to prove this late in his life, yet he spent hours with charcoal in hand, dragging it across the surface of the paper, erasing, making the gesture over and over, because the integrity of the moment was all that mattered. In front of those yellowing 100-year-old drawings I understood something about being an artist that I never learned in all my years in art school. Revelation is where you find it.

Barbara Buhler Lynes

Although, as has already been pointed out, much of what comes into museum collections is through gifts and bequests, many museums have varying amounts of monies allocated for acquisitions in their annual budgets through which they can augment their permanent collection regularly.

I was a member for several years of an acquisitions committee at a major East Coast art museum whose role was to evaluate the spending of such monies for adding to the permanent collection according to the collecting guidelines set forth in the museum's mission statement. Members of the committee included, among others, the head of the board, the museum's chief curator, local collectors, and community leaders. Its membership was highly coveted, and although I can't speak for anyone else, I was never asked nor was I expected to contribute money to it.

At meetings, museum curators made compelling arguments for the acquisition of works that were displayed to the committee, with curators in white gloves often walking the objects in question around the room so that each committee member could look at them closely. Clearly, the curators had selected these works for very specific reasons, and their arguments demonstrated not only their in-depth knowledge of the works in question, but also the nature and significance of the museum collection and how such works could either augment specific components of the collection or chart new paths and directions for it. For the several years I served on this committee, its members could vote not to approve the acquisitions of works curators proposed, but none did, because it was so obvious that the curators knew more about the work, the collection, and how it should grow and move in new directions than anyone else in the room.

In such situations, are not curators the most sophisticated arbiters of what the museum should collect? So what if their knowledge and ideas about quality and taste ultimately shape the nature and character of collections. Who else knows more about what the museum has collected, what its needs are, and what it should collect?

Karen Mary Davalos

To Mark: Museums are more than places of private contemplation. First, the experience can be part of a collective experience—see Michele's example of children asking to view *Tar Beach*. The museum visitor can have an experience that is certainly private but not actually contemplative. And what of the praying and crying I witness at exhibitions all over the United States that celebrate El Dia de los Muertos/The Day of the Dead? Prayer, the completion of a pilgrimage, and commemorations for the dead can involve contemplation, but it is so much more.

Then of course we have action that is produced from looking at art—take the recent controversy at the Museum of International Folk Art in New Mexico when it exhibited Alma Lopez's digital print of Our Lady [of Guadalupe] wearing roses instead of a robe. The museum and curator as well as the artist were accused of being heretics, evil, and godless. The threats against the artist have not stopped.

And the point of one of my last posts was to describe the ways in which a museum visitor can have a very special relationship with the object on display because of a larger collective history, experience, or memory. That is, museums can be communal spaces.

In short, the viewing of art can have so many meanings and responses that I am not willing to use some presumed universal as a measure of what museums are and should be.

And for those individual curators, making individual decisions, trying to avoid or live with the "chain of command": How long do they hold their jobs? How long does that one individual shape the collections? What is the racial, gender, ethnic, etc., diversity inside the museum staff? For me this is not just a mater of identity politics. All collectors are products, shapers of their own cultural heritage. Whiteness is rarely acknowledged—and thanks to Maurice for naming what I danced around because I feared the other panelists would write off my comments as oppositional, etc. and it appears one did. My point is this: a majority of the last posts made collecting sound sterile, simple, and apolitical. Just individual human action, good hard work, and all that neo-liberalism. As if individual collectors exist in a vacuum away from the relations and webs of power that were previously discussed in the conference. Yes, yes, we are to believe that they can rise above, see more clearly than the rest of us, but how do they achieve it? From viewing lots of art? Really? The same eyes looking at the world from the same perspective, no matter how big that world is made, will always see what they want to see.

I think Maurice is closer to an answer when he addresses self-actualization—to invoke a term of Paulo Freire.

Sorry if the post is too late—in California the night is young.

Edward Rothstein

It's a little awkward leaping into such a highly developed series of conversations so late, so apologies to all. In this case, coming in at the close of the discussion of the politics of collecting also makes it clear how much of a minority view I seem to hold about these issues.

I don't agree that collecting is a variety of colonialism or has its origins in colonialism. I don't believe that art museums in recent decades go out of their way to shun or hide works based on race, gender, or sexual preference of their creators. I also don't believe that an art museum receiving public funds has any kind of an obligation to shape its collection according to representative demographics of the local community.

This doesn't mean, of course, that there aren't cases of discrimination or abuses of power. Nor does it mean that there aren't ways in which such factors enter into the mix. Sometimes, it may even seem as if race is the determining factor in a museum's collections, without it being so. If we think of the art museum as a creation of the 19th century—resembling in many ways, the concert hall (which I'll have something to say about later)—it reflects some of the ideologies of the 19th century.

The traditional art museum is self-consciously mythic: it tells the origins of Western society in its collections, which often begin with objects from Greek and Roman periods. The imperial project, of course, enabled the collection of such objects. But the impulse to recount mythic origins in a display of objects–and this display having some relationship to the demonstration of the power of a society—is common among all cultures.

What made the Western art museum so distinctive and important is not the display of objects but that this display also coincided with two other kinds of impulses that also became paramount in the West: 1) The development of science: the belief that what was true in one place about the universe was also true in another, that there were laws and principles that applied across space and time. Though we are all used to adding on qualifications to these beliefs, the development of science and medicine is linked to them. It is also evident in the universal ambitions of the museum, the attempts to display, in some way, a complete vision of the world—including objects from other cultures. This is related to 2) The development of cultural anthropology: the belief that other cultures were also shaped by organizing principles and bounded by the discoveries of science. The West, as far as I know, is the only arena in which cultural anthropology developed. This is not, as is so often asserted, a mere imperial enterprise. We are all its beneficiaries; now so is the multicultural world.

If the art museum developed so largely based on the works of Europeans, it is no accident. The development of aesthetics is also a European idea. Some of the arguments being made are that that should no longer be the premise—and indeed, in many instances, it no longer is.

Consider two examples from outside the visual arts that may help explain why I think the race/gender/imperial model is so limited. One of the great challenges in every

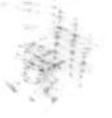

natural history museum (also a Western creation) is how to establish the categories under which objects are organized. As one philosopher once asked: In a supermarket are canned peaches to be stacked next to peaches or among canned goods? The natural history museum evolved out of the "curiosity cabinets" of the 16th and 17th centuries—cabinets stocked by collectors who were astounded by the range and variety of human and natural phenomena: seashells, dissected lizards, fetal skeletons, etc. . . . Early cabinets might group all body parts employed in motion in a single cabinet: function was the order.

But with the onset of evolutionary theory, the modern natural history museum came into being, completely reorganizing what was on display and why. Now, another kind of principle is at work in natural history museums: ecological diversity. This again reorganizes what is displayed and why. In many cases, the human observer, who began as the center of the collection, creating its order, has turned into its outsider, the disrupter of order. (Take a look also at the Rose Center at the Museum of Natural History in New York: the planetarium makes every effort in its displays to show the miniscule irrelevance of the human—precisely the opposite of the feeling cultivated in the old planetarium.) My point is that these changing models of interpretation are attempts to comprehend something about the world. And while one can tease out attitudes toward race and other cultures (and sometimes too much teasing is required), it would be a mistake to see those factors as the guiding ones of the enterprise.

Another example: when I used to review classical music concerts, I often complained that the concert hall, with its sclerotic repertoire, was turning into a museum. True. But I'm no longer sure that that's a problem. The orchestral concert, for example, developed at a certain time, along with certain repertoires, and served a certain social function. It still does. And as long as that function is important—and I believe it is—and as long as the repertoire is powerful and important—and I believe it is—the orchestral concert is doing its job.

The failure of the orchestra to attract large numbers of minority players, or the fact that so many audiences have so few minority listeners, is no longer due to anything resembling racism. And those failures are not addressed by asking the orchestra to transform itself into something it isn't. There are any number of cultural preferences and distributions at work in different fields;

we can't ask such enterprises to reflect some ideal cross-section of society. But we can say that the failure is significant if we believe that what is being offered in these concerts (or museums . . . or whatever) is so powerful and important that the opportunity to be exposed to them should be available to all. And that we have not done, because that conviction has been jettisoned in the educational system. It is no longer considered important to teach children (of whatever origin) about the European and American art-music heritage because (we say) there are so many other traditions they can learn. As a result, we end up teaching nothing and there is no conviction that anything is important. We are so focused on certain forms of cultural/racial/political distribution that the result is a false homogenization.

That is one reason I am heartened by the educational programs of some museums. I have gone to family educational events at the Metropolitan Museum of Art for years and it is phenomenal to see children taken around to the galleries and being taught how to see what they are looking at.

Anyway, this brings us to the democratization issue. I agree with Olu Oguibe that museums are not democratic institutions. But I don't agree that the acceptance of public funds means that they are accountable in a democratic fashion as currently defined. Or I should say that in the current atmosphere, public funds are a problem. Those funds are ideally made available to the museum to support its function and achievements. What would it mean to make a museum accountable to its community as some fellow contributors have argued? It would not just be a matter of diversity and representation; that is only a single idea of accountability that reflects a particular set of political beliefs. What about museums in communities that are not diverse? Should they, too, have such an obligation to their local community—or not have it? Who decides? Government statisticians? What about publicly funded exhibitions that are offensive to large portions of the local public? Is the democratic argument that [Robert] Mapplethorpe et al. should not be presented in such cases? My own sense is that until these issues are made more clear, until the differing interpretations of "democratic accountability" are understood, public funding will remain a land mine. It is one of the peculiarities of our democratic culture that democracy can end up stifling certain kinds of culture.

I don't have complete answers, and can't post often, but

I'm eager to know how this discussion and others evolve.

Carol Duncan

I agree with Michele Wallace, Olu Oguibe, Jennifer González, Alan Wallach, and others concerning the "whiteness" of art museum exhibitions and collections. However, we should also recognize that that whiteness was much more the rule, at least in the prestigious, big-city museums, 10 or 15 years ago than it is today. I remember walking through the then-new installation of early 20th-century art at the Art Institute of Chicago (this was around 1993) and noticing works by African Americans, women, lesbians and gays, and they weren't ghettoized—they weren't put into separate galleries or second-class spaces like hallways, where I have often seen works, especially by African Americans.

There were also other unusual things about the hang, at least unusual for a permanent collection (if not for temporary shows), namely, there were galleries with themes, and galleries that made the point that the conventional museological ways of packaging the past into relatively neat classifications (styles, movements) give a fictional account of what were complex and messy art-historical moments. The whole impression I got (compared, say, to what you could see in most modern collections) was that modern artists were not only trying to be Cubists, or This-ists or That-ists (although such questions of art language were on their minds), but also they were men and women who loved and hated and thought about the world they lived in, the political and social world they lived in as well as their particular sexual, emotional, and psychological experience.

Not incidently, I also noticed lots of nonwhite people in the galleries, and they were addressed not as outside others, but directly as part of a broad, inclusive public. Maybe I was being too utopian, but it was one of the first times that I experienced a big, important museum throwing all the weight of its prestige into the idea that we can actually identify with each other across all the lines of race and gender (the class issue was not as clearly present). Nowadays, there is more of this rethinking, but from my experience, it seems to happen more often and more thoughtfully in places that are just outside the dead centers of high prestige: Newark or Brooklyn (rather than the Met) or Oakland, Cal. (rather than San Francisco's Modern Art Museum). The pressure of having to generate higher attendance among the people who live in the surrounding neighborhoods (we are far from 5th Avenue), no doubt acts as a spur to this development, especially since granting agencies now want to see such figures.

Just one more thought: Michele describes especially well the infrastructure of the art world, in which collectors, dealers, critics, and publishers play significant roles in the elevation of artists' reputations, a requirement of their becoming visible in museum collections. But there is also a counter to this, and that is the movement of scholarship and university culture and criticism that goes after the criteria and categorical thinking used by the art establishment to maintain its values and myths as authoritative. Museums, after all, are a variety of public space. They may be controlled, but they are not absolutely controlled.

■ ■ ■

Maurice Berger

Every time I walk into a museum I do so as a passionate observer. Foremost, I come to look at art. But for as long as I can remember, I have been fascinated with something else about the museum experience: my fellow viewers. I am a committed observer of the observer. Watching people look at art has taught me a few things about the ways museums undermine or facilitate the experience of art. It is always a joy, of course, to read the signs of awe, fascination, and intensity on the faces of viewers. All too often, however, I observe another, more troubling sign: the expressions of confusion, bewilderment, or disinterest on the faces of viewers who have lost confidence in the experience of a particular exhibition.

There are many reasons for this problem. Sometimes viewers are turned off by "difficult" or conceptually challenging art. (On a recent visit to San Francisco Museum of Modern Art, for example, I observed a number of bewildered viewers quickly make their way through the remarkable Philip Guston exhibition; one flight up, at the dreadful Marc Chagall extravaganza, most viewers seemed utterly transfixed and captivated.) Sometimes viewers are turned off by the museum's inability to help them make sense of difficult or challenging art. Many perfectly fine exhibitions, in my opinion, are undermined by didactic materials—text panels and wall labels, for example—that are so poorly written or riddled with jargon that they defy comprehension.

For many Americans, if not most, the art museum remains off limits—an irrelevant world of abstruse, elitist game playing. I would like to devote the next two days to the topic of "audience."

Who is the audience for art museums? How can museums maintain the audiences they already have? How can museums expand their audience, thus making art available and important to a broader range of people? To what extent do museums ignore the cultures and interests of the communities around them? Should museums compete with other, popular forms of cultural "entertainment," through expanded public relations and marketing programs? To what extent should museums piggyback onto other cultural forms in order to build audience, such as concert series and film festivals? What is the museum's responsibility to its audience, both in terms of education and advocacy? How can museums facilitate the experience of art? And what of the potential of the museum to enhance and edify the viewer's experience of art by connecting it to the collective history, experience, or memories that underwrite it, the "communal" experience that Karen Mary Davalos so eloquently describes?

And . . . yes . . . I do understand that the notion of "audience" can differ widely from one type of art institution to another. So we may need to get fairly specific here.

Sylvia Yount

I'm entering the fray rather late—having been out of the country—and wanted to say at the outset how refreshing it is to hear such a range of voices in this critical dialogue. Maurice's questions about the art museum's current and future challenges, the reality of corporatization, and the politics of collecting have all hit home as I've been processing my recent trip to Spain and France.

Having now seen for myself Gehry's spectacle in Bilbao, where the building's contents truly seem beside the point (though the current [Alexander] Calder show, displayed in that space, was refreshingly revealing, if only in formal terms), and having wandered through the Musée du Louvre's galleries close to midnight on *la nuit blanche* with hundreds of other visitors, the most powerful—if often stated—recollection remains the markedly different ways that Europeans and Americans value culture. And yet the issue of museum audiences—building and maintaining them, pleasing and challenging them—is an increasingly shared concern for institutions on both continents. This seems to me to be the crux of the matter. (By the way, I began this as a response to the last session, not knowing that it was locked and that our next topic would be audiences.)

Gate or no gate, ultimately, we're all dependent on our publics on one level or another. As difficult as it may be—for curators, especially—to gauge if our work is engaging anyone, I think it's safe to say that most of our colleagues are not interested in speaking only to one other.

Earlier participants have touched on the importance of producing smart and responsible exhibitions and installations for a variety of visitors—from the critic to the child. Let's hope that as curators we can maintain our intellectual and institutional integrity in the face of all the challenges of current museum practice, and continue to do substantive work.

Returning to the High Museum of Art this week, I couldn't help but fantasize about a time—perhaps just two years hence—when a striking new addition designed by a sexy international architect [Renzo Piano] (but one more attuned to modes of contemplation than pomp) might entice crowds of individuals to the museum on a regular basis. Whether drawn by the buildings, the special exhibitions, the newly reinstalled permanent collection, and/or the public programming, I hope we can offer them a variety of experiences that will reach them in meaningful ways. As clichéd as that may sound, I think it remains a common goal for most of us.

Finally, a few questions:

Alan mentioned the problem of "democratized" art; what, exactly, do we mean by that term? Does J. Seward Johnson at the Corcoran qualify? What happens when art museums operate outside of established hierarchies and taste? Is the critical or public response different if the initiative is known to have been spearheaded by a curator rather than a director or trustee?

And to Barbara's question about curators as the shapers of permanent collections: How many acquisitions committees function as more than a rubber stamp? With most proposed acquisitions fully vetted by directors before they ever appear before trustees, how great a role do curators play in the overall definition of a collection? Will aspects of collections continue to be identified by the names of philanthropic patrons? What does this signify to most museum-goers who often have little idea how decisions are made about what art goes on display?

Alan Wallach

Sylvia asks what do we mean by "a democratized art." She also asks: "Does J. Seward Johnson at the Corcoran Gallery of Art qualify?"

Since I deployed the term "democratized art," I will attempt to sketch an answer to Sylvia's question.

As most participants in this symposium would probably agree, the art-and-museum system is profoundly hierarchical. Indeed, "democratized art" can be considered an oxymoron. For as Bourdieu and others have argued, Art in our society is not simply a thing but an institution that reflects and reinforces existing social hierarchies.

When I use the term "democratized art" what I have in mind is art that is accessible to all members of society. By that I don't mean that everyone would like the same objects—or worse have to like the same objects. And I most definitely do not mean various forms of corporate or state-sponsored kitsch—e.g., an ersatz "folk" or "people's" art, or the various industrialized "realisms" of, for example, the former Soviet Union. Nor do I have in mind the work of J. Seward Johnson, to go back to Sylvia's example, which, in its thoroughly creepy (necrophiliac?)

way, is designed to appeal to a debased, blockbuster-inspired taste. Seward's gloss on Gift Shoppe Impressionism is exactly the opposite of what I intend when I think of a democratized art.

To make clear what I mean, I should say that the underlying premise of the argument is real democracy, which means a thoroughgoing social transformation—one that would eliminate the forms of social and economic exploitation characteristic of late capitalism and which would thus do away with the material bases for hierarchies of race, class, and gender. Such a vision of the future may seem hopelessly utopian, but I believe real democracy, which means above all a plebian democracy, is the one long-term historical goal worth considering. Consequently, arguments about museum audiences and the future of the museum need to be made in light of such a goal.

As things now stand, only about 20% of the U.S. population ever goes to an art museum voluntarily, which is not to say that the remaining 80% is unaware of museums—far from it. Art with a capital "A" is a pervasive social fact. No doubt many of those who are excluded resent their exclusion—and for good reason.

Fred Wilson, in the introductory video he produced for *Mining the Museum*, repeatedly asked, "Where am I in the collection?"

That question could be a point of departure for a discussion of a democratized art. For if we are equal—if every member of society has an equal dignity and an equal say—then we have an equal right to look for ourselves in the museum, or whatever institution would replace the museum in a fully democratic society.

I am not arguing—nor was Wilson arguing—for a solipsistic definition of art. But, as *Mining the Museum* demonstrated, he was calling for a history of art quite different from the redemptive history that is usually presented in the museum: history may be a nightmare but the history of art represents a form of salvation. Exalt the "genius" of a Leonardo and forget the *ciompi*—the starving wage laborers of Florence's wool industry. A democratized art history could take as its point of departure something by Walter Benjamin: "There is no document of civilization which is not at the same time a document of barbarism. And just as such a document is not free of barbarism, barbarism taints also the manner in which it was transmitted from one owner to another."

Two final points in this by now overlong post:

First, a democratized art is not necessarily a different art—I'm not saying, for example, do away with Impressionism—but an art that is seen and experienced differently. Thus exhibitions of Impressionist art would no longer be occasions for nostalgia for the (imagined) lifestyle of a defunct upper class. They would not, in other words, continue to succumb to what might be called the Master Race Theater syndrome.

Second, the struggle for a democratized art is part and parcel of the struggle for a democratic society. On a practical level that means calling for an expansion of the museum audience, for a far more serious commitment to art education, for more access, for far greater diversity, and for critical-historical exhibitions like *Mining the Museum* as well as engaging in unrelenting criticism of our society's dominant, Eurocentric definition of Art and the institutions, especially museums, that sustain that definition.

Irving Sandler

A belated comment. In his introductory remarks, Maurice asked us to show-and-tell. I am an art critic and historian. Aside from that, my main concern has been the welfare of artists and their community. Among other activities, I ran the Abstract Expressionist Club in the late 1950s, served on NYSCA and NEA committees and panels, co-founded Artists Space in 1972, and now chair the Artists Committee of the Marie Walsh Sharpe Foundation which has been responsible for the 1-800-Artists-Help line, the book *A Visual Artists' Guide to Estate Planning*, and the Sharpe Studios in Tribecca.

Michele Wallace raises an important issue that involved literally thousands of artists. Of the some 250 artists of the New York School, many of them superb painters and sculptors, who showed downtown in the 1950s, only a half-dozen continue to command any art-world attention. The rest may have had a gallery show or so, placed a work in some museum or other, or shown in a Whitney Annual. Check the old catalogues of Whitney Annuals of two or three decades ago, and I bet you won't recognize the names of 5% of the exhibitors, if that. But, aged as many have become, they keep on making art. The neglect rate since the 1950s has worsened considerably. This is the reason I cofounded Artists Space. Can museums help solve this problem? The Museum of Modern Art's partnership with P.S.1 Center for Contemporary Arts offers one solution. Are there others?

Maurice Berger

Alan, you wrote: "Second, the struggle for a democratized

art is part and parcel of the struggle for a democratic society. On a practical level that means calling for an expansion of the museum audience, for a far more serious commitment to art education, for more access, for far greater diversity, and for critical-historical exhibitions like *Mining the Museum* as well as engaging in unrelenting criticism of our society's dominant, Eurocentric definition of Art and the institutions, especially museums, that sustain that definition."

First, I think your post is very important to this discussion, honing in, as it does, on the very nature of the museum's relationship to audience. Second, I wonder in a practical sense, how the changes you suggest can actually occur. Do museums really want to open themselves up to this kind of democratization?

And Irving: good question. May I ask that we hold off on answering it at this point? It speaks less to audience than the issue that will be the subject of our next topic: exclusion, inclusion, and the boundaries that museums establish for "appropriate" content, acquisitions, and programming. In other words, how things—even important things—get left out of museums and why.

Jennifer González

I loved Mark Alice Durant's description of his revelation in front of the Degas drawing. Anyone who makes art, or studies art practice, understands the labor and attention of this meticulously dogged search for a line. I had a similar experience of surprised, elevated epiphany seeing Richard Serra's *Torqued Elipses* on a solitary afternoon in Manhattan. Awe arrives in unexpected ways, and remarkable works of art often lead us into this rare and significantly human state of mind. The fact that it was a small drawing by Degas for Durant, and a towering Serra for me, indicates the wide variety of forms and objects that might elicit this response—a response that might be either private or collective. (Who among us has not experienced some form of collective awe, as Karen Mary Davalos suggests?)

I was concerned, however, about the either/or perspective taken by Durant in his suggestion that his revelatory moment in front of Degas might be more important, more significant, more sophisticated, more worth preserving and protecting than a similarly revelatory moment audience members may experience encounter ing explicitly activist, critical, or "edgy" art exhibitions. I find it remarkable that the much-maligned Whitney Biennial of now a decade ago (1993) is still producing such backhanded hostility. Does Durant protest too much?

Emerging from this discussion is an all-too-familiar pitting of politics (perhaps even democratization) against the incredible—and truly precious—experience of awe in front of great works of art. Is it possible to avoid this simple, indeed simplistic, dichotomy?

Who will say that Picasso's *Guernica* is not both political and deeply moving? Few. What about Fred Wilson's *Mining the Museum* (since Alan Wallach has brought it up again today)? This work was both political and deeply moving. It certainly produced vociferous ire in several white museum patrons and profound joy in several black museum patrons—as the audience-response testimony indicates. By breaking with traditional forms and taxonomies of museum display, Wilson's installation also broke the Maryland Historical Society's narrow concept of its audience, which was utterly transformed by the exhibition's unprecedented popularity with the citizens of Baltimore.

Edward Rothstein accurately points out that "The traditional art museum is self-consciously mythic." He also points out that, although all peoples collect, the current museum tradition is a uniquely "Western" epistemological project. I am quite familiar with the history he provides, and I agree that "Western" museums have always sought to display current knowledge about the world, including its aesthetic achievements and its diverse peoples as seen through an anthropological lens. When considering why museums (or concerts) attract some audiences and not others, the question for directors, curators, and educational programmers must be not only: How can I make my institution available to all? but also: Whose myth am I presenting?

Bruce Altshuler

A number of years ago Stephen Weil wrote an article entitled, I believe, "From being about something, to being for somebody," suggesting that museums—as recipients of public support—must change from an inward focus on collections to directing their efforts outward, toward serving actual and potential audiences. For me this phrase does not imply that the collecting, display, and interpretation of artworks is not done for the benefit of the public, but it sets these central museum functions alongside other activities that connect museums with multiple constituencies and a variety of communities.

These relationships extend beyond educational programs-the most obvious connection—to include, for instance, recent efforts to make museums sites of public assembly and discussion (and more than cultural malls with theaters, shops, and restaurants encircling galleries). When the Japanese-American National Museum in Los Angeles staged forums to discuss discrimination against Arab-Americans after September 11th, or when the Lower East Side Tenement Museum brought garment workers, management, and union organizers together on the neutral territory of the museum to discuss a labor dispute, these museums were reaching out into social and political territory of a kind not often associated with the museum (but essentially connected to the content areas of each of these institutions, one dealing with the difficult history of Japanese Americans, and the other with the struggle of immigrants on New York's Lower East Side).

Similar opportunities for art museums to become such places of community interaction (and healing, as people found in New York after September 11th) readily present themselves. And an emphasis on audience does not imply a reneging on the commitment of art museums to collect and display outstanding objects of significant visual interest, but rather to see this as an obligation to someone, to in fact multiple publics worthy of respect. As Donna De Salvo mentioned in an earlier post, the kind of exhibitions criticized for "dumbed-down" content and interpretation often are a consequence of a lack of respect for the audience, a condescending attitude lacking faith in the viewer's ability to rise to (excuse the hierarchical metaphor) the experiential and intellectual opportunities presented by the exhibition of works of art. Of course none of this settles the particulars concerning what to collect and display, and how to do so, but I think that it is an attitude essential for the creation of what Alan refers to as a "democratized art."

Maurice Berger

Jennifer, you wrote: "Emerging from this discussion is an all-too-familiar pitting of politics (perhaps even democratization) against the incredible—and truly precious—experience of awe in front of great works of art. Is it possible to avoid this simple, indeed simplistic dichotomy?"

Great point. Indeed, if we were to transpose your argument to a discussion of film, for example, this dichotomy might not exist at all (especially in work of the more progressive film critics and curators). There is this long-standing sense in the art world of the danger of diluting the awe-inspiring potential of art with "politics." Yet, as you rightfully point out, ideology is often a part of great art, from Goya and Picasso to [Robert] Motherwell's *Elegies* and Fred Wilson's *Mining the Museum.*

Inherent to the museum's—and art world's—social removal is the danger of marginalizing ourselves out of existence for most people. Mary Kelly's imperative to recover from the horror of the Terminator's victory in California through the awe-inspiring qualities of great art rather than by watching *The Simpsons* (Mary's dichotomy, not mine) strikes me as a self-defeatist position (though, I too, have gone to the museum many times in difficult periods in my life). *The Simpsons* is an example of great art that is also profoundly "political" (no other work of art has more dramatically questioned and attenuated the myths of middle-class, white normalcy, and the manipulative sham of "family values"). Matt Groening, however, understands something that many of us clearly do not: that great art can appeal to more than just a tiny elite *and* that its message and ability to awe can move people deeply and even sway public opinion.

George Bush's victory in 2000 and Arnold's big win last week yet again remind us that the message and its ability to reach and move its audience is everything in politics (and not unimportant in art, either). W. and his crew are not as dumb as many of us think.

Dan Cameron

Although contemporary art with roots in the historic avant-garde may not seem the ideal vantage point from which to discuss the question of art's public, I have often come away from the experience of lecturing to museum or college audiences feeling a sense of amazement at the power of personal intervention to connect audiences to what artists are trying to communicate through their work. The same people who stand unmoved in front of a work by, say, Felix Gonzalez-Torres can suddenly become deeply engaged if there is someone present to help them explore the different ways of looking at it. Talking about artwork, even in the form of the humble gallery walk-through, can sometimes make all the difference between opening a viewer's mind and heart to experimental art practices and leaving them out in the cold.

This observation makes me reflect on another aspect of the museum experience: art is, first and foremost, a social practice. You or I might have profound experiences of solitary contemplation while visiting a museum, but these moments are predicated on years of training in visual reception and literacy that are sadly absent from most people's lives. Furthermore, I would suggest that if I had nobody in the world with whom I could converse about my experience with Joan Miro's art, and no books to read on the subject, my deep connection to his paintings would soon wither and disappear. Because a community already exists that is defined by its passion for art, we constantly seek affirmation and solidarity within that community, whether we see it in those terms or not.

When visitors' eyes glaze over because they feel confused by contemporary art, this is also a way of saying that they feel excluded from our community. Because of this feeling of being excluded, I believe that one of the most important commitments any museum professional can make is to try to reach out and connect to the public through continuous lectures, gallery tours, workshops, and the difficult but necessary writing of readable wall and brochure texts. A startling number of the New Museum of Contemporary Art's most passionate supporters today are people who started out feeling a degree of hostility and resistance to new art, but were able to overcome those barriers because someone on the staff took the time to talk to them in plain English about what the art on view might mean to their lives. And, as anyone who has been involved in museum education can attest, once you have guided someone two or three times through the process of opening themselves up to new art, they can usually go on to make those connections by themselves.

Alan Wallach

Maurice, you "wonder in a practical sense, how the changes [I] suggest can actually occur. Do museums really want to open themselves up to this kind of democratization?"

I'm afraid I can't speak for museums, but it seems to me very unlikely that museums would want to open themselves up to democratization—certainly not the big universal survey museums such as the Washington National Gallery of Art and Sculpture Garden, the Museum of Fine Arts, Boston, or the Metropolitan Museum of Art—since those with real power are usually loath to give it up.

Democratization might mean adding community representatives to a museum's board of trustees. The Metropolitan Museum's board, for example, consists of members of the "community" of the Wall Street wealthy. Would the Met allow non-wealthy New Yorkers to join or even dominate its board?

I'd be interested to know what Maxwell Anderson and David Ross think about the possibility of changing the membership of museum boards so that they more fully represent the communities they claim to serve. Can we imagine a Whitney Museum board that is not a rich man's club?

Irving Sandler

There are diverse museum audiences. A significant constituency consists of artists. They need what they see to make art. In talking to artists, at least of my generation, everyone has told me of the importance of the Museum of Modern Art's permanent collection in the development of their art. I would hope that museums could serve all of their diverse audiences, but the health of art and its future depends on how they meet the needs of artists.

Maurice Berger

Dan, you wrote: "Because of this feeling of being excluded, I believe that one of the most important commitments any museum professional can make is to try to reach out and connect to the public through continuous lectures, gallery tours, workshops, and the difficult but necessary writing of readable wall and brochure texts."

This is a very important point, yet I suspect that you may be the exception rather than the rule. All too often, I have found (as a consultant to a number of museums) resistance on the part of many curators to examining and improving their pedagogical skills. Indeed, education departments are often marginal to or left out of the curatorial process. On Thursday, I will open a two-day session on museum education, public address, and pedagogy.

Irving, you wrote: "A significant constituency consists of artists. They need what they see to make art. . . . I would hope that museums could serve all of their diverse audiences, but the health of art and its future depends on how they meet the needs of artists."

A very important observation—the museum as a space of education, inspiration, and motivation for other artists.

Maxwell L. Anderson

Alan asked about the possibility of opening up major museum boards. It took me quite some time to persuade the Whitney Museum board that it would be logical to have a seat for an artist. I was lucky enough to have three artists on the board of Toronto's Art Gallery of Ontario, a much larger museum spanning from the Renaissance to the present with a budget comparable to the Whitney's.

The concern expressed by the Whitney's board was that having an artist could create conflicts of interest. I noted that it might well be a conflict of interest to have trustees who actively collected in the general areas that the museum does, but that I trust members to recuse themselves when discussions warrant it.

Eventually, I was given the green light by the Nominating Committee to invite Chuck Close, who graciously accepted over a bottle of Glenlivet in his studio, and proved to be a superb trustee. Chuck has helped keep the conversation alive and focused on the museum's mission. His term was up this June.

My nominee to succeed him would have provided a return engagement to mine a museum, in this case the Whitney, but that was not to be. Chuck's term has been extended, and he will be terrific as long as he cares to stay on. My preference was to alternate, at the end of each three-year term, between a more senior artist and a midcareer artist.

As far as other positions on boards, the prevailing desire of most nominating committees is to have trustees with the means necessary to fuel a campaign and support the annual fiscal burden of the operating budget. One can understand the impulse. On the other hand, across the nation there is still an unfilled need for greater ethnic diversity and better representation of various segments of an artistic spectrum—in the Whitney's case, for example, for more collectors of contemporary art.

For the makeup of a board to change, there has to be an overarching will to do it. That is not the impulse around the United States today. When times are tight, whatever will there might be is put to the side in a quest to find people with proven capacity to give.

Mary Kelly

Over the years, I have noticed how the same work, shown in different contexts, draws vastly different audiences, in terms of numbers and responses, and perhaps this is why I placed emphasis on the issue of reception in my earlier remarks. Of course, in making a work, there is a subjective investment that presupposes an audience, or put another way, the desire of the other. I think artists are always speaking, consciously or unconsciously, to very specific people—friends, lovers, patrons, collectors, and sometimes to certain communities—professional, political, social, generational, or geographic, but this is never the same audience constructed by the exhibition. Considered as a "statement," you could say an exhibition is formulated by a curator/author who is given the

The public for this exhibition is not only the dependable busloads of children who are brought to the museum by regional schools, but also, perhaps more important, families who bring their children to the art museum on weekends and even Thursday evenings.

Now, just a few months prior, we had an outstanding exhibition of photographs by Robert Frank called *London/Wales*. It was beautiful, moving, intellectually rich, and provocative. The exhibition told a story through pictures of bankers and miners in Great Britain after WWII as seen through the eyes of a preeminent photographer. This was a very important exhibition, and the first time these photographs, which just preceded those of the renowned series *The Americans*, had been on view. By the way, I was also not the curator of this exhibition. It was the work of Philip Brookman, our senior curator of photography and media arts. I don't know the actual attendance figures, but I think it's safe to say that the Frank exhibition was seen by relatively few people; by which I mean, the galleries were not always full, which surprised me. In N.Y.C. there would have been lines around the block. In Washington, this was not the case.

I don't think I will ever understand the Washington audience, in part because there are so many museums drawing on and distorting a given institution's view of that audience. Indeed, this may be the main reason why the galleries were not always full during the Frank show. For a metropolitan area with a population roughly equal to that of St. Louis, there is more going on here than could possibly be seen by the 20% Alan Wallach mentions. If this were St. Louis, Seattle, Atlanta, or Denver, and we were the only major art game in town, the situation would be very different. Moreover, the Corcoran is one of the very few art museums in the city, and maybe the only one, that does not get one dollar of federal or District funding. As a result, it dramatically affects our bottom line when people don't visit, or if we consistently lose visitors to the National Gallery, which gets about 100 million dollars a year directly from Congress.

The Johnson show is reaching the farthest edges of our public while the Frank show touched and was deeply admired by mainly our core constituency. It is important to note here that, at the Corcoran, our core constituency is not only deeply committed to artists like Frank but also to reaching out and grabbing the farthest reaches of our viewing public, which includes importantly the region's children, and literally pulling them in. The idea is that if they come while they are young, they will hopefully come again as they grow older. So, they come, get their pictures taken while sitting among [Pierre-Auguste] Renoir's *Boating Party*, and they take the photo home and put in on their wall. (Art with a capital "A" in their bedrooms?)

This is the institution's thinking and its strategy. The Corcoran is overtly civic-minded and strives mightily to achieve a democratic representation of visitors in its galleries. It sees itself as committed to the District and its inhabitants in ways that other art museums in the area are not. It is also appropriate here to consider that exhibitions like Johnson help pay for exhibitions like Robert Frank, or my recent biennial, *Fantasy Underfoot.*

Maurice Berger

Jonathan, you wrote: "It is important to note here that, at the Corcoran, our core constituency is not only deeply committed to artists like Frank but also to reaching out and grabbing the farthest reaches of our viewing public, which includes importantly the region's children, and literally pulling them in."

Apropos of what Dan and Mary said about actively teaching the public about the art it is seeing: Why couldn't you bring in this "diverse" audience, including school children, by animating (through all forms of pedagogy) the best possible exhibitions, including your own biennial?

I think we might want to wait until Thursday/Friday—when the topic will center on museum education–to answer this question.

Stefano Basilico

I'm going to jump ahead, Maurice, and try and address the question of education and audience now, since I think they *need* to be linked.

As Maurice already highlighted, Dan makes a very important point, and one I would like to second and expand upon.

Dan's quote: "Because of this feeling of being excluded, I believe that one of the most important commitments any museum professional can make is to try to reach out and connect to the public through continuous lectures, gallery tours, workshops, and the difficult but necessary writing of readable wall and brochure texts."

Before taking my job at New School University and the Milwaukee Art Museum, and therefore being able to claim the title of curator, I was something which I suspect nobody else on this panel was, I was a dealer. Oh, the Shock, the Horror! But seriously, I want to address the educational role of art dealers, at least of some, and the importance they play in building audience for contemporary art and ways that museums (BTW all museums) could benefit from their model.

Before opening my own gallery, I worked at Sonnabend gallery, New York, for many years. The most important lesson I learned there was the need for the dealer to transmit his or her enthusiasm and understanding for the art, and artists, that were on exhibit. Antonio Homem, the then and present director, was and still is available and will to talk to anybody about the work on view, when he's not on the phone. Naturally, one of the reasons he and many other dealers do this is to make a sale, but what also happens is that information is distributed to many, many people who will never buy a work from a gallery. Artists, as Irving said, are an important audience for museums, and for galleries too. As a young dealer, who was showing even younger artists, I spoke to as many people as I could about the work I was showing. It was my job to be an advocate for it, and I took that job seriously—actually, it was the part I enjoyed the most. Lest anyone think I am presenting too rosy a picture, let me say that unfortunately things are changing and have changed (the architecture of Chelsea is not the architecture of SoHo, where Leo [Castelli]'s desk was in plain sight and in shouting distance to anyone who entered the gallery, while Matthew Marks's desk is not visible and cannot be found unless you pass through various doors and sentries—and Matthew is just one example). The exception that confirms the rule is that Antonio is still visible in the new Sonnabend gallery with nary a velvet rope blocking the way. Younger dealers are by necessity more accessible; they need to be since they are trying to convince an interested audience that the unknown artists they are showing are worthwhile.

Museums are, or should be, when it comes to contemporary art, in the same position: that of convincing an audience that these artists are worthwhile. Museums suffer from an even greater obstacle, which is that their audience is not necessarily interested, nor do they see the value of contemporary art to their lives. Now, I'm not proposing that curators hang out in their exhibitions and talk to everybody that comes along, but the fact that most museums have separate departments for education and curatorial is an indication that they are seen as two separate activities, as opposed to two different tools to be used at different times to achieve the same greater goal.

I will not make specific structural suggestions now; mostly because I think they would need to be customized on a case-by-case basis, but I believe that already diminishing the conceptual barrier between curating and education would be a good start.

Raina A. Lampkins-Fielder

I'm heartened by this discussion about audiences, but am reminded again how far museums still need to go to identify and serve their perceived audiences. I'm an idealist and truly believe that what I do in museums can resound broadly and make the world a better place. When Sylvia Yount states that we do what we do to make museum experiences meaningful even though that sounds "clichéd," I say, hear, hear! We don't actually say that enough . . . and mean it. We have to admit to ourselves, though, that our audiences come to the museum for various reasons, some of which may not be in line with what our preconceptions of what a "meaningful" audience experience might be. It is crucial that the museum be willing to provide audiences multiple access points for engagement while simultaneously acknowledging the various ways that people learn.

Although educational programming—for the novice museum-goer to the expert—is the most obvious medium for engaging audiences, I would argue that audience needs, expectations, and modes of acquiring information be infused into the preliminary conception of an exhibition (and the definition of an institution, for that matter), exhibition interpretation, and its supporting design as well. Look, I've been in enough exhibition meetings where the question: Who is our audience for this exhibition? or better still: How will this exhibition engage various audiences and who are these audiences? is never asked. Or, often, the audience is considered initially but, when the practical demands of mounting an exhibition loom large, the audience is systematically carved out. Where there was once an exhibition design that allowed for a variety of physical engagement with the work, be it speedy or slow, interactive or introspective, there is now a claustrophobic labyrinthine space; where there was once a resource area integrated into the exhibition experience that broadened its contextual potential, there is now a single shelf at the exit of an exhibition with a copy of the catalogue perched on it (you've seen the movie, now buy the book).

It's difficult to have the much-needed discussion about the quality of the content in wall labels when on a very practical level, the text in wall labels is often too small—

and too long—for the average viewer to read comfortably. And there remains the perennial debate about the amount of appropriate seating in the galleries. While we all must be mindful of the presentation of the object and insure that it is presented in the best manner, we must also accept the fact that we have real audiences with real needs—not conjectural ones who we imagine engage with us philosophically and intellectually only and who reside in bionic bodies that can read miniscule wall text with minimal lighting through the backs of the visitors crowded around it; audiences who never need to sit to either contemplate what they've just seen or just to take a load off. When we are both sensitive and responsive to these realities then we can begin to be honest with ourselves about who the audiences are for art museums and how we really want to serve them.

The museum has to have a common goal throughout all of its programming and define for itself what audiences it wants to continue to serve and the new audiences it wants to cultivate. These discussions should not be restricted to individual areas of the museum nor to the education department—which often serves as cleanup crew for exhibitions that do not actively provide access to multiple audiences with various needs. These should be institution wide discussions that include education, curatorial, exhibition design, development, marketing, and human resources departments. (I include H.R. because, well, let's not fool ourselves, if the employees of an institution do not accurately reflect the community which it attempts to serve, we are seriously compromised, no matter how well-meaning we may be. I am acutely aware that my presence simply as an African-American woman in a managerial position in a museum changes the culture of that institution and the type of programming that it will do.)

That said, I appreciate that Maurice states that he is a committed observer of the observer. If museum professionals would spend an hour a week (hey, an hour during an entire exhibition run) on the gallery floor really observing the public, listening to the types of questions that they ask guards or docents, watching how a multigenerational family group moves through an exhibition or participates in a gallery program, following the person in the wheelchair and watching how she/he negotiates a corner or around a three-dimensional object, we would be moving quickly toward making ourselves actually relevant both to the intellectual and the practical needs of the public. After all we all want our visitors to "get it" and to be as excited and critical about the artists and their work as we are.

It is now customary when we speak about audiences to also speak about community. This is an even more illusory term in many ways than audience, in that implicit within community is the idea of social interaction. Many of the participants speak of the museum and art itself as a "social practice," a "communal" experience, and as socially transformative—sentiments with which I wholeheartedly agree. I do believe that the museum is both an educational institution in its commitment to enabling people to learn and a community resource in bringing people together. But it is a struggle, and I'm afraid that museums may be reluctant to open themselves up to a democratic notion of community. The question of community/communities and engaging them has certainly been circulating around museum education tables for awhile. Sorry to say that we haven't come to a conclusion yet, but there does seem to be a distinction between "community" and "audience" in museums.

George G. King

As a practical aside, we are an institution situated in what is considered a destination-location for tourists with the four seasons experiencing their more or less predictable peaks and valleys in attendance. We know the museum's primary audience, 85% in fact, is made of tourists planning to spend a few days in the area. As a single-artist museum whose mission is to contextualize Georgia O'Keeffe while framing a discussion and program for defining American Modernism, we also have exhibited the work of over 155 other artists, 15 of whom are living. A good portion of our permanent collection remains on view for the out-of-towners because we know they expect to see O'Keeffe works and, in fact, are disappointed if most of the galleries aren't devoted to her work. So, for our audience, and like many other institutions, there must be a balance with our programs—one that extends from and for the broad range of international visitors to one that examines the lingering contextual concerns and discussions of American Modernism.

In our case, because O'Keeffe was admired not only because of the enduring and universal appeal of her images, but because of her role in the larger development of modernism and her identity with much of the same landscape that endures today, the audience for her work, her life, her legacy, appears to be sustaining itself.

Not only Santa Fe, but more broadly, the unique landscape that first attracted her here in the late '20s is still doing the same thing today for the same reasons even with the proliferation of casinos.

Maurice Berger

I find Stefano's, Raina's, and George's personal discussions—as museum professionals—both very enlightening and important. A great pendant to some of the theoretical issues we've been discussing.

Stefano, you wrote: "Antonio Homem, the then and present director, was and still is available and will to talk to anybody about the work on view, when he's not on the phone."

Antonio, alas, is a very rare presence in the gallery world—a dealer, intellectual, facilitator all in one person. Leo personified this type of dealer. So, too, Paula Cooper, Illeana Sonnabend, and Marian Goodman. This kind of dealer scarcely exists in the ranks of the new generation.

Raina: Your post is astonishing in its honesty and incisiveness. I can't wait for our discussion on education and pedagogy on Thursday and Friday.

Barbara Buhler Lynes

In many ways the problem lies in the fact that American museum audiences, for the most part, are completely unprepared for the experience of looking at and responding to works of art—much less understanding or feeling passionate about them. Even those who come to museums fairly regularly to take in what they want to see, or more often what the media has promoted as worth seeing (indeed as Mary has pointed out, critics exert a huge influence over what people want to see or think they want to see), most know almost nothing about either the art on the walls or the artists who made them. Thus, as Dan has pointed out, the experience often leads to feelings of exclusion.

No matter what museums do to learn about their audiences, no matter what they provide visitors in terms of information about what is on view through wall texts, exhibition brochures and catalogues, lectures, tours by curators and docents, and audio tours, they confront the reality of having to begin at the beginning, as most people have had no training with respect to looking at works of art. Almost no elementary or secondary schools in this country include the study of art history as a component of the curriculum, and thus, if children aren't lucky enough to either be so curious about art that they pursue its history on their own or have parents, relatives, or friends who know and teach them about this history and take them to museums, they have no way as either children or adults of coming to terms with experiencing the art on museum walls.

I can't remember who suggested earlier on in this conference that if monies were allocated to teaching elementary and high school students about looking at and feeling comfortable with looking at art, and in turn teaching them the realization that the power to come to terms with the work of art and their feelings about it lies within, but I concur, and feel that if this were the case that the 20% figure that Alan has cited as being representative of that part of the population visiting art museums in this country would escalate dramatically.

Sylvia Yount

Since I first raised the specter of J. Seward Johnson at the Corcoran Gallery of Art (the latest of many such case studies), I wanted to speak to Jonathan's candid and thoughtful response, particularly the significant point he makes about museum programming and the ideal of diversity and balance.

It may seem obvious, but is worth repeating that at most art museums the crowd-pleasing exhibitions help pay for more scholarly or challenging projects, not to mention acquisitions. (This is the case at the High Museum of Art, where revenue from a string of popular exhibitions—Impressionism, Picasso, Matisse, Norman Rockwell—fueled the establishment of an "enhancement" fund used for the purchase of a significant array of historical and contemporary art over the last few years.)

Like Maurice, I'd argue that it would be better to approach all thoughtful projects as potentially popular—at least with some component of our audience—but let's be clear about what informs such programmatic decisions. Focus groups and marketing surveys have become a central component of exhibition planning at most art museums, sometimes outweighing curatorial expertise and passion. It seems to me that the real danger lies with those directors and board members who become addicted to the content-free blockbuster, losing their compass and forfeiting responsibility for the institution's supposedly primary educational mission.

Raina's point about the tension between notions of audience and community is also important here. Yes, museums need to be sensitive to their core audiences while looking further afield with an eye to cultivation. But it's also incumbent upon us—as public educators—to introduce fresh and relevant material to our visitors, lest we succumb to the "give the people what they want" consumerist syndrome.

The Museum as Gatekeeper

14–15 October 2003

Maurice Berger

One of the museum's most important responsibilities is that of cultural gatekeeper. Museums make decisions about what's in and what's not—in terms of collection, permanent and temporary displays, and programming. Cultural decision making, of course, is never truly "objective": the gatekeeper makes decisions based on subjective understandings of taste, quality, relevance, and cultural and historical significance.

The problems inherent in cultural gatekeeping became clear to me in a two-part project I completed for *Art in America* in September 1990: "Are Art Museums Racist?" The answer then was to a great extent yes. And while things have improved over the past decade, the museum's decision making continues to reflect a range of biases and hierarchies. The role of gatekeeper, of course, extends far beyond the issue of identity. Museums must make decisions about disciplinary boundaries (what constitutes "Art," for example), the period, nationality, and type of art they are mandated to exhibit and collect, the audience they are trying to reach, the architecture of their buildings, and the tastefulness, beauty, and importance of the objects they sanction and acquire.

In 1992, curator Donna De Salvo, then at the Parrish Art Museum in Southampton, New York, organized a remarkable exhibition at that institution: *Past Imperfect: A Museum Looks At Itself.* I can think of no exhibition that more incisively and honestly self-examined the hierarchies, motives, and sensibilities of its sponsoring institution.

Past Imperfect was neither accusatory nor tendentious. Its curator meticulously and open-mindedly excavated the museum's storerooms and archives to build a complex historical picture of a century-old institution in constant flux. More than anything, her inquiry—which culminated in an exhibition and catalogue that were at once innovative in design and rigorous in execution and content—revealed the reasons for a particular institution's policies of inclusion and exclusion, from the changing fortunes and demographics of the Southampton community aroundit, to the ascendance of new directors and curators, to the influence and power of the museum's wealthy patrons and founder.

In this two-day session, I would like to explore the museum's role as gatekeeper. To what extent should museums "look at themselves" in an effort to self-consciously examine their own history of exclusionary decision making? Who traditionally has made these decisions? What effect have these choices had on the museum's relationship to audience, collecting habits, and the art world as a whole? To what extent are restrictive decisions about "appropriate" content a form of cultural censorship? To what extent do standards of "artistic quality" reflect cultural biases and ignorance? To what extent can the museum's audience influence these processes? How does economic class shape the museum's role as an arbiter of taste and aesthetic respectability? How have certain "alternative" institutions undermined, altered, or defied the museum's role as gatekeeper? What do you see as appropriate changes in the museum's gatekeeping role?

Joan Rosenbaum

Dear Maurice, what a huge topic. Taking a highly practical view, I'll start by saying that it is possible, alas, for a museum to have fascinating exhibitions or wonderful collections on view and have very few people walk in the door. There can be multiple reasons: no money for marketing; image of museum mysterious or confusing to public; huge competition in a city with many museums; no press coverage; no evening open hours. These, I know, sound very mundane when you are bringing up issues of class and standards of beauty, but they are very real issues.

On the positive side of your large question is the fact that museums, except in the rarest of cases, are always in flux. It's very difficult in fact to keep museums from changing, unless you are a Barnes Foundation or the Isabella Stewart Gardner Museum. New trustees, curators, directors, educators, marketers, and fund-raisers influence the hierarchies of taste; competition, demographics, politics, and world events also influence institutional change. (Some obvious examples are the exhibitions that were created post-9/11 [in particular the push-pinned photo show in Soho]; and the tightening of NEA and NEH funding for any edgy shows during the Cheney/Helms era and even more recent times.)

That said, I feel the most important resource for a museum—to reach an audience, to excite them, present new ideas, inspire them to think in an atmosphere that doesn't feel excluding, etc.— the most important resource is imagination. Imagination balanced with a decent amount of managerial expertise is what indeed brings in the money, press, and audience. It is what creates a transformative experience in the galleries. Fabulous scholarship on an artist or group of artists is lifeless without it. This isn't just the creative imagination of the curator, but also the imagined experience for the audience and the imagined encounter with the institution and the art.

Maurice Berger

Let me restate the central question of this topic (to make things simpler): How and why do museums make decisions about what they will sanction and support and what they will not, and how do these decisions lead to exclusionary practices? Why, for so many years, did most art museums ignore women and people of color? How do cultural conceptions of taste, quality, or elitism inform these exclusions? When are these exclusionary policies censorious, or racist, or sexist, or delimiting?

So the real subject of this topic is the politics of *Exclusion*. How and why it operates within the museum. And how these policies can change.

Carol Duncan

In 19th- and through most of 20th-century museum culture, education was a pivotal value. Liberal ideology assumed that people were or could become reasoning individuals, responsible citizens who, by exercising their individual rights, contributed to the self-realization of the state. Citizenship—the exercise of freedom—was premised on the ability to reason. Going to a public art museum was one of the cultural experiences that engaged, developed, and affirmed this "civilized" self. Even when museums lacked formal education programs (which, in any case, were usually addressed to genteel or wannabe-genteel audiences), the museum collections and presentations were thought to be inherently uplifting and educational. The model of the "aesthetic museum" that developed in Boston in the early 20th century is a variant of this: it addressed a "cultivated" viewer and provided an experience that affirmed the visitor's sense of being civilized, of being able to partake of the proffered spiritual fare set before it, and therefore worthy of leading in the political realm. And, as we can now see, the museum also authoritatively located civilization as an attainment limited to particular groups, namely, those familiar with Western European high culture.

What I want to stress here is a set of linked liberal assumptions: that a reasoning individual is the museum's target audience, that this reasoning individual is the same one who knows how to exercise his (later, hers too) freedom to act politically, and that familiarity with museum culture, including knowledge about how to be aesthetically uplifted (usually a class-based learned skill), is a demonstration of one's self-realization as civilized. It's important to remember that this very forceful and compelling liberal ideology underwrote the dominant museum ritual for two centuries, and even today it still provides formulas for museum collecting, organizing, and display.

Our world today—in the U.S. and elsewhere, but nowhere more than in the U.S.—is saturated with a debased and empty rhetoric of liberalism, even to the absurd point of being told that bombing Iraq (and killing an estimated 10,000 civilians) was necessary to protect our freedom—this at a time when we no longer enjoy even the pretense of fairly electing our chief executive. Where does all this take us now? The whole long history of the public art museum was predicated on an Enlightenment concept of "the public," of the existence of a public sphere. This suggests to me two very contradictory things: that what we have been seeing (as many of you already pointed out very well in the introductory session) is museum culture trying to compete with mass media in some way (alas, it sometimes betters it in mindlessness); but also that museum space is one of the few kinds of places we have in which to think and feel and get some perspective on our existence. Maybe I'm saying Down With Museums and Long Live Museums.

Karen Mary Davalos

Carol Duncan's post is exactly what I have been hinting at these past several days. Exclusion operates because it shores up liberalism. So that in order to open up the museum—and I wrote and lost a post last night about why it is economically necessary to open up art museums—we must get beyond the liberal assumptions about public institutions and private citizens.

This will change art history, notions about a public, audiences, collecting, exhibition interpretation—the whole *tamal*. Inclusion requires a reformulation of the museum's own hierarchies and departments.

This would also include a rethinking of what we mean by inclusion. As others would suggest, to date we have a mutation of multiculturalism, and the type that only reinforces exclusion, or an open-then-shut-gate policy. One or two exhibitions of artists of color, one curator of color, one initiative that reaches out to communities of color—these are the types of open-then-shut-gatekeeping practices that have marred the museum since the 1980s. That is, I am not confident that current understanding of people of Mexican descent will aid in the opening up of the museum world. Museums just don't have a clue about this population. I say this because the university world has yet to get a firm grasp of the scholarship in Chicana/o Studies—we read ourselves, but few others do—and thus, how could we expect museum staff to know this material if it has yet to circulate in the conventional disciplines. (I am not blaming Chicana/o Studies scholars for their exclusion within academia.)

Imagine my surprise, then, when the Los Angeles County Museum of Art (LACMA) opened an exhibition that echoed the mythic and discursive counternarrative of Chicanismo. *The Road to Aztlan: Art of a Mythic Homeland* (2001) claimed that people on both sides of the U.S./Mexico border are of a shared cultural space and heritage. It appeared as if Chicanas/os had stormed the museum and won, but this was not the case. In fact, the museum did not anticipate two things precisely because of the mutation of multiculturalism/inclusion: 1) that the Spanish-speaking audience would attend in large numbers, breaking attendance records that year, and perhaps the following year, and 2) that another group of visitors would protest against Yolanda M. Lopez's painting, *Nuestra Madre,* which fuses the Mexican diety, Coatlicue, with the Virgin of Guadalupe. Some Mexicans/Mexican Americans found the image to be sacrilegious, while another group of feminists found it liberating. LACMA curator Virginia Fields knew that her audience would be Spanish-speaking and she insisted that all text be presented in Spanish and English, but I doubt that Dr. Fields and the other museum departments knew what to make of the ritual performed there to bless the space. And that is my point. It happens, but the precious little moments of beauty and awe are lost, misfiled, or ignored.

The opened museum would be able to anticipate and design programming to enhance and support these types of ritual performances simply because it would comprehend the deeper cultural meanings that people have about art. It would not be embarrassed or apologetic. It will have expanded its notion of art in order to make such connections and collaborations with alternative arts centers, artist collectives, and community-based organizations. Again I suggest that the future of the large metropolitan museum depends upon the alternative arts spaces that have a longer and more significant relationship in the communities outside the museum's doors. The politics of exclusion currently shapes these relationships and collaborations between alternative arts centers and museums, but this will not last.

Long live the OPEN museum!

Maurice Berger

Karen, you wrote: "Again I suggest that the future of the large metropolitan museum depends upon the alternative arts spaces that have a longer and more significant relationship in the communities outside the museum's doors."

This is especially true given the polyglot nature of the urban environment. But as you yourself so eloquently point out: the politics of inclusion as we now know it in most museums is shallow at best, disingenuous at worst. And we must also consider the inherent elitism (not to mention snobbery) of the mainstream museum: How many traveling shows organized by small, alternative institutions ever make it into the hallowed halls of the mainstream Museum?

Most art museums, almost by their very nature, continually reinforce this exclusionism. They take their role as gatekeeper *very* seriously.

Carol and Karen's point about the liberal ideologies that underwrite the museum is very important to this discussion. I hope we will have follow-up by other panelists.

David A. Ross

I think that there are few, if any, museum professionals who remain unaware of the role that their institutions play as "gatekeepers." The extensive self-examination that nearly all museums have undertaken during the past decades has made substantial changes in the ways that the men and women who direct and staff our museums understand their constituent communities. If this is the product of liberalism, than I for one applaud this seemingly disgraced ideology.

Perhaps the reason that this topic has attracted so few posts is that it presents itself as a rhetorical trap rather than a celebration of change taking place in a wide range of art museums.

The idea that Los Angeles County Museum of Art can now be seen as a model institution is no surprise to anyone who knows its dynamic and creative director, or who understands the changed demographics of California. Other major encyclopedic museums—most notably the Museum of Fine Arts, Boston, and the Metropolitan Museum of Art—have also made enormous strides towards embracing their changed audiences—changes that have come about, in part, because of three decades of patient and steady audience development work.

So, yes, the museum retains an unusually important and powerful role in both shaping audiences and reflecting the nature of their changing communities. The work is ongoing, far from done, but worthy (and in need) of our continuing constructive criticism.

Maurice Berger

David, you wrote: "Perhaps the reason that this topic has attracted so few posts is that it presents itself as a rhetorical trap rather than a celebration of change taking place in a wide range of art museums."

I think the questions I ask are both complicated and difficult. I also think there is a good deal of grey area, vis-à-vis the question of expanding the museum's cultural purview. Rhetorical trap? No. Just my own voice and opinion (shaped by personal experience) on this issue calling out for other voices—to agree, parse, ruminate, or disagree as you have done.

Barbara Kirshenblatt-Gimblett

Might it be helpful to identify exemplary instances of alternative spaces, artists' projects, independent curation, and the like? We pretty much know the problem as it manifests itself in major metropolitan museums. I'm interested in responses to the limitation of major museums—whether within them or elsewhere.

Maurice Berger

Thanks, Barbara. Good point. Some of the most important boundary-breaking work being done in museums today is occurring in alternative institutions—small museums, certain university galleries, etc.

I have a question for you, Barbara (as well as the other panelists): As a longtime observer of the museum, what institutions do you think are exemplary in this regard—i.e., "alternative" institutions advancing new ideas about the museum, its boundaries, and its role in society?

Donna De Salvo

It has been over ten years since *A Museum Looks at Itself* took place, an exhibition that grew from my desire to understand a museum I had just begun working for. At the time, there were many other projects that sought to make visible the museum and its methodologies. Most of these were undertaken by artists at the invitation of museums, including Fred Wilson, Judith Barry, Joseph Kosuth, and Barbara Kruger. Our project involved Barry and Wilson, both of whom made brilliant contributions to the exhibition.

However, I suppose what was different about *A Museum Looks at Itself* was that the bulk of the "looking" was undertaken by the museum staff, that is, from inside the institution. I think this is a very important distinction. Did the project change anything? Did it make a difference? I cannot attest to its long-term impact, but I can say that at the time it energized the entire institution, at every level. It also created an important context for an exhibition program that was about to make a far greater commitment to contemporary art, with all the challenges this implies. Most importantly for me, it was a way in which to make the historical as much a part of the present as the past. By unraveling the past, including Southampton's historical relationship to England, attitudes towards its African-American and Native-American populations, and to challenging art itself, it was possible to see how much of that past was, in fact, still present. It was a way of stimulating an honest public conversation about the present, and a future.

Barbara Kirshenblatt-Gimblett

The events of 9/11 and their aftermath generated some extraordinary responses that might be useful as a way of thinking about alternative practices. I've written about some of them, as have others. Have a look at: http://www.nyu.edu/fas/projects/vcb/case_911/pdfs/kodak.pdf. Two projects in particular impressed me: *Here Is New York: A Democracy of Photographs,* http://www.hereisnewyork.org/ and *Exit Art's Reactions,* http://www.exitart.org/reactions/front.htm. But there were others, even in major museums such as the National Museum of American History (I found their Website even more powerful and interesting than the exhibition), *September 11: Bearing Witness to History,* http://www.americanhistory.si.edu/september 11/index.asp. I find these examples illustrative for a variety of reasons, not least of which is their highly participatory nature and the way they put art and curatorship into question and into play.

Maurice Berger

The Parrish Art Museum, of course, is a relatively small, regional institution (albeit with strong New York art world connections). Apropos Barbara's question: Could such an elaborate and rigorous self-inquiry undertaken by museum *staff* (as opposed to inviting Fred Wilson, say, into the mix) take place in a large mainstream museum? Would such a project be too "inside the beltway" or disruptive to the delicate balance of funding, trustee support, and attendance that all museums face?

Could the Corcoran Gallery of Art undertake such a project (Jonathan), or the High Museum of Art (Sylvia), or the Tate Modern (Donna)? And would such institutions even want to or need to?

Simon Leung

It's hard to keep up with the dialogue while teaching during the first half of this conference and traveling during the second—as I am now—but here are some scattered thoughts on the museum as "gatekeeper."

In a 1977 essay on the old J. Paul Getty Museum in Malibu, Joan Didion astutely pinpoints an ironic secret at work in the enjoyment of museums. She begins the essay with a description of reviews of the museum in the bourgeois press, reviews which render the museum as an ostentatious display of one man's vulgar wealth; as a simulacrum of "real" high culture; as "Jewish" even, if she "did not misread the subtext in 'like a Beverly Hills nouveau-riche dining room' or 'gussied up like a Bel-Air dining room.'"

She goes on to describe the tension between the museum ideally conceived as the imaginary inheritor of a truly aristocratic attitude—the one which stood in contrast to the perception of the old Getty. "Something about the place," she writes, "embarrasses people." The old Getty, she claims, offended because it showed "Ancient murals (that) were not always bleached and mellowed and 'tasteful.' Ancient murals once looked as they do here: as if dreamed up by a Mafia don." In other words, the old Getty laid bare, perhaps unintentionally, mythic notions the educated middle class have about the past, about the foundation of society, about the reason we go to museums in the first place—to "elevate" our sensibilities as bourgeois sophisticates.

What J. Paul Getty built, however, was immensely popular: "As a matter of fact large numbers of people who do not ordinarily visit museums like the Getty a great deal. . . . On the whole 'the critics' distrust great wealth, but 'the public' does not. On the whole 'the critics' subscribe to the romantic view of man's possibilities, but 'the public' does not. In the end the Getty stands above the Pacific Coast Highway as one of those odd monuments, a palpable contract between the very rich and the people who distrust them least."

This observation of the distance between our desires for the museum to be an instrument of the social good (be that spiritual uplift or social activism) and the attendance of a museum audience not predisposed to such desires could have been put forth by [Michel] Foucault or

Bourdieu. The disciplining of taste and class, political and social distinctions that constitute the jouissance of museum attendance is at the heart of why anyone goes to a museum in the first place. People (we) go to museums because they (we) want to partake in a pleasurable fantasy (and yes, I include in this an enjoyment of a political spirit of whatever persuasion, be that Chicano identity, the Russian avant-garde, or the Situationist sublime). The enjoyment of this fantasy is by definition a psychic enactment of constraints—that is, we know our desire to see "beautiful," "extraordinary," or "challenging" objects/propositions/events in the museum because these objects/propositions/events are isolated from the polyphony of the world outside the gate. Psychic constraint is the precondition for any form of desire—we set up criteria to limit the object of our wanting. We may not even know what "it" is, but we know that the subtle contour of this object/subject is one and the same as the delicate constraint, the frame if you will, of our desires.

Since I raised the specter of "conflict" as a possible retooling of our understanding of the false binary logic of an either/or (serious reflection/easy fun, enlightened preserve of learning/corporate monstrosity…) dynamic of the museum, I want to apply this generative notion of conflict to the moral, analytical problematic of museums "looking at themselves."

The problem of "cultural gatekeeping," it seems to me, is not necessarily "exclusion" in the simple sense of keeping the less powerful outside the hallowed gates of the museum. Tokenism, as you pointed out Maurice, does not solve a problem of gender, racial, or ethnic exclusions, because they are stop-gaps of larger problems.

What I wish to briefly outline here are the lessons from and constraints placed on art practices that examine the borders within a museum's self-conception. In other words, I propose that the genre of art practice we call institutional critique, growing out of site-specific work, has always worked on the tenuous edges of an institution's (often a museum's) self-conception, and that it derives its power exactly from the conflicts that arise from within the institution. Historical examples abound: Hans Haacke's *MoMA Poll*, Mierle Laderman Ukeles's maintenance projects, Michael Asher's subtle interventions, etc., depended on exposing the site of such work as a site of political struggles. The generation that followed, say Fred Wilson and Andrea Fraser, further complicated the ideological pretenses of the museum by implicating themselves as desiring subjects in performing services which not only reveal the economic differences and power dynamics, say, between the interests of a trustee, a curator, and a guard. . . . In short, the artists working under the rubric of institutional critique are contract players, shifters performing an often well-intentioned, often necessary service within the same ideological given.

Now, I think it is worthwhile for us to think of these moments of "the museum looking at itself" along with the ideological given of the museum, that is, as a parallel analogue to what several of us here have termed the public sphere. But for me, what is at stake is the way in which the museum inherits a particular kind of subject formation apparatus that no matter how much it tries to divest, how well intentioned it is about "inclusiveness," it cannot fully do so exactly because of what we, as artists, curators, museum directors, etc., want from the museum. As various panelists have pointed out—we actually *want* the museum to be that Habermasian post-enlightenment entity that guarantees a ground for reflection in the promotion of the social good, that allows for an educated public debate of this good. Whatever we want the museum to be—less "elitist," more "accessible"—I think we have to get real about this: these places are rare—there are so few places in contemporary capitalist society where spectacle and economics don't dictate the flow of traffic and the expenditure of money and time. The museum, as the official repository of cultural capital, has always implicitly maintained a contract with artists: within its institutional walls is where the fantasy of the autonomous subject can be played out. Put simply: the logic of the condition for institutional critique is no different from the logic of any other form of modern patronage—it depends on artists reframing the institution in a way that does not perturb the role of the institution as the granter of privileges for the artist, the guarantor of bourgeois subject formation in society.

This became palpable for me in the 1990s, when it became common for museums to commission site-specific/institutional critiques of themselves. This was at times institutional narcissism, sometimes the enactment of the conflict I spoke of earlier (say a curator with a progressive agenda). Sometimes they produce lasting works like *Mining the Museum,* but I honestly do not feel that museums can change that much as a result.

This leads us back to the "corporatization" of the museum.

As many have noted, what we speak of as the corporatization of the museum met in this time a flurry of other corporate formations. Nothing is exempt from this, not our favorite bête-noire, television (how many local TV stations once owned by cowboy millionaires are now owned by Rupert Murdoch?), and not our cherished exemplar of creative autonomy, the artist (what are Matthew Barney and Damien Hirst if not corporations that bump up production costs by 20, 50, 100 times to wipe out competition?). We can say that there is nothing new about artists "incorporating" themselves as well. The phenomenon that I think is more interesting is how museums interface with artists who function as corporate entities and what claims are made for them. For example, Jorge Pardo at the Dia Center for the Arts—but that's another discussion.

The heart of the matter is this: I would not like to lose the museum as the imaginary site where democracy is enacted. But as a model of the ground upon which subjectivity is questioned, I would like this ground to sustain a discourse of conflict, of disruption, one resisting the oppressive cohesion that forms under the united banner of corporations interfacing with one another—be that business as usual before the politics of difference challenged the status quo, or the return of the *Gesamtkunstwerke* genius demonstrating a show of force in the gleaming trophy-building that has lost any sense of the public at all.

Irving Sandler

In making their decisions about what to show, museum curators keep an eye on the activities of certain artists, dealers, art editors, art critics, etc.—that is, the art world. Actually, museums generally tend to be rather late as gatekeepers. New artists first achieve recognition by being talked up by fellow artists, then by dealers who give them shows early on, followed by critics who review these shows and write articles. The museum tends to serve as validator of art-world opinion, for better or worse. However, curators have tried to shortcut this process by getting to studios first. Nevertheless, their role remains validation, and as validators their influence is tremendous.

The question, as I view it, is: Does this process result in the recognition of the most vital new art? In my opinion, it has, on the whole.

Maurice Berger

Irving, you wrote: "New artists first achieve recognition by being talked up by fellow artists, then by dealers who give them shows early on, followed by critics who review these shows and write articles."

I would add "alternative" spaces to this list, like Artists Space in New York, for example.

Dan Cameron

Rather than attempt a coherent reply to Simon's erudite and provocative post, I'd like to take a different approach and propose that one of the ways that museums act as gatekeepers is not simply by challenging themselves, but by challenging other museums, and by implication the art community, in the process. One way to consider the origin and growth of New York museums like the Museum of Modern Art, the Whitney Museum of American Art, and the Soloman R. Guggenheim Museum is as correctives to a situation of perceived absence or neglect: not enough modern art, not enough American art, etc. Once these missions are established and the health of the museums defined according to how they achieve these goals, the incentive for radical self-examination largely vanishes.

We could say that the ideal remedy to this process of enforced stagnation is for major museums to commit themselves to drastic programs of soul-searching, but I'm not really sure that this is the best solution. Institutions like the New Museum of Contemporary Art, the Studio Museum, and El Museo del Barrio seem to thrive in part because the built-in resistance of larger museums to substantive change creates a vacant cultural space, one that is being filled by a different generation of entrepreneurial museums. Perhaps other museums will in turn open the way to different audiences that are each, in their way, a kind of niche market within the general museum-going public.

But even these institutions are faced with serious obstacles in their efforts to break new ground. I feel a bit guilty always referring back to the New Museum, but ever since the mid-1990s, when we consciously shifted our focus to a more global program—one that focuses more on new art from Africa, Asia, and South America than any other contemporary art museum in the country—we've met with extremely mixed reactions from the press and public. At times the hostility and neglect—largely from critics who have very little interest in or knowledge about the art world outside the U.S.—results in an exhibition getting largely ignored by the public. This situation highlights the fact that even when museums organize programs that explore new ground, they can only accomplish so much if their constituents reject the new models in favor of programs that are more local, more biased toward the known and the familiar. In this sense, for better and for worse, museums are reflections of the communities they serve.

Maurice Berger

Thanks for your honesty, Dan.

You wrote: "I feel a bit guilty always referring back to the New Museum of Contemporary Art, but ever since the mid-1990s, when we consciously shifted our focus to a more global program—one that focuses more on new art from Africa, Asia, and South America than any other contemporary art museum in the country—we've met with extremely mixed reactions from the press and public."

You should *not* feel guilty about referring back to your own institution and situation. It's the practical application of theory and ideas to our everyday experiences as curators, directors, writers, scholars that makes these issues come alive. It is crucial that we talk these questions through on a personal scale, lest we risk meandering into abstractions and distortions.

Mark Alice Durant

To state the obvious, institutions such as the New Museum of Contemporary Art, the Studio Museum, and El Museo del Barrio exist to address the aesthetic, cultural, and political issues that have been ignored by design or by default by mainstream institutions. It is a good thing that artists/curators/activists band together to create alternative sites. I believe that every community and every generation must, to a large extent, take care of its own, because to expect to be invited to the party is a sign of naiveté or evidence that you already belong to the club. To expect the *museum* to address the real needs/desires of working people is just a daydream at best.

I have conflicting feelings about the band-aid attempts to address issues of inclusiveness. While I fundamentally abhor the real inaccessibility of most art to working people, I have found most attempts made by museum outreach efforts at "community" and "inclusiveness" to be patronizing and ineffective. There is also that persistent presumption (as suggested in earlier posts) about the "civilizing" responsibility of the museum. As if to say that if only these unwashed masses could bask in the edifying glow of our cultural treasures that somehow our social ills might be lessened.

Sylvia Yount

Maurice: You ask if the High Museum of Art would (or could) ever engage in a self-reflective project along the lines that Donna produced at the Parrish Art Museum. First, let me say that although I've heard much about *Past Imperfect*, I did not see it nor have I read the catalogue. However, I gather that it was akin to *Mining the Museum*, with the important exception that the investigation was performed from within, by the museum's own staff. I also gather that it was more critical than celebratory of the Parrish's history on many levels.

I'm intrigued by Donna's statement that this exhibition was done when the Parrish was repositioning itself as a primarily contemporary art institution, and wonder if that shift in mission (if that's what it was) may have accounted for the project's timing and success. By exploring the highs and lows of the Parrish's history (and, by extension, its historical collections) the exhibition, I presume, threw into sharp focus the challenges and goals of the present.

Would such a project be possible at the High—a comparatively young institution (technically founded in the 1920s, but not really "on the map" as a professional museum till the advent of Richard Meier's building in 1983), located in a complex region of the country that due to major social and political upheavals throughout its history embraced Culture later than most metropolitan centers?

In many ways, the examination and redefinition of the High's collection and institutional identity is an ongoing project. Successive directors have shaped it in distinctive ways (particularly Ned Rifkin, who established curatorial departments of photography, folk art, and media arts). Curators have developed holdings that reflect their particular expertise, interest, and taste. Transition is a fact of life at the High, particularly as we draw nearer to an expansion—designed by Renzo Piano—that will more than double our size.

We also have recently undertaken a reinstallation of the permanent collection—reintroducing a historical chronology to our galleries and dismantling what was, at the time, a groundbreaking thematic installation (again, spearheaded by Ned Rifkin) that had lost its focus and relevance. While this earlier installation began with an investigation of the various donor collections that formed the nucleus of the High, as a "permanent" collection display it was hardly presented critically—

as it would not have been in most municipal museums. As others have noted in this conversation, the larger the institution, the harder it is to issue such a public statement about the "past imperfect."

Indeed, in my previous curatorial position at the Pennsylvania Academy of the Fine Arts—a smaller, older, quirkier institution with a more venerable history, scrupulously documented in its archives—I regularly gravitated toward this type of investigative project. Whether focusing on the firing of [Thomas] Eakins and its repercussions for the Academy's collection and identity, or exploring the hits and misses of its exhibition and acquisition histories—for example, saying no thank you, at different times, to [Thomas] Cole, [Frederic] Church, [Mary] Cassatt, Whistler, and Albert Barnes—I found that such efforts were generally embraced both inside and outside the institution.

While this type of analysis may not be as common at larger institutions, I believe that questions about why certain patrons collected what they did—or, more broadly, the issue of gatekeeping—can and should be explored in long-term displays through didactic material (text and/or audio) and guided tours. It's certainly a point I like to raise in my interpretive labels and gallery talks.

In closing this long, drawn-out response, I'd argue that a growing self-awareness about institutional histories and identities is just one of the things that distinguishes the current generation of curators now working at a broad range of institutions, large and small. Perhaps it's just a matter of time before more directors (and boards) follow suit.

Maurice Berger

Sylvia, you wrote: "While this type of analysis may not be as common at larger institutions, I believe that questions about why certain patrons collected what they did—or, more broadly, the issue of gatekeeping—can and should be explored in long-term displays through didactic material (text and/or audio) and guided tours. It's certainly a point I like to raise in my interpretive labels and gallery talks."

I actually find this idea rather extraordinary. I wonder how many institutions, curators, and directors would sanction this kind of information in wall labels. I hope you will bring some of your ideas about didactic materials into our next two-day session—on museum education and pedagogy.

Edward Rothstein

I've been wanting to jump in a few times, so this post refers to some issues raised in previous sections on audiences and on gatekeepers.

One of the issues that Maurice has raised and that has come up again and again in other posts is a question about the restrictive quality of museums, the extent to which museums exclude. And this, of course, means that the museum excludes particular audiences as well as particular works of art. There seems to be very little disagreement about this, though it is usually described in political terms as a manifestation of anything from cultural blindness to racism.

I think the description is correct but the analysis wrong. Yes, museums exclude. They exclude by definition. That is what any collection does. By making certain selections of objects according to certain standards, it necessarily rejects others. It demarcates the world. And though Carol Duncan argues that the emphasis of the traditional museum on an ideal of reason was bound up with the notion of an attainment limited to particular groups, I think reason is precisely what is behind the claims of a museum—any museum—because the archetypal act of reason is the act of demarcation, the act of making certain distinctions, finding certain qualities in one thing and not in another.

Of course, this can lead to unpleasantness. Almost anything can. Reason has been misused to create categories that are now justly shunned. Reason can literally turn into "rationalization"—a justification of prejudices and unexamined passions. And in the act of distinction and selection there is always someone who feels wronged. Nevertheless, we all depend on selection and all museums must do it—or why else should they exist?

My guess is that often, in discussing this notion of exclusion, the issue of democratization gets brought in, as if they were inherently contradictory and that the values of democracy are incompatible with any forms of exclusion. But I don't think they are, unless democratization is treated as an ideology in which all reflections of human enterprise are required to "represent"—to embody a statistic ideal. This is far less liberating than it may seem. The requirement is all. And exclusion is just as endemic to vulgar definitions of diversity as to arbitrary and unreasoned doctrine.

The question is the nature of the criteria for the exclusion—or, to look at the glass half-full—the selection. Many of the museums that have been discussed, including those that are ethnically based or based on a time period or a particular cultural or political taste, are simply defining the selection according to different criteria. These museums, incidentally, will also end up selecting their own audiences as well.

Returning again to a parallel with the art-music scene: There are concert halls that are perfect for certain kinds of music (chamber, solo, orchestral, vocal, operatic), concert halls that are perfect for certain periods (much 16th- and 17th-century music should be heard in a church), organizations that specialize in one thing or another. And there are world music groups that also have their own specialties. We don't require a diversity of attention from each group, nor do we chastise their exclusionary principles. Stories are told by different groups in different ways. Diversity is not an internal characteristic demanded of each group, but one successfully nurtured by a few—a very, very few—societies as a whole.

Perhaps the real object of contention is not the issue of selection, then, but the fact that there is, in museum culture, a certain priority traditionally given to ideas of aesthetic selection. This claim of a certain "objective" aesthetic quality is often challenged for its supposed exclusionary character, as if the notion itself were a form of delusion. But what, after all, is the thrill of the museum that we are all talking about? What Simon Leung calls the "jouissance" of the museum is the reason for the art museum, and it is largely due to the aesthetic power of the object.

Anybody who has felt this knows its character. And it cannot be easily reduced to another category or turned into a superstructure. It is not something class-based. And education is something that only expands its horizons, not something that makes it possible. The aesthetic is felt by the untutored. It crosses cultural and educational boundaries. And it is the reason, I would guess, why many of us became interested in museums in the first place.

It is also, of course, selective, relying on a certain talent of perception (there are aesthetic gifts on all sides of the creative process), and it is also a form of knowledge. Incidentally, one thing that seems to me paramount about the art museum as it developed in the West (and that is now under heavy criticism by many in this symposium) is that under the best of circumstances, the act of selection and inclusion is not limited to particular groups; the selection criteria are not mainly political or even cultural. As far as collected art objects are concerned, recognition of other civilization's aesthetic attainments is one of the triumphs of the great Western art museum.

The aesthetic has not gotten its due in recent years. It is generally pushed aside for political reasons, discarded because of disagreements, shunned for its supposed non-democratic character, treated as an ideology that is a mask for more ugly sentiments. But the aesthetic is a perfectly good category for exclusion and selection and needs to be examined anew. If it can lead to unjustified snobbery, it can also lead to democratic possibility. And to matters even more important. I think it's a worthy form of exclusiveness.

■ ■ ■

16–17 October 2003

Maurice Berger

George Baker, in the first post in this conference, alludes to an issue that has become one of the central themes of our dialogue: the museum as educator. George theorizes an art museum that could exchange the interests of the corporation for "other, older functions: pedagogy, research, and public education." "There are exceptions of course," George continues, "but never has the split between the museum and the university seemed stronger, a split echoed all the way down the line between the museum director and the art historian, the curator and the art critic, the museum public and the art student. Museums seem today in danger of abandoning their possible role as an institution for the education of a public."

The museum's relationship to education and pedagogy at this moment appears to be paradoxical. Never before have education departments been so actively engaged in strengthening the museum's public address—in creating strategies that help its audience to better understand and enjoy the visual culture that it is engaging. Yet some curators remain indifferent to their education departments, thus failing in certain ways to enhance their ability to reach, move, and engage the public.

The subject of this session is museum education and pedagogy. What role can education departments play in the museum of tomorrow? Is the central function of the museum that of educator or something else, such as the archival and art-historical preservation of visual culture? How important are the didactic components of the exhibition—wall labels and texts, context rooms, docent and recorded tours, and even exhibition catalogues? What of the relationship between curators and education specialists—what can they teach each other? And what of the role of new media—particularly of the Internet—in advancing the educational and aesthetic messages and ideas of the art museum?

Once again, there are many kinds of art museums with multiple and divergent missions. So please be specific and feel free to address these questions as broadly or narrowly as you like. And for those of you who are museum professionals, you might want to discuss your own personal stake in these issues.

Jonathan P. Binstock

Last night I attended the unveiling, so to speak, of a remarkable DVD about the life and work of Joseph Cornell. It's not a movie, or what one might normally associate with a DVD, but rather a world of information to which one gains access through "browsing," that is, computer browsing. The DVD works like a CD-ROM, but it is definitely *not* a CD-ROM.

The DVD documents many, if not all (I'm not sure), of Joseph Cornell's boxes in various useful, cross-referenced, and absolutely compelling ways. It features volumes and volumes of material (maybe six very thick books' worth), including factual information; Cornell's films; video commentaries by academics, curators, dealers, collectors, friends of the artist, etc.; source material from art history books and the Cornell Study Center at the Smithsonian's American Art Museum; and, get this, extensive video imagery that convincingly conveys what it is like to look closely at and handle the actual boxes. I've never picked up a Cornell box and jiggled the stuff inside or opened the drawers, etc. Even curators are discouraged from doing this. But I now feel as if I have. I have never seen anything like this DVD in the art world, and I believe it is the first of its kind to appear.

The project is the brainchild of Robert Lehrman, Chair of the Board at the Hirshhorn Museum and Sculpture Garden in Washington and a renowned Cornell collector. It comes with a book titled *Joseph Cornell: Shadowplay . . . Eterniday*, which is now available. Suffice it to say I recommend you pick this up at your local bookstore. Lehrman produced both the book and the DVD—he spearheaded the entire project; it was his idea—but he also worked with many scholars and academics, such as Cornell expert Lynda Roscoe Hartigan, now at the Peabody Essex Museum in Salem, Mass., which gives the project its serious academic heft. It is a lovingly and carefully made thing, a remarkable resource that will benefit people of all types and backgrounds for a long time to come.

My experience last night leads me to believe that I've gotten the first whiff of what art education, publications, and, in particular, a successful digital museum educational experience might look like in the future. In fact, in some ways I think this DVD has surpassed the museum experience. The DVD offers an intimate experience of many art objects, even though the art in question is not actually present. (Well, it was present last night, in the other room, but I dared not touch it nonetheless.) The DVD enabled me to get closer to Cornell's boxes—and a lot of them!—than I had ever been. Granted, Cornell's art is the right candidate for this digital medium. Even the computer screen's luminosity contributes to conveying some of the aesthetic sensibilities Cornell was after, for example, a glowing night moon behind an owl. Rather than distracting one from the actual art, this technology brings one closer to it. Even I have a hard time believing the previous sentence, and I wrote it.

How might an educational experience that puts one into contact with the object, if only virtually, help people to connect with not only art but also museums and what they do? Websites don't do this, nor CD-ROMs. I am encouraged by the Cornell DVD. It is not a toy nor a distraction.

I think Mark Alice Durant is correct when he writes (in the previous topic) "that most attempts made by museum outreach efforts at 'community' and 'inclusiveness' [are] patronizing and ineffective." His comments, in the context of the present topic, make me think of young adults rearranging magnets on a board, wearing 3-D eyeglasses, or pushing a button to change the lights in a room to yellow. Then, of course, there are the patronizing exhibitions to consider. The solution to "patronizing" and "ineffective" lies in the objects in museums, the ones they already have, and fully conveying all that these objects are in their material glory.

One last comment, Stefano Basilico's idea (posted in the "audiences" topic) is a good one, that "diminishing the conceptual barrier between curating and education would be a good start" to expanding audiences and improving the situation in general. Indeed, I think that this DVD is a prime example of this. Educational imperatives—communicating ideas to and establishing the potential for revelatory experiences in the visitor/user—must be included in the germination of an exhibition or project idea.

Maurice Berger

Jonathan, you wrote: "One last comment, Stefano Basilico's idea (posted in the 'audiences' topic) is a good one, that 'diminishing the conceptual barrier between curating and education would be a good start' to expanding audiences and improving the situation in general. Indeed, I think that this DVD is a prime example of this. Educational imperatives—communicating ideas to and establishing the potential for revelatory experiences in the visitor/user—must be included in the germination of an exhibition or project idea."

I could not agree more. In practical terms, how might some of this intermingling occur?

Dan Cameron

Museums really ought to be dedicated, first and foremost, to making a convincing case for the seriousness of art's role in relation to the rest of society. If they fail to do this convincingly, they will be unable to attract a dedicated public. On the other hand, if they can demonstrate that the quality of civic life is severely impaired when art has no place in people's lives, the public will beat a path to their door. The problem with this hypothesis is that most museum directors and curators seem comfortable with the notion that while art may be important to their lives, its impact on the rest of society is not really an issue of compelling interest.

I believe that the only way to bring pedagogical and curatorial practice together within a museum is to have them working together from the beginning. Most museums squarely locate their brain center in the curatorial desk, and educational initiatives are usually tagged onto the final result as a kind of afterthought, or at best, as a parallel stream of ancillary activity. But if educators are bodily present and encouraged to participate while curators are weighing their choices and making their decisions, the results are strikingly different than when curators are left to work things out in isolation. I don't think it's so much a matter of making the curatorial process transparent to the public (whatever that might mean), but of making curators accountable to the museum's public in a way that emphasizes quality of experience over quantifiable results. I'm not sure it's something that can even be tested, but all of us know that when we have an unsatisfying museum experience—from an institution that's too greedy, too stingy, too insular, or too self-satisfied—we can perceive the absence of communication in every nuance of the visit.

Stefano Basilico

As Dan said: "The problem . . . is that most museum directors and curators seem comfortable with the notion that while art may be important to their lives, its impact on the rest of society is not really an issue of compelling interest." True, true. And the issue goes deeper than museum directors and curators, since as a culture we don't privilege the study of art—as a few people have mentioned already—and as a result, while some people find great importance in the contemporary, they usually feel it is an example of their sophistication, not a basic human necessity.

I, too, think that in order to be an active citizen (of any nation) one has to be aware of and engaged in contemporary art, if for no other reason that to be a better informed political actor. Mass media is an insufficient forum for debate and consideration of complex political issues. Critical thinking, a skill that good art history teaches, will be constantly honed as one encounters the new and constantly shifting practice of contemporary art.

Practically speaking, this shift needs to occur outside the museum, not inside. The museum can point in the right direction, but the real success would be for the culture to embrace this notion.

Barbara Buhler Lynes

Having spent many years as a college professor prior to my current work as both a museum curator and director of a museum research center, I have long been committed to the importance of creating situations in which people have the opportunity of becoming excited about art and want to learn more about it. Although preparing courses and lectures for college students is certainly different from organizing exhibitions for museums, the goal remains the same: awakening and enriching people's sensibilities to the complex forces of the creative process with the hope of their becoming more aware of this component of themselves.

Because those who help run the education department at the Georgia O'Keeffe Museum are responsible for training docents, who generally conduct most of our group tours, as well as organizing outreach and teacher programs both within and beyond the immediate community, they ultimately have more contact and direct experiences with our audiences than me and staff members from other areas within the museum. As a result, they develop particular sensitivities to how audiences respond to what they see, from which everyone associated with the museum can learn; nonetheless, museum education departments are often marginalized.

In addition to developing the usual materials for museum visitors—brochures, exhibition catalogues, audio guides, and wall text—the curatorial department here collaborates in a variety of ways with the education department. We plan the kinds of lectures that will accompany exhibitions and discuss how the subject of exhibitions can generate different types of in-house and outreach programs for both adults, children, and families. For example, in conjunction with the exhibition *O'Keeffe's O'Keeffes: The Artist's Collection*, which explored the dynamics of O'Keeffe's management of her own career from the death of Stieglitz in 1946 to her own in 1986—she owned nearly half of her output at the time of her death, which she consciously kept for a variety of reasons—the education department sponsored a workshop on estate planning for artists that was extremely well attended.

While some of our galleries are always filled with works by O'Keeffe, we often organize or host exhibitions of works by O'Keeffe and her contemporaries, or by artists she knew and from whom she learned, to acquaint our audience with the history of American Modernism and O'Keeffe's place within it. In response to this component of our exhibition program, our very creative director of education proposed sponsoring what has turned out to be a very popular series of concerts that provide visitors with the opportunity of experiencing seldom-performed music by a variety of modernist composers. On another note, the education department has organized a highly innovative and very successful program for girls in their early teens—an age when they often confront extremely challenging identity problems—who are interested in becoming artists, based on the profile of O'Keeffe's remarkable commitment to personal independence and self-realization as an artist: "The Art and Leadership Program for Girls." Interest in this program has been so enormous that it is being expanded to include programs for boys, men, and women.

Jonathan P. Binstock

At the Corcoran Gallery of Art we give our educators the title of curator, a nominal distinction that is meant to encourage collaboration between the two departments; and it does. Even if discussion of education programs enters later than sooner into the development of a given project, not a label goes on the wall before the senior curator of education reads it. In the end, we struggle together with the task of writing the labels. I sometimes find that label writing is my most challenging and rewarding task. I take it seriously and try never to pass along the responsibility. Wall text can make all the difference to our visitors, and they go out of their way to thank us when they appreciate it.

But there is a third component that is essential to realizing the much talked about connection between the education and curatorial departments, and that is design, both graphic and exhibition. Regrettably, we don't have an exhibition design department at the Corcoran, which makes securing the ideal collaboration among all three components difficult. We work with freelance exhibition designers who don't have the same integral relationship to the institutional process.

So, ideally, curators, educators, and designers work hand-in-hand to make a unified exhibition product that begins with great ideas, includes great work, and that is successfully conveyed to visitors through smart didactics, exhibition displays, etc. However, I've seen many shows in large museums that do this well and still lack something that the best exhibitions at the Corcoran—or other similar, more nimble institutions where curating is a sort of do-it-all job!—have. Here I'm referring to a distinct, personal, and creative voice that can give an exhibition personality without getting in the way of the art. When too many cooks are in the kitchen, it becomes more difficult to create something gutsy, something with a discernible voice that is both institutional and personal. Exhibitions that reveal how a curator is thinking (and the thinking is clear and smart) are the ones that inspire me the most professionally. It is very difficult to strike a keen balance between the fantasy of ideal, objective institutional product and an exhibition with soul. I have never really been moved by the work of Gerhard Richter, but I think Rob Storr achieved what I'm talking about in his Richter retrospective at the Museum of Modern Art. Indeed, it can happen at large institutions.

George Baker

I'm very interested by the discussions happening here involving the imperatives and projects of different museum education departments. When I raised the specter of pedagogy however, one of my main concerns was the place of art history within the museum of today and of tomorrow. For I don't think this place is secure anymore, and I wonder if others share this concern, or perhaps feel that the changed relations between museums and the field of art history (as it exists in universities) is a good thing.

For example, to speak to Jonathan Binstock's most recent post, I too found the recent Richter exhibition at the Museum of Modern Art to be a profound experience. However, this profundity for me was gleaned from the art despite what I took not only as a terrible job of curation, but a rather violent one. This exhibition was curated in a manner that attempted to do violence, specifically, to the art historical discourses and investigations that have formed around Richter's oeuvre. When, in a critique of the exhibition, Rosalind Krauss raised the question of whether we could have imagined a previous MoMA curator such as William Rubin operating in such a relationship to art history, the distance that we and that the museum have traveled today became clear to me.

So the difference between Rubin's Picasso or Cubism shows and this Richter exhibition is the one I'm asking us to think about. For whatever else its achievements were, and whatever might have been its drawbacks, the MoMA Cubism exhibition transformed the very status of art historical debate upon that movement and on modernism itself. The Richter exhibition, in its violence, has sparked almost nothing new in terms of art historical discourse or debate; it provoked a kind of bored shiver.

I am polarizing; I am exaggerating; but it serves a purpose. I feel that museums and art history stare at each other today over a growing, often hostile divide. The art historian used to be the preacher of the museum (what was the curator then? Missionary?). Now the art historian is like a raving lunatic on the subway (to be ignored), or the homeless person on the street (to be pushed aside, or, perhaps, thrown a stray nickel of support).

I am always amazed by all the catalogues that I see for exhibitions, especially on contemporary art, in which art historians are not called upon at all. This seems a growing trend—the curator writing about the exhibition is enough, other artists writing about the art is enough. We have nothing more to learn from art history or art historians. And they have nothing more to say within museums.

There are exceptions. I've just been involved in a two-year project with the National Gallery of Art, as part of a think tank involved in assisting the curators of the forthcoming retrospective of the Dada movement. This collaboration between curators (most of them trained art historians) and researchers in the art in question has pushed the level of debate to unheard of highs and has produced remarkable insights. I wait now to see what form of exhibition such intense dialogue will produce.

Do people working within museums feel this split that I've just described? Why have our two fields split, in function and in aim? I feel that the museum without art history is like a boat without a rudder.

Maurice Berger

George, you wrote: "I am polarizing; I am exaggerating; but it serves a purpose. I feel that museums and art history stare at each other today over a growing, often hostile divide. The art historian used to be the preacher of the museum (what was the curator then? Missionary?). Now the art historian is like a raving lunatic on the subway (to be ignored), or the homeless person on the street (to be pushed aside, or, perhaps, thrown a stray nickel of support)."

I, too, have sensed this divide. But not just "today," as you suggest. When I was a graduate student (in the 1980s), I found myself being asked to make a rather strange, ultimately polarizing decision: Are you an art historian or a curator? But I suspect that my training (not that different from yours, George) in theoretical art history—my mentor was Rosalind Krauss—made this divide seem particularly exaggerated, given the early resistance of many curators to these kinds of methodologies (structuralism, poststructuralism, neo-Marxism). Yet, I fundamentally agree: there remains an unspoken resistance, *but* I think it works *both* ways.

George, I quoted you at the outset not just for this reason (i.e., the more self-reflexive issue of the art world division of labor) but also because of your fear that "Museums seem today in danger of abandoning their possible role as an institution for the education of a public."

So how might the art historian help improve the museum's relationship to its public?

Olu Oguibe

The responsibility of "educating the public" is a very grave one, indeed, and from the outside one is often left with the impression that museums now approach this task rather mechanically, that is to say, in very predictable ways with methodologies that seem coded in a universal handbook. The effect is that the bar is leveled, not raised, and as has been pointed out already, the goals become more volume—rather than quality-oriented. As Dan pointed out, the curatorial department takes the lead and the education department is brought in to "outreach" the show, and most such departments, it appears, simply bring in the template and at most stack the numbers.

There is often little creativity or element of risk in evidence because, again, often the stakes are too high, the wrong stakes that is. One senses that the internal conversations invoke too many don'ts and often end at meetings after which each department retires to carry out its assignments. In other words, there is little real or truly sustained collaboration between the curatorial and education departments, and little mutual oversight. This is exacerbated when the curatorial initiative or input is from the outside, when the museum is working with an independent curator especially on themes that appear exotic to the normal museum program, and everyone seems at a loss what to do or how to present the exhibition to the public. In such instances there is almost always already a rift between curator and education department, not antagonistic, no, but simply one of unfamiliarity, and ideas have to be passed and filtered through so many channels and layers of communication that there is little left to do but fall back on the method handbook: how many workshops are arranged, how many talks, how many storytellers should be brought in to speak to children on weekends even if storytelling sessions have not a thing to do with the theme of the exhibition.

In one's experience working with major museums and institutions, rarely are curators consulted on how best to outreach the show and very rarely are they allowed to help supervise the more brass-tack aspects of museum outreach, such as accurate titling and dating on wall labels even if these are considered of less consequence. Of course, the larger the institution, the worse the problem. At one such exhibition at a major museum in New York in 2002, there were four inaccurate dates on labels in one small room, which is not to belabor issues.

Artists are another resource that museums seem always very reluctant to involve in their education and outreach. Sometimes this is because artists are considered extraneous to the museum process beyond sending in their works, filling out insurance papers, and, budget permitting, showing up at the press conference and the rowdy exhibition opening and after party. Again, once the provisions in the guidebook have been met, vision and involvement stop. Rarely are artists approached with the question how best to get their work across to the public. Instead things are put to them: "It would be a really good idea if you could come down and do a workshop for the neighborhood kids." Often the artist doesn't really care about a workshop for the neighborhood kids and might not consider that the best way to educate the public on his or her work. Sometimes the museum or institution is simply too frugal to provide for adequate artist involvement in the education and outreach process. However, that is a resource that ought to be harnessed more imaginatively, more meaningfully.

The key here, as has been noted, is greater collaboration from initiative to realization, not only between curators and museum educators but also artists, consultants, designers, marketers, at least at an ideas level that does not muddle the process or results.

Periodic outreach, of course, is only one of the museum's educational roles. There are also more perennial, institutional research and pedagogical roles and in this regard most museums seem to be up to the task and willing to be of service. Museums with collections routinely open their collections to researchers and those that can afford it even institute their own funded research programs that allow scholars and other professionals to take advantage of their resources. How much scholars and other researchers take advantage of these resources is another matter.

Sometimes the results of such research are buried in low-circulation, college tenure-oriented trade journals that, though not entirely inconsequential, are of little overall value to history or the public. Optimistically, one should presume that the results are filtered into college classroom lectures and seminars, visual resource libraries, and graduate advising, from where they may not be visible to the museum, but nevertheless are of immense value. Not everything is instantly quantifiable.

The perceived divide between museum and academy has been raised here, but if the above is taken into consideration, it may be apparent that the divide is perhaps not so acute. Group museum visits are still a routine aspect of the art history syllabus when convenient. Internships are still routine. College-resident museums are still the norm even if they have to struggle to keep their programming vibrant and engaging. The one area of disruption that seems in doubt is the prominent involvement of the art historian in the museum process. Many museum professionals would protest that art historians are still part of their process as consultants, catalogue essayists, visiting researchers, and occasional curators. And many traditional museums still draw their personnel from art history and museum studies. There is, of course, the emerging figure of the "independent" curator without an art history background, but this is neither a bad phenomenon, over all, nor significant enough as to displace the art historian entirely.

The question, though, is: How relevant to the museum are art historians willing and prepared to make themselves? How knowledgeable, how flexible, how versatile, how savvy, how forward-looking, how current, how imaginative, how visionary, how in with it are they? If the curator without an art history degree proves far more knowledgeable and savvy than the academic stuck in his or her graduate seminar notebooks, then, pray, what is the museum to do?

Of course, it would be wrong not to acknowledge that there is a trend within museums, in line with their market-oriented evolution, to fall for name-recognition when assembling their exhibitions, which means that celebrities are brought in to form the façade that sells the show. The Brooklyn Museum of Art took the plume in this regard by having David Bowie do the voice introductions for its *Sensation* exhibition, and as someone has pointed out, other museums now prefer such figures to art historians as catalogue contributors. There are two blades to the sword. There is no reason both blades cannot be put to use. Celebrity presence is a good marketing tool and will become more evident with the museum's transformation into a culture mall. However, unless equally knowledgeable, celebrity presence cannot replace the wealth of valuable knowledge that the art historian offers to the museum and its public, even as the art historian no matter how exciting and knowledgeable may not be able to provide the appeal that the celebrity brings. The winning route, it seems, is not either/or, but both, and the museum should be able to utilize the specialist depth that the art historian brings and the marketing appeal that the celebrity curator, collector, director, actor, magician, stunt figure provides if it so chooses.

George Baker

I have resisted until this point, but can no longer: I just want to register my doubt about the ideal of the "culture mall," an idea inserted repetitively and masochistically in this discussion, as a viable future for the museum. This utter capitulation to the logic of the market and to its rhetoric is a form of coercion that we are subjected to everywhere in our daily lives; I hope this discussion and the museum itself can be places where we might have other rhetorics to explore. How boring and predictable this neo-liberal utopia is. It is no accident that the culture mall ideal now adds a cruel parody of the academic to its arsenal, for this too is an anti-academicism that we hear everywhere around us in our culture, with its current idolatry of the market. The market is not democratic, as we have been exhorted to believe again and again in this discussion. It is, instead, sadistic—as will be the museum that conforms to its dictates under the guise of "populism."

Needless to say, I don't think the "winning route" is to have David Bowie and supposedly "savvy" art historians in new collaborations. I don't think we have to submit here to a sword that works "both ways." I don't think we need to submit to a sword.

I will go back to Maurice's turning of my question back on me: What can art historians do in the transformed museum situation today? I am increasingly convinced that art history, especially that of modern and contemporary art, has abdicated its function of providing compelling narratives—stories—of the development of art itself and its trajectory into our contemporary moment. This failure is echoed, I think, in what I would call the rudderless rethinking of museum hangs that we now see increasingly in modern art museum collections: I am thinking of the series of hangs that the Museum of Modern Art did before its Manhattan site closed for renovation; I am thinking, too, of the Tate Modern hang. We need new stories (histories if you like) for why art matters, and traditionally it was the art historian who told these, both to a museum and to a public.

Maurice Berger

George, you wrote: "We need new stories (histories if you like) for why art matters, and traditionally it was the art historian who told these, both to a museum and to a public."

I think this dichotomy is too rigid. What of the curator who is also an art historian? And what of the curator/intellectual who serves as far more than a high-end arbiter of the art market? (After all, where would we place Alfred Barr in the sharp dichotomy you draw?) As a cultural and art historian who also sometimes serves as a curator, I'm also aware of how much I've learned from my colleagues in the museum. Curators of contemporary art, at least, usually spend more time with artists than art historians. They handle the art object at close range (and are less apt to subjugate it through theory). They figure out ways to make art come alive to the public.

I did indeed turn your own words back to you, but strangely you misquoted my quote of your post. The operative word in my question to you, vis-à-vis *your* post was "public." In the best of circumstances, the museum should serve the interests of art history as well as those of the public. Maybe art historians need to think of the public, too, if they are to better serve the interests of the work they write about. Thus, I would like to quote another post, that of Barbara Lynes above: "Although preparing courses and lectures for college students is certainly different from organizing exhibitions for museums, the goal remains the same: awakening and enriching people's sensibilities to the complex forces of the creative process with the hope of their becoming more aware of this component of themselves."

An honest and provocative post, George.

Alexander Alberro

I think that this topic is a particularly thorny one and gets to the heart of several of the issues raised thus far in the conference. As has been noted by Stefano Basilico and others, there still exists a significant "conceptual barrier between curating and education," despite a variety of strategies to bring these two groups together and foster a dialogue (as suggested by Dan Cameron) between them. This division between curators and educators is not unique and is related to the divide that exists more generally in academia. I am referring in particular to differences between the training received in a School of Education versus that received when working towards a Humanities degree. The former is often geared towards future primary school educators, whereas the latter focuses on higher education. This structure establishes and maintains a two-tier/class system. Those pursuing a Ph.D. degree are expected to specialize and to achieve the highest possible level of expertise, whereas those working towards a graduate degree in education are expected to think more in terms of a popular or conventional middle ground to which to pitch their knowledge. The same then is often true with art education professionals who take into consideration the "average" museum-goer. In so doing, they risk becoming populists, alienating and rejecting both more specialized curators and art historians.

I believe that the gap between curators and educators starts early on during the education process when the latter are not encouraged to take advanced courses in art history. Unfortunately, these courses are all-too-often deemed impractical or too difficult because of their theoretical content. A pity, for I wholeheartedly agree with Stefano's assertion that "mass media is an insufficient forum for debate and consideration of complex political issues. Critical thinking, a skill that good art history teaches, will be constantly honed as one encounters the new and constantly shifting practice of contemporary art." Unless this position is reinforced at the most basic level of education, art historians will be positioned as hopelessly elitist, obscurantist, or as George Baker has concisely put it, "lunatics."

There is much truth in George's exaggerations, truths that

sadly extend beyond the parameters of our immediate topic and point to the larger state of intellectuals and critical thinkers in society (here we need only think of Andrew Ross's prescient observations in *No Respect: Intellectuals and Popular Culture,* or more recently to the public ridicule that the prose of great thinkers such as Judith Butler has encountered). Often the value of art historians and intellectuals in general is reduced to our ability to produce sound-bite statements. Yet, like their corollary in the context of art production, complex thoughts and complicated arguments require the public to work in order to comprehend what is being communicated. And all too often it is assumed that the public is unwilling or even worse unable to perform such labor. The result is that writers are often sought to produce texts that are easily consumable, and educators are expected to reduce complicated exhibitions and artworks to their simplest level of meaning. The art historian is marginalized, or if she or he is sought by the museum as a writer or lecturer, it is often because she or he also has experience and a well-established reputation as a critic and not just as an academic. Of course I'm making generalizations, but I think that what I'm suggesting isn't that far from the mark. In order for the situation to move beyond this schism between an educator and a curator, and between art historians and museum professionals, I believe that fundamental changes need to occur at the basic level of educational training.

Maurice Berger

Alex, you wrote: "And all too often it is assumed that the public is unwilling or even worse unable to perform such labor."

I find your point a bit overstated, even if I essentially agree with it. The public is not stupid, even if mass culture (and, I might add, academics) sees it as such. But no form of discourse can serve everyone. Yes, I am a *big* fan of Judith Butler's extraordinary work. But do I see her rhetorical tropes and complex writing as something most of the "public" can handle? No. Not even the so-called smart people we're taking for granted.

That being said: theory works on multiple levels. I have actively observed the trickling down of critical theory into the culture at large. This is a good thing—and not necessarily about dumbing down. Thus *The Crying Game, Middlesex,* and the work of Lyle Ashton Harris and Cindy Sherman all can be seen to represent a "theoretical" point of view exemplified (and even pioneered) by Butler's incisive, if sometimes inscrutable texts.

There is nothing wrong, by the way, with intellectuals being agile and good writers. As Roland Barthes taught us—much can be communicated in the style and resonance of the text itself.

Mary Kelly

Something Maurice said in the introduction to the discussion of audiences about being a passionate observer not only of art, but also of other observers, has stayed with me. I found it very moving and profoundly "ethical." I realize the question of ethics is not exactly the most pragmatic take on the topic of museum pedagogy, but it might be a provocative diversion. I have often thought about it in relation to making work, but come up against the stumbling block of "passion," that is, whatever drives an artist's truth procedure verges on a certain kind of terror, I mean, the fidelity to an idea that is necessary to enact it in some form. Yet, this seems to be precisely what I need to relinquish in order to be a passionate observer of art. Passion here implies a suspension of aims. Nothing is being produced. I am just looking (trying not to read the wall text), making myself vulnerable or open to "the situation" as Giorgio Agamben calls it, and this includes as Maurice says, other viewers. So, unlike a critical engagement with the work (which is another and equally important issue) the ethical dimension of museum-going experience resides in neither judgment nor decipherment, but in anticipation.

What relevance, if any, could this have for museum education programs? In the case of exhibitions, perhaps, the Doctrine of Preemption is not the best way to go. Often, there is too much information too soon. Like the good-enough mother who can't bear her child's frustration, it cancels out the viewer's demand before he or she makes it. What's more, the public has come to expect it, but once the work has been framed by an introduction, especially the biographical narrative (replete with traumatic incident), the ethical gesture is almost impossible.

Of course, the importance of interpretation is not in question; it is more a matter of where and in what form it appears. This has been addressed intelligently by several contributors already, but what I might add, from an exhibiting artist's point of view, is that when it comes to wall text, one size does not fit all. The tendency, call it corporate, to design and display signage in the house style does not acknowledge the diversity of visual and subjective experience the artworks invoke. Fine tuning fonts, color, scale, placement, and amount of text in relation to individual artists' work, on the other hand, cannot make the viewer "ethical," but does seem to produce a sort of vulnerability to difference. And then, there are events that occur in the gallery space as an integral part of the work exhibited (live performance), or as an intrusion (conference, panel, tour), or a simple interaction (viewer and museum guard). In unpredictable ways, they forge a sense of community out of human ephemera—looks, sighs, shuffles, poses—and open us to the situation, however you want to think of that, philosophically or politically. I imagine it as a place of empowerment without prescription.

Alexander Alberro

Maurice: Yes, it seems that we agree that one of the greatest dangers in the administration of culture or education is to think or presume that the public is stupid. Quite to the contrary. And there have certainly been enough examples in the 20th century of intellectuals who have used culture pedagogically and produced astonishing results. This has often involved engaging the public actively in constructing meaning and/or in coproducing work. Perhaps this might be a direction museum education departments could take: to move the public from passive to active consumers of knowledge.

You state that "no form of discourse can serve everyone." To that, I would add that no form of art serves everyone. Is it our (i.e., artists, art historians, curators, museum professionals) aim, then, to produce art, discourse, and culture that serve the largest amount of people, or would we do better to target a more selective audience? Even though the prose of Judith Butler may be largely inaccessible to most people, isn't it still necessary to get it out there for those few on whom it will have an impact and enable what you refer to as the "trickle down" process to take place? I guess the question that needs to be asked is where in the process does the art museum see itself today—at the top or at the bottom of the trickle?

George Baker

Mary's is a beautiful set of thoughts. But I disagree with her in one respect: I think her reflections are intensely pragmatic. They should be taken as a recipe. And typically, Alex's thoughts too bring us back to the root cause of surface problems we now face.

I don't have anything new to add yet, just a clarification: Maurice, I didn't misquote you; I was restating a question. And I surely have not issued a call for the museum to begin to see its function as serving art history. But when did serving the interests of the public and those of art history become mutually exclusive? *That* is an interesting discussion to have.

The narratives of which I was thinking were in the past more the province of art historians than curators, whose labors often shaped the art historical narratives, but were not given in the same form nor pitched to the same level of generality. I am thinking back to figures and to stories told by people such as Ernst Gombrich and Vincent Scully, or if you like, more recently by Rosalind Krauss (but it wasn't that recently that she wrote a "survey" narrative) or Kenneth Frampton. We've gone a long time without narratives like these being reinvented for the changed times we now face. (Of course, of the people participating in this conference, I have to exempt Irving Sandler from this claim, and I gladly do so.) We've been told—it was one of the founding tenets of postmodernism—that now such narratives are no longer possible. But I think we (art historians) need to resist that "tenet." To do so would serve the museum, it would serve the public, and it would serve art history as well to reinvent the bases of its own research and the pathways that need to be explored in the future. Art historians do need to think of the public, Maurice, and at least that was what I was trying to communicate.

To return to Mary's post, though: Do museum curators and educators see their work in any sense as ethical? What would it mean to do so? To construct the museum as an ethical space? What would it entail, besides the framing advice and strategies about which Mary speaks? I want to hear more about this. I think we need to hear more about this. For me, it could ultimately be what separates the experience of art from other forms of culture or entertainment, and the museum from other public spaces and "mass media."

Joan Rosenbaum

Maurice, you have generated so much interesting conversation here. I don't know that there is anything untouched really.

But I will give my perspective as a long-time museum director on a few points. One, that the ideal indeed is to bring together different voices in putting together exhibitions, and prior to that to include these voices in defining the institution's goals over a period of time. The different voices are curatorial, education, marketing, and outside expertise. Shows are indeed best done as Dan comments with the combination of these elements as well as design. At The Jewish Museum we never take on an exhibition without a "scholar's meeting" prior to the show. Included are people who can inform the topic and the presentation as well—people from all disciplines, including educators. That said, the curatorial voice does ultimately dominate, and it is something that a director has to manage.

Regarding what we want people to learn, I'd just like to go back to two early posts: one regarding the Cornell DVD and this "surpassing the museum experience" because of the ability to "hold" the object, etc. A DVD just isn't a work of art, and it's not what museums are made for, and it's not what our whole challenge and mandate is about. With a DVD, no matter how awesome the experience, the actual work is not in front of you. Art exhibitions with real objects are far, far more selective. They are curated more finely than DVDs, which tend to present more information than any human could possibly absorb.

Finally, regarding Dan's remark about presenting art that is important to people's lives. How can we really do this? One artwork can allow a person to truly identify with it; another can just seem awesome; another can make a person remember their dreams. The latter is a particularly great achievement if it can be accomplished.

I do think that brilliant curating—meaning a highly developed concept, sounded out with colleagues from varying but connected disciplines, and the means to offer a variety of educational mediating strategies all combine very well to make a wonderful educational experience. Put such a presentation in a space that feels respectful to the visitor—respectful either in its imaginative theatricality, deliberate calmness, or just in its clarity.

Raina A. Lampkins-Fielder

As the sole museum educator represented in this discussion, I'm pleased to hear that my colleagues are of a like mind with what many in the museum education field have been saying all along—that it is through the spirit of collaboration across departments that we will have a greater and truer impact on our audiences, our profession, and each other.

Maurice asks whether the central function of the museum is that of educator or of something else. The American Association of Museums task force report "Excellence and Equity: Education and the Public Dimension of Museums" asserts that "Museums can no longer confine themselves simply to preservation, scholarship, and exhibitions. . . . They must recognize that what we are calling the public dimension of museums leads them to perform the public service of education—a term we use in its broadest sense to include exploration, study, observation, critical thinking, contemplation, and dialogue." This statement does not dismiss the importance of object care and display but rather, I think, folds it into a larger realm that includes "the users of the object" (i.e., museum public) with various models of access.

I would suggest that curators and educators are primary to the development of the various "products" that museums offer to the public, with the curator responsible for the choice of object and its display, and the educator responsible for how a variety of intentions are communicated to the public. It's no wonder that questions of territory come into play. As many others have noted, curators and educators would benefit from closer and more sustained interaction—something more than the add-on mentality that so often characterizes the curators' approach to education, or the idea of education departments as a kind of cleanup crew.

George Baker's concern about the place for art history in the museum is certainly one that I've grappled with. At the Whitney Museum of American Art, and with Irving Sandler's encouragement, the education department has recently created a scholars' roundtable—a think tank of sorts composed of art historians and studio art professors as well as members of the museum's education and curatorial departments. The group meets occasionally to discuss what we perceive as the current state of affairs in the museum and in the academy. One of the goals of these meetings is to insure that the museum is being responsive to some of the practical issues of the academy, including how our exhibition and educational offerings can augment academic course offerings. Another goal is to have a reciprocal idea exchange about art, art history, the academy, and the museum—an exchange that may influence both the academy and the museum in our conception of programming and our contribution to an ever-expanding and revised "canon." We hope that these roundtables will prove to be a good first step in traversing the boundaries between the academy and the museum. It is this sort of behind-the-scenes programming that I would encourage every museum education department to engage in.

Olu Oguibe speaks perceptively of the reluctance of many museums to involve the artist in their educational programming and outreach. One of the many ways that I've tried to infuse the artist's voice both practically and conceptually into the education programs that I oversee at the Whitney is to have artists on my Education Committee. We have three artists on our Education Committee, all of whom are represented in our permanent collection. We also strive to maintain a balance between scholars/art historians, community advocates, officials representing the N.Y.C. Department of Education, schoolteachers, trustees, and education patrons. In this way, we try to be as ecumenical in our approach as possible.

On a "real world" note, however, many times the artist is made unavailable to education departments by curatorial departments. I've experienced this in some other institutions in which I have worked, and it is certainly a primary complaint of many educators in other museums. Too often curators erect a hermetically sealed bubble around "their" artists, and artists are allowed to assume that educational programming is of the Popsicle stick, pipe cleaner, and Elmer's glue variety rather than integral to the formation and execution of the exhibition and its ideas.

I will say though that many educators need to assert themselves more and get over their inferiority complexes—particularly in their relationships with curators—and demand greater input and integration. However, as I stated in my audience post, diminishing departmental barriers is assisted when it is a stated institutional goal. It is true that many education departments are ghettoized within their institutions, even though the idea of education is lauded in mission statements as well as grant proposals for exhibitions. Often education departments are physically isolated. How many education departments are within a stone's throw of curatorial departments? How many education departments or workshop areas are in the lower level of museums? I've worked in many subcellars in my time. We speak of the benefits of greater intra-institutional collaboration and exchange, but what of the actual buy-in? It takes work, commitment, and structures that support it.

So, I will end on a practical note. As an educator, I am constantly looking at best practices in museum education and viable models that will help to instruct what I do on a daily basis. Though there are few models for curatorial/educational teams, one that I find particularly instructive was published in the *Journal for Museum*

Education. The model was developed by Jeanette Toohey and Inez Wolins who envisioned a 12-step program for curatorial and educational turf-battle recovery. I will quote liberally from this model, which I think is a sound one and may be instructive in our endeavors to diminish the curator/educator divide.

The following is fairly consistent with what Toohey and Wolins described, although I have taken the liberty of rethinking certain steps along the way.

1. "Communicate what you believe your territory to be and agree on the 'givens' of the project and working relationship." This demands that we be honest about the role of the content provider/object protector (the curator) and the audience advocate (the educator). Roles need to be clearly defined.

2. "Acknowledge your starting place." Partly this is about describing your background and your intellectual or pedagogical foundation. Both educators and curators feel, in some way, invested in education and think of themselves as interpreters (and experts) of a collection, era, aesthetic strategy, etc. On a more practical level, I know that it has been beneficial for my curatorial colleagues to learn that I've done curatorial work. It gives me the additional "street cred" that, sadly, is needed to establish a museum educator's credibility as a peer.

3. "State the assumptions you bring to your work, and challenge each other's assumptions."

4. "State the defining principles of a project and what has brought both parties to that point." This is an extension of the previous step. What are the bottom lines for each party, and how are they articulated? This is the most challenging step because this is where listening to and informing each other is replaced by true collaborative thinking.

5. "Recognize the validity of the kinds and levels of education and experience that each brings to the joint venture." Partnerships assume equality.

6. "Come prepared with the materials needed to begin a substantive dialogue." We're talking some practical stuff here. For instance, sharing, at every stage, the evolution of an exhibition checklist will aid in this discussion.

7. "Build a climate for expression by creating or taking advantage of structures and vehicles for communication."

8. "Be a change agent and model best practices to other staff members."

9. "Provide opportunities for the extended staff to 'own' a piece of the product."

10. "Identify yourselves as a team. . . . The partnership

reminds the institution that decision making is shared, and that contributions are jointly made."

11. "Allow additional time for each aspect of the project." And be respectful of each other's timeframe for creating the best possible product. What one often sees—particularly in less-than-inspired educational programming that has a decidedly cookie-cutter feel to it—is that the education department receives information at such a late date that it cannot respond creatively to what has been given to it, and regresses to a tried-and-true model that may not represent the curatorial, artistic, or even educational aims and intentions in the most stimulating and accurate manner.

12. "Celebrate each other's strengths publicly." Stick up for each other's disciplines and promote each other's point of view. Why not?

Maurice Berger

The preceding chain of posts is extraordinary. They raise fundamental and important questions about the museum's (and the art historian's) relationship to the public as well as to the question of the museum's methodologies and discourse. I, too, agree with George that Mary's sentiment is beautiful. I have been pondering it this afternoon—the idea that art cannot be defined by a one-size-fits-all form of museum pedagogy. Her desire—as a groundbreaking visual artist and theorist—to imagine the museum "as a place of empowerment without prescription" is admirable.

As for Joan's remarks about "scholars' meetings" at The Jewish Museum: I can personally attest to the importance these discussions place on art historians. Ditto Raina's observation in her excellent post: "At the Whitney Museum of American Art, and with Irving Sandler's encouragement, the education department has recently created a scholars' roundtable—a think tank of sorts composed of art historians and studio art professors as well as members of the museum's education and curatorial departments."

I sense that we are in a period of great struggle vis-à-vis how we construct the kinds of narratives that George [Baker] speaks of (or whether they are even necessary). Once again, I think we need to be careful not to generalize or exaggerate the problem re: the interface or lack thereof between curators, art historians, and their methodologies. I have seen the art historian banished from the curatorial process; I have seen the art historian embraced by the museum, too.

Irving Sandler

Problem: What should a museum's education programs communicate? What the viewer should see? The artist's intention? The art-historical and/or contemporary-art backgrounds? Art-theoretical issues? The social and/or political contexts? With this in mind, does George Baker's contention that Rob Storr's presentation of Richter does "violence" to the artist, or does Rob's interpretation differ from George's? Certainly, Rob's art-historical knowledge or commitment to scholarship is no less impressive than that of George (or Rosalind Krauss).

Are art historians necessarily the best interpreters of art? I have found the commentary of artists as (and often, more) interesting and useful. I agree with Olu Oguibe that artists should be used more in museum education.

Problem: Who are the audiences? Grade-school children? The general public? Graduate studio or art history students? Etc.? They all have different needs.

Obviously, museum curators and educators should collaborate, as Dan Cameron and Raina Lampkins-Fielder say they should. But it should be kept in mind that they have different skills and functions. Curators know the art (or ought to). Educators know their audiences and their requirements. A critical priority is to build bridges between curators and educators.

We need various approaches to museum education, for example, wall labels (with Mary Kelly's thoughts in mind) for the general public (with Maurice's assumption that it ain't stupid), and for the studio and art-history constituency, lectures and symposia.

Olu Oguibe

In a review published 12 years or so ago that permanently changed the way contemporary African art is curated, historicized, and packaged—and indeed triggered one of the stellar careers in contemporary art, not mine, I hasten to add—I wrote about "nostalgia for the good old days of art history when Bernard Myers or Herbert Read could efficiently plough through several epochs in very modest, three-shilling paperbacks and still give you a good body of text and enough fair quality reproductions for your money." That sentence was written in response to an exhibition catalogue, and I should hasten again to add, the nostalgia that it spoke about was relative if not sarcastic, and was hedged with reservations. I was not ignorant of the fact that the art history that I appeared to invoke with a sense of loss was, after all, the very art history that we all have come to acknowledge certainly fell grievously short on innumerable counts.

To read George moaning about the supposed demise or relegation of that art history is a bit of a surprise, not only because the idea of "a growing, often hostile divide" between museum and art historian is a fallacy since, as I and several others have pointed out, art historians are still very much part of the museum process, but also because it seems to place the art historian on a pedestal that is certainly groundless.

As a practicing art historian—of contemporary art, no less—I do not dismiss the profession or its place in the work of the museum, but I definitely would not want to return to that period when the art historian was "the preacher of the museum," because that's an era that I cannot recall without a shiver. Perhaps George forgets because he can afford to forget, but there are some who cannot. We need not feel nostalgic for that era in order to underline the crucial role of the art historian. If there are chinks in the works regarding education and pedagogy in the museum, it cannot all be put down to an imagined, fantastical rift valley between the museum and the art historian. The latter is only one of many whose services and expertise are useful in this regard, but not a prima donna.

At a moment when the contemporary art world outside the museum is worried sick of the figure of the curator as god, to espouse the return of the art historian as deity is neither proper nor realistic. Besides, as I already pointed out, there are people in the art world who have no professional qualifications in art history, but nevertheless are immeasurably knowledgeable in their areas of interest, and it would be wrong to imply that their involvement in museum pedagogy is questionable or any less valuable than the art historian's. I believe that museums are wise to explore various possibilities and sources of expertise in putting their programs together. That, certainly, is the way to go.

Sylvia Yount

It's been exciting to follow the lively exchanges of the past few hours. What I find most extraordinary is the different perspectives on the curator/educator schism as well as that of the curator/art historian. Just wanted to pose a few questions.

The main problem I have with the ongoing debate regarding the divide between curatorial and education departments is the underlying notion that the latter is primarily responsible for "interpreting" or communicating the ideas of exhibitions and permanent collection installations for and to a public. The notion that the curator's voice needs to be translated or mediated before it can reach a viewer is something I do not fully accept. It's a very different matter to engage in a dialogue—sharing ideas and seeking feedback—from the outset of a project with colleagues—be they educator, designer, marketer, fund-raiser, etc. As others have noted, that is the best recipe for public success and personal gratification, not to mention collegial respect.

Granted, I'm of the generation of Ph.D.-equipped curators trained in more critical approaches to art history and museology. As a result, I take my job as a public educator and historian very seriously—from explaining the thought process behind an installation and writing substantive wall texts and labels to providing audio commentary, training docents, and giving public lectures and gallery talks. I also believe the burden is on curators to make their work relevant, intelligible, and accessible to a wide range of viewers with different learning styles and levels of knowledge. We hold privileged positions within our institutions and fields and should approach our work responsibly as well as, in Mary's word, ethically.

As Alexander has noted, curators and educators generally bring different training and expertise to their jobs. It goes without saying that's there much to be learned from each other. However, the notion that we don't share the same concerns and goals is, in my experience, simply false—even if we approach them in different ways.

Now, to George's [Baker] posts. I assume the discussion about the curator v. art historian is mostly directed to the field of contemporary art and theoretical methodologies. I don't believe I could name one colleague in my field—historical American art—who does not consider themselves an art historian first, curator second. Moreover, many of us are drawn to our careers by the challenge of exploring historical narratives with tangible art objects, keeping the primary focus on the material at hand. (The American reinstallations at the Brooklyn Museum of Art and the Newark Museum of Art are good examples of this.) The growing phenomenon of exhibition catalogues devoid of "art history" is also something foreign to my specific field.

I feel that this kind of mindset—one I met frequently in graduate school whenever I expressed my interest in pursuing a curatorial v. academic path—is incredibly damaging and only fuels the Great Divide between the museum and the academy that, in my area, historically has not been as pronounced as in others. Moreover, setting up such a dichotomy certainly does not improve the art-historically trained curator's standing and ability to affect change within our own institutions. If curators need, on the one hand, academically based art historians to conceive of the projects or flesh-out the ideas and, on the other, museum educators to present or communicate the arguments, where does that leave the curator?

Maurice Berger

Sylvia, you wrote: "I assume the discussion about the curator v. art historian is mostly directed to the field of contemporary art and theoretical methodologies. I don't believe I could name one colleague in my field—historical American art—who does not consider themselves an art historian first, curator second."

Good point. But I believe what you are saying is true even in modern and contemporary art. Many of the curators I know in the field (myself included) consider ourselves art historians first, curators second.

18 –19 October 2003

Maurice Berger

The past 12 days of conversation have been rich and productive. In the end, we may have raised more questions than we answered. But in the process we have exposed some of the central issues facing art museums—from the corporate culture of many art institutions to the museum's understanding of its role as repository of culture, educator of the public, and forum for the study of art.

We have also contributed to the kind of "interdisciplinary" discussion that is all too rare in the world of the art museum—a discussion that permitted theorists to dialogue with practitioners, art historians with curators, artists with museum directors.

I would like to devote the next two-day session, the final topic of this conference, to concluding statements from each of its participants. I ask that you try to address the following three questions, though you should feel free to limit your responses to any one: What issues discussed in the conference have emerged as important to you or have altered your thinking? What is your personal vision of the ideal art museum of the future? What changes, if any, do you think the art museum needs to make to strengthen its programming and standing in society and culture?

Alan Wallach

I am primarily interested in the history and operation of larger museums in the U.S.—the Metropolitan Museum of Art, the National Gallery of Art, etc.—so I will confine my observations to institutions of this type.

The history of art institutions is inseparable from the history of the society that creates and maintains them. Right now we find ourselves in an unprecedented moment in U.S. history. We face the prospect of endless war abroad and economic depression at home, not to mention the real possibility of economic collapse (see Paul Krugman's latest). The future of U.S. art museums is obviously bound up with these unpropitious circumstances.

In trying to imagine the museum's future, I see three more or less possible scenarios. The first might be called "utopian": a democratized museum in a more democratic society—a museum in which the lines between professional and non-professional were blurred and there really would be some sort of "dance" involving curators, artists, and an audience that would be equivalent to the whole of the population.

The second scenario can be called "dystopian" and would

involve an intensification of current trends toward corporatization.

The third, which barring economic collapse is probably the most likely, at least for the immediate future, represents some sort of muddle or compromise between the two. Thus we would have, on the one hand, continuing corporatization, which means a museum in which the bottom line determines programming, curators find themselves increasingly subordinated to administrators, and the museum more and more exclusively focuses on bland, money-making entertainments that appeal primarily to what it takes to be its primary or core audience: white, middle-class suburbanites—an audience very much in the mold of the liberal, *bien pensant* viewers of PBS. On the other hand, some curators and administrators will bravely persist in their efforts to mount imaginative, innovative, and art-historically critical exhibitions, to collaborate with artists, and to engage "non-traditional" museum audiences. More power to them!

Miwon Kwon

I have not posted for several days because I feel depressed for two reasons. One, I don't doubt or disagree with the prognosis that the "culture mall" is the future of the museum. It is not far off the mark in my view; we are already halfway there. But the fact that many feel such enthusiasm and hope regarding this prospect underscores my sense of despair (if not anger) over the absolute erasure of all spaces that could provide, even if provisionally and imperfectly, a reprieve from the rationalized, instrumentalized, commoditized experience of social life. If the terms of marketplace consumerism (going by whatever other name, as "democracy," for some) are to be the basis of determining the success or failure of a museum, I personally don't want to have much to do with it. This isn't to deny that the museum is part of the market economy (of course it is) but rather that precisely because so, it should seek to do more than capitulate to, or worse celebrate, its logic. I can get my shopper's fix at the real mall; I want something else from the museum.

In terms of museum education, I think perhaps the issue isn't so much curator v. art historian (for certainly there are few curators invested in a critical historical project and plenty of art historians disengaged from the same) but the ways in which the primary institutional context for each—the museum, the academy—pushes for certain types of pedagogical work from its employees. Museums today are not as supportive of a critical, skeptical engagement with culture (high or low, historical or current) as universities still are, no matter how compromised this commitment might be. Further, as the museum's mnemonic function splits from its investment in the visual, with the latter trumping the former, museums are not really invested even in art anymore but simply visual content (or rather art is viewed as visual content, and art that affirms this bias is favored). As such, the kind of education that is possible and desired in a museum is precisely the kind that we have, by which I mean no education at all.

Having worked in museum education for a while, I can say quite simply that I am against it. With the excuse of making art accessible, legible, familiar, and democratically available to as many people as possible, museum education often domesticates art and diminishes and contains the art-viewing experience as a programmed sequence of people-moving sound bite "captions" (audio tour, wall text, brochure, etc.). Inculcation of what to think, how to look, where to stand, why bother is often mistaken for education, by which I mean, following Elaine Scarry's work on beauty (though I'm going to paraphrase badly here), the opening up of a path toward the desire to struggle, to seek conviction, to face error.

Museums underestimate art, artists, and most egregiously the audience, and self-aggrandizingly overestimate the value of their paternalistic "educational" effort as a form of generosity and public do-gooding. Museum education is often a euphemism for efforts to increase its market share/audience base and, along with development and promotion departments, really runs the museum and its exhibition programming.

This brings me to the second reason for my depression and silence. This very symposium, sponsored by a museum, reinforces my growing suspicion that with all my knowledge and experience and critical perspectives on contemporary art, I am a mere, though privileged, "content-provider." Does it really matter what I have to say so long as I say something, evidence "participation," lend my presence (i.e., my cultural capital) to affirm the project, in turn elevating the status of the sponsoring institution?

Maxwell L. Anderson

The last few days found me (offline) at the Castello di Rivoli in Turin, teaching a master class as part of a course on "museology." There I found 20 graduate students in the field of contemporary art yearning for a position in a profession that awaits transformation in

Europe, but has changed notably stateside. For these students from across southern and northern Italy, the art museum is a place for support of living artists, for the embrace of risk as an antidote to the toxic sameness of market-driven media and museum fare, and for a pause from the modern-day, celebrity-mad culture that is Berlusconi's version of the California political scene.

Returning to New York, and its perpetual marathon for the biggest, toughest, and newest, I felt a familiar tug to gainsay the superficial. Miwon's post questioning the legitimacy of museum education hit a chord. But there is a problem inherent in indicting efforts to make the mysterious power of art less mysterious. We all have to start somewhere. And for many people, there has been no permission extended in their lives to look beyond the necessities of life on to the possibilities of the imagination. Those of us invited to participate in this forum live in a stratosphere of permission, and it can become all too easy to forget that children are growing up in a society that makes precious little room for anything but the quest for money and celebrity.

Alan's prognosis that we are entering a compromise between the utopian scenario and the dystopian corporate one seems on the mark. As ever in human history, the beliefs and actions of a few individuals can disrupt the momentum towards an ever-more predictable program. These individuals must be generous, enlightened patrons who can, through unrestricted endowment, insulate museums from the trap of earned income, as well as museum curators and directors who are prepared to take chances.

Barbara Kirshenblatt-Gimblett

Reflecting back on the discussions of the art museum's role, curatorship, audience, and educational mission (and in light of the changing media/technology environment in which the museum, artists, and visitors operate), it might be worth thinking about the museum as a ramified site that is bigger and more dispersed than its physical location, however spectacular the architecture with which the institution identifies itself. Terms like "outreach" don't begin to capture the distributed nature of the institution at all levels. Where is it? This question prompts not only the familiar answer of traveling exhibitions, franchising (Guggenheim), outreach, and web presence, but also encourages us to rethink the "location" of objects, information, activities, functions, processes, experiences, and persons. If, for example, "educational" objectives can be pursued in many "places"—and not only or even primarily in the gallery—what does that free the gallery exhibition to do?

Let's not confuse "educational" and "didactic" and either term with "learning." Think rather of the art museum of tomorrow as a space of soft mastery, to take a page from Sherry Turkle, in contrast with hard mastery, which is more like systematic instruction that proceeds in linear fashion, step by step, from simple to complex, formally through logic and calculation. Soft mastery proceeds laterally, associatively, non-hierarchically, through trial and error, flexibly and informally. It is the difference between the way most artists work and the way a student in a language class is taught. The difference is one of style. Both styles have their value, their place, and their adherents, just as there are various learning styles. Learning may be a better term here than education because it makes us place the learner first and imagine an active learner, rather than think in terms of a target to be educated.

Following this line of thought, one might say that there are two basic paradigms for thinking about "learning" in relation to the museum—art making and art history. The soft mastery paradigm, as already suggested, is related to the way that artists proceed, particularly if one takes the position that artists in their creative process are engaged in a mode of inquiry. A hard mastery paradigm is that of art history as it is conventionally taught—just think what art history might look like if a soft mastery approach were taken. Art history might look more like visual culture or performance studies (and in some cases that is exactly what is happening). Modes of inquiry are pursued in more than one style, though judging from the transformations in my own pedagogy as new generations of students come my way, the active learner and emphasis on soft mastery have gained much ground, even in the university.

What then is the relationship of the art museum to art knowledge? The history of museums, art museums included, but perhaps even more dramatically museums of natural history, is a history of increasing misalignment of knowledge formations and collections. There was once a close fit between the institution, the knowledge it produced, and the collections that it formed. As knowledge formations changed, museums became custodians of the collections of outmoded disciplines. Many fields that began or were located primarily in museums formed collections in the course of their research and depended on them to further their work. As those fields migrated from the museum to the university, they left the collections behind and museums became custodians of the outmoded knowledge formations that gave rise to their collections in the first place. As museums largely abdicated the creating of new knowledge to the university, they focused more on educating the public, however that task is understood.

For these reasons—and because of a shift more generally away from an "object lesson" pedagogy (that's a topic unto itself)—some museums began to see collections as a liability. In some cases, collections were no longer central to the fields that created them. Or, exhibitions were being driven by a concept, theme, or narrative rather than by a collection. Such exhibitions did not require a collection per se and exhibition planners saw no point in limiting themselves to objects to get their message across. Last but not least, museum pedagogy is changing as museums find themselves in evolving high-density information and high-intensity media environments. The place of the object in museum pedagogy cannot be assumed, if indeed it ever could, notwithstanding the confidence in object lessons.

Where do art museums fit in this picture? Exhibiting art is what they are about, but unlike museums of natural history, technology, and culture, much (though not all) of the art that art museums show is complicit with—if not subversive of—the circumstances in which it is shown. It was made to be shown. To the degree that contemporary art engages the conditions of its display—even attempting to destabilize them—it is a catalyst for the transformation, however slow, of the institutions in which it appears. We might want to look at art museums (new ones and ones focusing on contemporary art), new art, and the "new art history" to see the degree to which they are mutually constitutive of one another. To what degree do knowledge formations and institutions (museums, universities) transform in relation to the unfolding of their emergent subjects (new art) and alter their relationship to all that went before in the history of art and the collections that sediment that history?

Where in the mix—in the actor-network, to use the language of Bruno Latour—is the lash-up that will give museums of art in the 21st century their efficacious forms? We would need to look at the relationships of emerging art practices, new knowledge formations, changing pedagogies, and responsive institutional forms. We would need to consider transforming information and media environments and their impact on the sensorium and learning styles of new generations of visitors.

Barbara Buhler Lynes

The impressive and thought-provoking dialogue that has taken place here over the last two weeks has provided a rich and stimulating resource for rethinking the complex issues museums are confronting with respect to their future, as well as the roles directors, curators (who are often art historians), artists, educators, and those in the development and marketing areas of museums can and should play in shaping the museum of tomorrow—ranging from how it organizes exhibitions, collects, cares for, and displays objects, communicates with and educates the public to determining the kinds of buildings and spaces that will house its collections—in hopes of not allowing its degeneration into a culture mall, or worse yet, a discount culture mall.

The conversation has poignantly demonstrated how infrequently academics and museum professionals have a chance to talk to one another about these pressing issues in any kind of forum, as well as how important such exchanges are to the issue of self-examination in the academy and museum and to that of how individuals within these entities could more effectively interact and rely on one another as resources. Whether in the format through which this discussion has taken place or, as Joan suggests it should also occur, in the more traditional bringing together of people in actual rather than cyberspace, I hope the future will offer numerous additional opportunities for discussions of this sort so that the issues raised here will continue to be discussed, developed, and expanded.

This dialogue has also made clear that in spite of overarching similarities between museums in terms of both structure and purpose, those working in them know very little about how other institutions function on a nuts-and-bolts level or what mechanisms exist by which different museum departments work together to exchange ideas easily and effectively. Hearing about such particulars provides models for encouraging and increasing collaboration between the various departments of the museum, which in turn could lead to deconstructing the ineffective components of museum hierarchies. But such collaborations are very hard to actualize because they challenge the hierarchy upon which so many in the museum have been nurtured and in which they by nature find comfort and safety. Yet, it is only through such collaboration that new, imaginative, and creative ways of thinking about all aspects of museum practice will materialize and through which—in spite of the pressing reality of market forces—the museum can maintain itself in the future as the kind of anticipatory and ethical space that Mary referred to and upon which so many participants in this conference place great value—one that provides both sanctuary and challenge for the passionate observer.

I also wanted to say that it has been a great pleasure for the Georgia O'Keeffe Museum Research Center to have sponsored this online symposium, and I want to extend my deep appreciation to everyone who has participated in it, and especially to my colleague Maurice, who has so skillfully and brilliantly moderated its amazing and invigorating discussion.

Carol Duncan

I see that some of my fellow symposiatistas are getting the blues. So let's step back for a longer perspective. For about two centuries, art museums have claimed to be sites of spiritual enlightenment, healthful pleasures, revitalizing communion with the past, and so on. To their users, they often delivered on these claims, but, as we also know, in addition, they functioned as sites of intense and elaborate ideological programming. They reinforced and will continue to reinforce the hegemonic powers that be. But let us not get too depressed. We should not expect art museums to transform the world or to tarnish the prestige of the powers that sustain them or to expose the injustices on which their power rests—at least we should not expect art museums to do these things outside of larger political, social, and cultural movements. And yet, as we sometimes see, they do, here and there, now and then, manage to mount shows or installations that look at things in a genuinely new light, and move people to think and feel in new ways. Actually, I can't remember a time when there was as much critical thinking going on inside of museums as there is today.

Jonathan P. Binstock

Let me attempt to further comfort our "fellow symposiatistas" who are getting the blues. I, perhaps like others, am thinking of Miwon Kwon's recent contribution, which is important and deeply moving, as have been all her posts. She derides so-called education programs and, as she writes, their "inculcation of what to think, how to look, where to stand, why bother is often mistaken for education." And why not deride such prescriptive notions of education? They are obviously antithetical to all of our (symposium panelists) relationships with the pleasures and challenges of the vast and open world of art, a world that is inherently antagonistic to attempts to codify and explain. Nonetheless, such educational strategies are, at times, the best ones to adopt. There have been at least a few times when I grabbed a museum visitor by the shoulders and said, "stand here; now look." A rare occasion, perhaps, but in those circumstances my efforts to lead a visitor to something more and, I hope, something lasting were met with success. I took a personal interest and showed that individual the pleasures and challenges of the vast and open world of art.

The art museum is an institutional enterprise, but the art experience is individual, unique. This is a structural problem. There is an inherent contradiction between who we are and what we ought to be doing, which is servicing the aesthetic needs, desires, and educational ambitions of individuals within diverse populations. People who work in museums may find pleasure, challenge, and value—including, perhaps most importantly, social and political value—in this contradiction. But the fact remains, however powerful the notion of the culture mall may be, both in concept and in actuality as capitalism pulls the art museum toward for-profit corporation status, the experience of art will, by force of its nature, resist this transformation. This is because art does not provide for, or have pretenses to offer, a uniform experience among people. Anyone who has ever witnessed a museum educator's last-ditch efforts to connect with a visitor knows this well. The educator almost always resorts to: "the work is what you want it to be; it is what you make it," or something to that effect. However institutional or "corporate" the museum may be, everyone who works there, from the top down, knows that in the end it's a question of the individual, from the individual aesthetic experience to the economics of the price of admission per head. The divide between curatorial and educational departments, or between academics and curators, is, in my view, nothing compared to the divide between the museum and who visits it, or may visit it in the future.

In thinking about the museum of the future, perhaps we should stop comparing it to the mall or the Gap or some other functional and solvent corporate entity that construes its public as an indistinguishable mass within a given demographic. The ideal museum is decidedly not this. Instead, we might look to another struggling and failing not-for-profit institution that is also essential to people and society (unlike the mall or the Gap), albeit for very different reasons: the hospital. This comparison is not meant to invoke the longstanding and deeply flawed idea that art is somehow essential medicine for the infirm or imperiled soul. Please put that entire can of worms aside for the moment. I raise the idea of hospitals because their purpose is to meet the needs and satisfy the demands of a public, but the public, as construed by the hospital, is above all a collection of individuals with unique needs and demands. There is no panacea for the would-be hospital visitor. While the Gap or the mall may offer a one-size-fits-all T-shirt that will appeal to a majority of shoppers, the hospital has to consider the needs of each and every individual who enters its doors.

Nobody would relativize the importance of hospitals to society, but they are shut down all the time. So, how do hospitals combat the threat of extinction? They focus on specialized care (heart, children's, and women's hospitals, for example); on being consumer friendly (nicer waiting rooms, private rooms, improve the look of the gowns); on switching to digitized record keeping (I can go to Japan and take cash out of an ATM, why do I have to tell my doctor my address every time I visit his or her office?); and so on. My museum of the future might learn something from these efforts. It would look to its public as a large body of individual constituents. For the person who needs literally to be positioned in front of a work and told how to look at it, a curator or an educator with passion and knowledge would be there to help. And for the critic who detests even the scent of wall labels, they would disappear upon her entering a particular gallery, the result of her museum (highway) E-Z pass being scanned as she approaches a given sculpture or painting. The art museum of the future will have someone or something greeting people at the door who/that actually understands them. Might such understanding be a solid step in the right direction, toward a more ethical museum practice?

Mark Alice Durant

I am again moved by Maxwell Anderson's observations, specifically his statement that we all have to start somewhere as we approach the mysterious power of art. I agree that most of us live in that "stratosphere of permission" and it is for some impossible to even imagine how far away the world of art can be from the daily lives of a majority of our citizens.

Although I have expressed some skepticism about museum educational outreach, I fully support the efforts. As I mentioned before, there has to be some kind of art "head start" program in public schools K–12, with the goal of not only teaching kids to make art, music, etc., but to prepare them to engage with what they encounter in the museum, whether it be Impressionist or Fluxus. The internal transformation that is required for this kind of awareness is every bit as revolutionary for the individual as the many calls for structural transformation.

As someone who came to art from the working class, I have struggled with class issues and associated feelings of guilt, envy, resentment, and have always felt as if (although it has lessened considerably) I was trespassing on the territory of the privileged. I do want social transformation; I do want public institutions to be aware and active in their role of the democratization of knowledge. Yet the ones who are to be "saved from their savagery" must want, desire, and demand their own transformation. I think art, in its slow, contemplative manner, can cumulatively nudge this change and occasionally provide life-altering epiphanies.

When public libraries close, which they are doing at an alarming rate, I despair. I used to think (silly of me really) that one day, those in charge of our government would wake up, look around, and see that the foundation of our democracy and the seeds for the future health of that democracy depend not on shrinking bureaucracies but on vibrant public institutions, schools, hospitals, libraries, museums, etc. The marketplace is not democratic (even if it is in some ways populist). It is the role of those who live in the "stratosphere of permission" to guard the old humanist ideals, especially if those ideals are under attack from a hostile government seeking to privatize everything. It is not hyperbole when I say that art saved my life and I will be forever grateful to the Museum of Fine Arts, Boston, the Peabody Essex Museum, the Isabella Gardner Museum, the Busch-Reisinger, and others for keeping their doors open and giving me the chance to experience the mysterious power of art. Finally, I do not think that the recognition and celebration of this mysterious power is somehow at odds with concurrent calls for democracy and accessibility, if ethics be served, they must be served simultaneously.

George Baker

I want to reiterate something that I implied Friday:

Mary Kelly's post on the museum and ethics is the most important thing that I've read while engaged in this conference. I think the silence in its wake is telling. No one has picked up on its challenge. No one has developed its terms.

Instead we read posts describing me as "moaning."

I want to sign off with a few, too-hasty thoughts related to why I find Mary's post so important but also so challenging. First, a fear—I think any discussion of either art or museums as ethical practices or spaces runs the danger of being compensatory: We elevate the ethical to the space of culture, where it becomes a passive spectacle produced by a society where ethics have all but disappeared. But that this thought of the museum and ethics occurs with increasing frequency now does register an important change, a shift: Art was precisely the space for many avant-garde artists that implied a release from ethics, a space for transgressions ("Beat up the Poor," Baudelaire's refrain, would be the model here). The turn toward the increasing marriage of culture and ethics perhaps also then parallels the transformed place of the museum in contemporary culture. We haven't discussed this so much, it has been taken as a given throughout the conference perhaps, a basis for why we are even doing this, but: museums used to be the enemy for most modernist defenders of culture. They represented a dead zone, a space of entombment, where culture went to die. Only within postmodernism would the museum come to be a central site of cultural aspiration, a place were culture "occurs" rather than is "preserved." Some will conclude apocalyptically from this that art and culture are thus now finished, museum products, mummies. Others will, more optimistically, see new futures for culture itself when its home becomes the museum, when its "death" becomes the precondition for a new, different kind of "life."

I want to sign off with a citation from one of these optimists. Paradoxically, it is a statement tied to the modernist moment, not to our own. Also it comes from a writer more often associated with cultural pessimism.

I'm thinking of Theodor Adorno. I've been rereading his essay on the museum, usually taken as pessimistic, the one—"Valéry Proust Museum"—that begins with the oft-cited lament that museums are the "mausoleums" of culture. But that essay ends, more or less, with the following thoughts, and I had forgotten this: "In a sense," Adorno writes, "works of art return home when they become elements of the observer's subjective stream of consciousness." Adorno calls for a museum where the interpenetration of art object and human subject could occur, where art could be returned, after a long detour, to its human meanings, the range of desires it can both embody and fulfill—but more often displaces. He continues:

> *Works of art can fully embody the promesse du bonheur only when they have been uprooted from their native soil and have set out along the path to their own destruction. . . . The procedure which today relegates every work of art to the museum, even Picasso's most recent sculpture, is irreversible. It is not solely reprehensible, however, for it presages a situation in which art, having completed its estrangement from human ends, returns, in Novalis' words, to life. One senses something of this in Proust. . . . where physiognomies of paintings and people glide into one another almost without a break and memory traces of experiences fuse with those of musical passages. In . . . the description of falling asleep on the first page of* Du côté de chez Swann, *the narrator says, "It seemed to me that I was the thing the book was about: a church, a quartet, the rivalry between Francis the First and Charles the Fifth." This is the reconciliation of that split which Valéry so irreconcilably laments. The chaos of cultural goods fades into the bliss of the child whose body feels itself as one with the nimbus of distance.*

Having recently been writing on artists who consider their work to be "institutional critique," artists like Andrea Fraser, whose project is not so different I think than the vision of Proust's cited above, it seems to me that the ethics of the museum must be found in this—admittedly wild—interpenetration. It must be found in an institution that allows the displaced social meanings and desires pent up in the object of art to be set free. The museum—from the very moment of its fraught origination in the cabinets of "wonder" or "curiosities"—is the place where we learn to care about things to which we have no inherent connection, not the place where we learn the "universal" value of some generality called "art." The latter was a distortion. The museum is a machine for producing a love and respect for the disparate. As such, the museum has become a singular space in our culture.

I want to become a church, a quartet, the rivalry between Francis the First and Charles the Fifth. I want to see paintings and people glide into one another; to feel the object of art as if it were a person, and every other person as if they were a work of art.

I will be misunderstood here, but that is okay, I'm not sure I understand this myself. But whatever measures we must take to defend it, whatever encroachments need to be repelled from other spheres of life with less utopian values, the museum of tomorrow must become a place where this possibility for caring becomes a reality more often than sometimes.

Michele Wallace

I don't know whether I am a cultural pariah or just a narcissist but in the past few days (as my body and soul have been preoccupied with the job I hold as a Professor of English, Women's Studies, and Film at the Grad Center and the City College of New York), my mind has been floating over a series of possible responses to the questions that have been raised during the course of this online conference on the future of the museum. For a little while I was pissed about issues of exclusion, and the feeling that they weren't being adequately addressed, and alienated by the assumption that there is such a thing as an exclusively Western (white?) tradition in visual art which automatically excludes the experiences and developments of many other cultures. But pretty soon the anger floated away as I realized that I am just one voice, and that howling in the wind isn't something that I can bear to waste my time doing at my age.

Gradually the prosaic impulse to be angry was replaced by a more philosophical and autobiographical bent toward thinking of the many museum stories I could tell about the crucial role that museums have played in my life as places of experimentation and liberation.

I wasn't born in some rural place, or in some remote part of the world. Therefore I never had the formative experience of coming from the comparatively uncivilized margins of our global societies to the museum in order to discover at a relatively mature age the wonders of the metropolitan center.

I was born in the metropolitan center (actually I was born in the Medical Center in Washington Heights) to a 22-year-old woman (the daughter of a sanitation truck driver and a fashion designer/garment district worker), who was, herself, a student of art and education at the City College of New York and who spent all her available time in the great museums and libraries of New York. This was in the '50s. I know you will be poised to point out that the museums benefited me because my family belonged to the bourgeoisie, but the truth is that I was born into the heart of a large, warm working-class family (with Floridian and Jamaican roots) in Harlem. Nonetheless, I have never experienced any aspect of the cultural deprivation that is assumed to be the common lot still of people born in my community in Harlem. Part of this was because I had extraordinary mentors in my Mom—Faith Ringgold—her siblings, and my grandparents, all of whom lived around me when I was a child.

But the other part of it was that I was born on the island of Manhattan instead of a place where there weren't any museums, or great libraries, or bookstores, or colleges, or parks, theaters, and opera houses, or subways and public buses to speed you to your destination for 15 cents. There are still many such places in this country, not to mention all over the world. I question the ideological and/or theoretical function of confining the history of the museum to the Western Europe (white) of the last 200 years. I strongly suspect that wherever there has been a process of successful urbanization coupled with a concept of education that requires one to make artifacts and documents of value available to the public and yet protect them from the vandalism and the shortsightedness of the greedy, the uncultivated, the angry and disillusioned, one will need a concept of a museum equal to the concept of a library.

The most convincing critique of the museum is the critique of enlightenment and democracy, specifically that it was never intended to include everybody, only those who had access to wealth and elite socialization. Some of us who won't stop wishing to see the last become first in our own lifetime would like to see the museum and democracy work in exactly the opposite manner to disenfranchise the wealthy and the elite. But, you know, quite frankly I don't see this happening no matter how much we wish it so. I don't like the idea of even imagining a world in which there would be no museums. I strongly suspect that the idea of destroying Afghanistan's and Iraq's museum-quality heritage was a major factor in our war against them. If it wasn't a factor, all the worse for us.

We know that the Philistines on the other side, such as the Taliban, were perfectly willing to blast every pyramid, church, synagogue, museum, library, and architectural wonder in the world into rubble in order to have their way. Their world would have no need of museums, unless it would be to display the bones of their victims. After all, a museum is a place in which strangers from different places, of different ethnicities and genders gently brush up against one another in an unregulated manner.

There have been in this horrendous country of ours such a thing as racially segregated museums, but I suspect it has always been a difficult concept, and that the museum in the South grew with the growth of the urban, and thereby, with the strengthening of the concept of racial integration and the successes of the Civil Rights Movement. Nor do I much like the idea of substantially dicking around with the organization of the present large, world-class museums. I think that the way to address the democratization of access to the universe of art would be to either make more museums, or better fund the more marginal museums that currently exist—i.e., The New Museum of Contemporary Art, The Studio Museum, El Museo del Barrio, as well as the so-called alternative spaces, some of which will, in time (if the right funding can be found), become museums as well.

There should be museums in every part of New York. There should be museums in every state, in every county, along with historical societies and libraries. Many religious institutions, in the U.S. and abroad, function essentially as museums, and it is the gallery system that should fulfill the weeding-out process in the present. Even as commodification, consumption, globalization, and computerization are turning almost every idea and concept into a yawning mediocre nothingness, it is the libraries, the museums, and the historical societies that must keep the historical record of our legacy as a coherent civilization. And I seriously doubt a thousand years from now that this civilization will ultimately be seen in the racist, xenophobic terms of a Western versus an Eastern civilization, whatever the hell that might mean. I suspect rather that our centuries-long struggles over a series of sacred texts (i.e. the Bible, Old and New Testament, and the Koran) will be read as permutations of a single schizophrenic civilization that could never have done without (and was perhaps destroyed by) its internal contradictions over enslavement versus liberty, equality versus deprivation, exploitation versus purification, the devastation of war versus the invisibility of the pursuit of happiness.

The distinctions between art museums versus historical societies, natural history museums, and libraries are less important than understanding the overall preservationist mission of such institutions. These are formations that are designed to outlast our lifetimes, to carry messages of what our values were into the future. It is interesting to me that you can't have much of a museum without a library, and that much of the key to how the collection works and makes meaning is archived in its library. So in this light, perhaps I can talk about one institution in New York which I have watched change dramatically in my lifetime. (Of course, they all have really, to tell the truth.) I have been going to the absolutely magnificent 42nd Street Library since long before I can remember. Because it was massive and unregulated, when we were children, my Mom was often tempted to take us to the main circulation room while she was doing her homework. We would have our books and our lollipops and paper to draw, etc. One very, very hot day in the summer when I was an infant, I managed to get all my clothes off and was running around the marble halls. My younger sister was in the process of imitating me. As often comes out in my Mom's story about our childhood, a man offered to catch Barbara, who was heading in the other direction, while she got me and my clothes and exited the library. The point of the story is that children don't know and couldn't care less concerning the conventions of appropriate behaviors in public. Often Mom's favorite stories, including the subject of her painting *Dancing at the Louvre,* are about how children are essentially savages, animals caught in the net of civilization, which is irreducibly dependent upon repression and restraint. Later on when I was older, and a student myself in the '70s, I can recall a point when I used to visit the library and notice homeless people snuggling up on the benches in the marble halls, the white marble now growing muddy and neglected. I never had the heart to wish that they were elsewhere because I understood the feeling of safety that these hallways provided to the desperate, but I wondered what would become of my library, how it would ever survive so many different agendas.

Well, I guess most of you know what happened then. We had a succession of really evil mayors and, in the process, a coterie of wealthy New Yorkers, including the legendary Brooke Astor and the designer Bill Blass, got together and poured money not only into rescuing the library, but also into completely redoing Bryant Park——which was right next to it—and turning it into a private park where the big fashion shows are annually held. The drug dealers and other less presentable constituencies were chased out to god knows where. The exquisite library facilities, its adjoining park, and a fancy new restaurant built into the back of the library, are policed by a force of private security guards, and the park, as well as the library, are firmly closed after a certain hour so it cannot become anyone's home. Nonetheless, in the summers, film screenings are scheduled to appeal to the many workers who come to the area daily to make their living in the surrounding office buildings. One can no longer borrow books from this library or any of the branches of what is now known as the research system (i.e. the Schomburg, the Library of Performing Arts at Lincoln Center). Yet would anyone dare to completely reject the extraordinary transformation of 42nd Street from what it once was (a truly terrifying place into which many children, male and female, disappeared into sexual slavery) into the tourist playground that it currently is. Every aspect of civility has its inexorable downside. It cannot be helped. It is part of growing up and getting on with it. I guess I said all this to say, I don't know how you are ever going to teach folk how to behave in museums (how to enjoy them) if you don't make sure they get to spend some time in them when they are children, even if they do spend the first time or two taking off all their clothes and getting shown the exit.

It isn't the kind of thing that you can learn much about or do much about in absentia. Museums may lend themselves to abstract discussion, but, in fact, the museum is a practice, not a philosophy. Museums have pretty much always been central in my life. Although I've worked in a few—for instance I participated in an internship program at the Museum of Natural History in which I was ostensibly trained to function as a guide in what was then "The Africa Room" (not sure whether it is still the same). This was in 1973 or '74 or so, at a time when both Mom and I were getting very interested in "traditional" African art of the kind one could find in abundance in "The Africa Room," along with a series of discrete panorama displays of Africans engaged in daily life, which I will never forget because I spent so much time trying to explain away their existence and to understand the necessity for their presence. A few years before that, the notorious *Harlem on Mind* exhibition put black artists and photographers on notice at the Metropolitan Museum of Art in 1968.

In the same year, as I recall, I can remember doing a protest-guided tour through the rooms of the Museum of Modern Art led by my Mom and Tom Lloyd, both of whom were working through the Art Worker's Coalition to open the museums to black and Puerto-Rican artists. They were then demanding a wing for artists of color. When Faith located a Jacob Lawrence hanging on the walls of one of the rooms, she chose it as the future location of the new wing, and she asked me to conduct an African ceremony to dedicate the room for that future purpose. Mortified though I was with stage fright, I led an African chant—a call and response—I had just learned as a student at Barbara Ann Teer's National Black Theater in Harlem. I can still remember it. We danced around the room and sang the words of the chant. It was one of a series of affirmations of my own relation to the museum that I will never ever forget. Also, I would be remiss if I didn't point my reader to some other writings that may help clarify some of my positions. These would be "The Mona Lisa Interview," which can be found at www.faithringgold.com, where Faith and I talk a little bit about the importance of the role of a 1961 family visit to the Musée du Louvre, and other European museums in her work.

Also, I think one may find much insight into my notion of family tradition and visual culture in "The French Collection: Momma Jones, Mommy Faye and Me" in *Dancing at the Louvre*, edited by Dan Cameron et al. I think Faith Ringgold's *We Flew Over the Bridge* (out-of-print but soon to be republished by Duke University Press), Little Brown, 1991, tells the story of her experiences as a student of Western Art and African Art and culture. I am looking forward to soon doing an intensive interview with Faith concerning my grandmother's trips to Senegal, Ghana, and Nigeria in 1973 and 1974, and Faith's trips to Ghana and Nigeria in 1976 to visit the museums and art-making villages there, and in 1977 in order to participate in FESTAC .

Sorry all for being so long-winded.

Alexander Alberro

Rereading the discussion of the past two weeks, I'm surprised at how much I disagreed with most of what was said. And yet, it was this very fact that made the online symposium an interesting one for me. All too often, conferences, institutions, editorial boards, and the like are comprised of individuals who share very similar perspectives and distance themselves from points of view that differ substantially from (let alone oppose) their own. How boring. How unproductive. How very conservative! Thus I learned from the diverse viewpoints, especially those that clashed or otherwise conflicted with my own.

This is after all what I like most about the context of the university—at its best, it is a site where a provocative clash of truly incongruous positions can take place—and the symposium was a success in this regard. Education departments in art museums would do well to provide more such contexts for genuine critical analysis and debate.

This leads me to one of the aspects that I would like to see emphasized more by art museums in the future, which is to provide a site for not only the production of knowledge, but also for the production of critique. Whether that criticality be activist, or reflexive, or even purely formalist, I believe that museums (and art more generally) should encourage skeptical thinking and question what is at any given moment taken for granted. Today's free-market model of art and museum practice values creative idiosyncrasy over critique, and I would like to see museums shift this set of priorities in the direction of the production of knowledge, investigation, and critical discussion.

But this is all within the horizon of possibilities today, and Maurice asks us to envision the ideal art museum of the future. So, let us dream. How about art museums that no longer collect unique objects? After all, doesn't the most interesting work of the past four decades throw into question the very issue of one-of-a-kindness, and of the collectibility of artworks? Or this could be phrased more proactively: If art museums stopped collecting objects, the way contemporary art is produced, distributed, and received would change accordingly. The contemporary art museum could free itself from the corporate shackles that increasingly restrain it and concentrate on its public role as a site of exhibition, contemplation, education, and study. There would of course be ample documentation in the form of books, catalogues, CD-ROMs, DVDs, and other multiples, but the role that the market plays in the contemporary art museum would be greatly diminished, and ultimately eliminated. And artists? Well, artists would be paid fees for their labor. They would stage exhibitions, carry out projects, make investigations, explore possibilities, push the boundaries, problematize the habitual. In turn, collecting objects (as with producing objects to be collected) would soon enough lose its prestige and eventually become obsolete. And while we're dreaming: How about the expansion of the very concept of the art museum into a fluid and labile institution, a fully deterritorialized practice? Practices that would encompass entire cities rather than attempt to contain culture within museum walls. Wouldn't the public greatly increase then? No more confined sites of culture! No more grandiose buildings by megalomaniacal architects! No more collectors who sit on museum boards stocking the institution with their prize possessions, or pestering directors and curators with their antiquated ideas of what art is! No more need for gallerists to lobby museum professionals to prop up the value of their wares! No more market for contemporary art objects! The world is already full of objects—why make more? Let's be realistic instead, and demand the impossible.

George G. King

This is the second online symposium that this young museum has organized, which has been masterfully moderated by Maurice. Thank you, Maurice, for your questions and for guiding and leading us through this important topic. I would also like to thank all of the participants for their invaluable posts.

When discussing this symposium with my colleagues in the art museum field as well as those in related fields, some individuals asked why it was that this museum was hosting the program. I was naturally surprised by these questions or remarks, and they lead me to further ponder the perception we have or don't have about ourselves or the museum field. It is terribly important we utilize some form of introspection (like this symposium) on a regular basis so that we are able to preserve and learn from our past in order to affect the future of museums.

Maurice, you asked the question of our personal vision of the ideal art museum, which reminds me of the founding director of the Newark Museum of Art, John Cotton Dana, himself a visionary of what museums could do and should be. Among the many important points he stressed in his writings was: "learn what aid the community needs" and "fit the museum to those needs." There is no question museums need to respond to their communities—they have and they should continue to do so. However, it is the museum-employed experts, particularly the curators and educators who are themselves part of the community, who must make the final decision on what the aesthetic presentation and programming must be. It is they who are charged to gather knowledge and expertise, organize, and disseminate it to their immediate communities, and others for that matter, in a manner that is relevant and cohesive and ultimately meaningful.

Museums of the future must not lose sight of this. Nor should the museum lose sight of creating an experience for the visitor, one of awe and inspiration and yes, one where knowledge has been imparted, and one which has been challenging and positive. In the end, it is the museum towards which the balance of authority should tilt in regards to its relationship with the community.

Whether we like it or not, museums of the future will come under increased pressure from their local or state authorities to provide taxable income to their local municipalities. Even though it might be that the collective cultural muscle is a major contributor to the local economies of one community, the need to create additional revenue streams for the government will always be in demand. Most recently here in New Mexico, authorities proposed a tax range from 3% to 6% on all income including admissions and grants. The tuition for the local private colleges would have also come under this tax. Fortunately, after a well-mounted campaign against this the authorities withdrew the proposal.

Because of the need to raise funds, some museums, as they have in the past, will form marketing alliances or relationships with for-profit entities. This will no doubt continue, and the more it happens, the more the core purpose of our institutions will be questioned and scrutinized. Perhaps a for-profit museum will emerge as a result of the increased corporate nature of our business. One hopes not, but who knows? I can only hope that discussions like this help underscore the long-term importance, need, and purpose of museums.

Sylvia Yount

Rather than thinking in terms of a utopian ideal, I'd like to ground my comments in the practical realm.

Unlike some, I'm hopeful that the current expansion fever sweeping the country bodes well for the future health of art museums, given the necessary reexamination of mission, collection, and audience that accompanies institutional growth and change. Perhaps the advent of additional gallery space will allow for a broader range of special exhibitions and installations—from the gate-busting variety to the more thoughtful, if potentially less popular, effort. Such concurrent programming should take some of the financial pressure off the latter and encourage museum staff to adopt a more holistic view of art production and reception.

The High Museum of Art's forthcoming Renzo Piano-designed expansion, debuting fall 2005, promises to transform the scale and profile of the institution. By ensuring enough space for the display of the full range of the permanent collection and special exhibitions as well as an entire floor devoted to museum education, we hope to provide visitors with different kinds of art experiences—from the inevitably quieter, contemplative moments spent with the collection and the theatrical buzz and hum of a temporary exhibition to more interactive, hands-on involvement.

I firmly believe that only by embracing this intellectual and aesthetic balance will we move closer to the "democratic" purpose of instruction and amusement that shaped the character of our country's earliest museums. Some 200 years later, it remains an admirable and critical goal in our ongoing efforts—personal and institutional—to make museums matter in these troubled times.

Bruce Altshuler

It seems to me that Mary Kelly's focus on ethics and the museum connects so much of what has been discussed over the past week and a half, from concerns about elitism and democracy to worries about collection and exhibition. And it is difficult for anyone working in an institution—whether museum or university—not to share Miwon Kwon's feeling that we all are cogs in a system able to assimilate criticism within an enterprise that basically ignores the transformational aspects of a personal engagement with art. But whatever the ethical shortcomings of museums, the fact is that museums increasingly expose large numbers of people of all ages to actual artworks, providing opportunities for the kinds of experiences that have brought each of us to this field, and allowing for the creation of the diverse narratives that have been called for throughout this symposium.

For there to be personal experiences of the artwork, however, works of art must enter the museum, and this brings the discussion around again to collections and acquisitions. For as long-term repositories of these objects—and the heritage (of many kinds) that they encapsulate—museums make them available for an unlimited number of presentations and interpretations, allowing (hopefully) these works to outlast all of our particular curatorial and educational strategies. I therefore am not at all attracted to Alex Alberro's ideal museum of the future as one that does not collect unique objects. For not only do particular artworks occasion critical experiences, they also connect us directly to the individuals who are central to all of this, people who often are ignored in institutional discourse. That is, artworks connect us to the artists who made them.

The centrality of artists to museum-goers, and the consequent importance of museums to artistic production, was raised by Irving Sandler, and there are other ways in which the artist has figured interestingly in the discussion. Barbara Kirshenblatt-Gimblett's distinction between educating and learning, and her linking the "soft mastery" of learning to the working process of the artist, suggests a deep connection between what is displayed and maintained in museums and what people take away from their time in them. With all of this talk about the (admittedly important) public—actually, publics—served by the museum, it is critical not to ignore the ultimate source of what museums present, which is the artist.

On another matter that has come up quite a few times, the relationship between the university and the museum, it is important to note the hierarchical structure within which members of these two parts of the art world relate to one another. While in actuality this is a dynamic system whose various elements interact in many different ways, in terms of status-allocation there basically is a three-tiered structure. Here the highest echelon is occupied by academic art historians, the middle level is that of museum curators, and the bottom rung not surprisingly is populated by denizens of the art trade (galleries, auction houses, etc.). This is a Platonic system in which those dealing with ideas are on top, and the closer that you get to the material world of objects and financial transactions, the lower your rank. In other words, the individuals most frequently having actual contact with art objects are accorded the least status. Of course there is one critical group that has not been mentioned, who in practice are shown the least respect because, perhaps, they are at the lowest scale of the Platonic system. They are those who make the stuff—the artists.

So my concluding suggestion—despite its problems—is to make artists more central to our art museums. This can be done in many ways (as others have mentioned), from involving artists in educational programs and in-house projects to their playing a greater role in museum governance. And this seems to me very much to be an ethical issue, for it has to do with our responsibility toward and respect for those without whom there would be no art, and therefore without whom there would be no art museums.

Edward Rothstein

I may risk violating the collegiality of much of this symposium if I say that the great art museum, in order to strengthen its programming and standing in society and in culture, should do precisely the opposite of what so many have been proposing. But my disagreement may already be fairly evident. I have sometimes even been a bit confused about how the reverence for the idea of the museum is combined with views that I believe would undo that idea's authority and its varied possibilities.

I have heard much I agree with, sometimes intermingling with things I do not, but if I had to articulate a conviction in this context, it would be something like this:

I have no problem with a thousand flowers blooming. I do have a problem if the few museums that have achieved greatness are thought of as promulgating ideas I do not believe are enshrined there, or if they are being asked to transform themselves in ways that will undermine the very aspects of the museum to which we all, in the midst of criticisms, ultimately defer.

By all means let criticisms be made: Let commodification be attacked when it corrupts the power of art; let corporate structure be challenged when it makes marketing a synonym for curatorship; let narrow-mindedness be assaulted when it asserts that there is something inherent in one's race, gender, or any other attribute that precludes the kind of achievements being celebrated; let diversity—yes, even diversity—be overturned if it insists that it should have the highest priority in an art museum's enterprise.

In their place, let us at least see *some* museums as magnificent repositories of mythic narratives and aesthetic achievements, which are, by their nature, both restrictive and expansive. And let us insist that in the midst of whatever programmatic and political ambitions exhibitions may reflect, that there also be room for exhibitions that try, very hard, to avoid preaching or telling viewers how or what to think about the world, and allow extraordinary artworks to exercise their inherently transformative powers.

If some space could remain for that sort of enterprise and if museum education and public education provided some understanding of it and reverence for it, and if parents believed in its importance as a necessary part of their children's lives—if all those conditions were to exist, then I think museums, in their varied shapes, would thrive. Such is the scope of my hope, which occasionally may seem to verge on utopianism.

In the meantime, thanks to Maurice and the Georgia O'Keeffe Museum for the opportunity to listen to and join this conversation.

Stefano Basilico

I've just come back from Milwaukee, where yesterday I participated in another symposium that I co-organized with Michelle Grabner, and therefore, I have been a little slow in posting. This forum has been challenging and surprising for me (I had not been part of a two-week discussion before and can honestly say it was enjoyable, informative, frustrating, confusing, encouraging, distressing—but never dull or depressing). It was a good thing.

I'm a little tired, but I wanted to post a final thought or wish for the museum of the future, which I hope will never be confused with a "mall."

The museum of the future will run with scissors in its hands, I hope.

The curator of the future will not know her or his role and will confuse it with the role of the educator of the future, who will also not know her or his role, and together they will make a big vital mess that will bring in 51% of all the population of the future, voluntarily.

This audience will encounter art that will challenge their culturally conditioned willingness to accept at face value the imagery they consume.

They will pay (a modest fee) for this experience, and they will feel it is a privilege. This privilege will be available for all.

Mary Kelly

I found the form of the symposium as provocative as its content. By that I mean the specific materiality of an online conversation, the way it erases almost all trace of gesture, prompting me to mime the voices of those I know and invent ones for those I don't. In fact, I suppose I was trying to animate the constancy characteristic of this medium with the contingency and sense of community that defines an exhibition in its phenomenal guise. But in the virtual space of the Internet, this animation seemed to foster a certain kind of psychologism or interiority predicated on singularity rather than the jubilant assumption of the collective pronoun "we." This is neither a good thing, nor a bad thing. It simply points to what is uniquely, perhaps perversely, pleasurable about the "outmoded" spectatorship of the museum. Of course, this is not an essential condition, but an historically determined one. It can be reactive or even redemptive as Walter Benjamin suggested, but its appearance at the present time is intimately linked to the question of ethics. George [Baker] made this connection lucidly in his concluding remarks. He called my attention to how close Adorno's "interpenetration of art object and human subject" is to Agamben's "liberation of image into gesture," in so far as both prefer the museum to be a place of epiphany rather than reification, yet the distance that emerges in the shift from "art object" to "image" and from "human subject" to "gesture" is indicative of the vastly different cultural realm we now inhabit, one described often in these conversations as a relentless flow of images and information, but just as often, followed by the ethical imperative "to keep going." In this much at least, I felt "we" were all on the same page.

Dan Cameron

I feel like the best way to respond to my colleagues at this final stage of the symposium is to emphasize that although I found many viewpoints here that I did not share, there were very few that I felt an outright disagreement with. In other words, in the face of all the legitimate reasons for feeling depressed or alarmed about the state of art museums in this country, I feel quite optimistic about the fact that museums today cannot follow a single path. Even the "culture mall" scenario, while disturbing on some level, is also liberating as a potential means of experiencing art within a different context. Perhaps the fact that I believe this phenomenon can easily coexist alongside the model of the experimental contemporary art museum as a laboratory for new ideas about art-making will be dismissed by some as the height of naiveté. After all, isn't the behemoth of consumerist culture relentlessly devouring everything in its path? Maybe so, but my faith in artists and what they do is such that I am convinced that once a museum-based model outlives its usefulness, it will be replaced by another, and then another, so that eventually museums will exist in every possible configuration, for every kind of viewer.

That said, I am equally un-worried about the relationship between the museum and the gallery system. I am as aware as anyone that the ties between blue-chip galleries and the boards of big museums are far too cozy, but I also see the roles of both parties in this relationship as having ossified a long time ago. Let them collect what they want—meanwhile, the smaller galleries that work with emerging artists are still changing the world that we live in, and the alternative spaces and "fringe" museums are doing the same. To suppose that museums would thrive in a world with no art market is to suggest that the only kind of art making that is valid is that which results in artworks that no one would ever want to live with. I for one find the notion of such a world far too bleak and monotonous.

My final note concerns the relatively loaded subject of museums, ethics, and class. I too come from a semi-rural working-class background, and there was absolutely no family background in art before I came along. I discovered art as a teenager, largely through the agency of an enlightened high school art teacher and a local museum that happened to have both an excellent Rembrandt and a first-rate David Smith in its collection. I have sometimes been criticized for my laissez-faire attitude when it comes to supposedly enlightened principles about art and ethics, and I suppose that my inherent flexibility has its roots in the fact that I am so deeply grateful to have found my vocation in the art world that I would no sooner exclude one way of looking at art than I would close the doors of the Soloman R. Guggenheim Museum just because their program seems so patently trashy to me. My philosophy at the moment is to permit everything and then make judgments based on the results. If this means going to malls to see what someone else considers the wave of the future, or looking at art in the middle of the desert, or on CD-ROMs, I'm afraid that you'll always find me at the front of the line!

Mary Karen Davalos

I came to this conference with some trepidation. I had an idea about the other participants, their cultural capital within museums and academia, and given the histories of museums and universities, their likely access to whiteness, masculinity, and authority. Not all of the participants, but the majority just by the nature of these institutions. My name does not carry that cultural capital nor does my expertise in Mexican/Chicano arts institutions and cultural production establish me as an expert in the world of art museums. Moreover, I am not the first woman of color to speak to such a group: What could I ever expect to contribute? What could or would this group hear from me? Did an online conference open a new space that would make listening a possibility? Would this new space assist in the creation of a democratic museum?

It was not refreshing for me to have my fears confirmed. The large, metropolitan, universal, or Western art museum is a space of exclusion. History provides one reason why it is closed, but not the only reason. I agree with Carol Duncan's assessment that we are witnessing an intense period of introspection within the museum, but this moment of questioning has not produced a space in which alternative perspectives—the critics of neo-liberalism, the critics of whiteness, the critics of capitalism, the critics of sexism, the critics of homophobia, the critics of empire, the critics of the West, the critics of the nation–are authorized, legitimized, and granted space at the table. For the future: the major institutions of art need to collaborate with the so-called alternative arts institutions. These collaborations must allow for equity, especially in areas of curatorial authority, labor, and decision making. Major museums should assist with funding of alternative spaces. And not in the model that the Smithsonian is using! The Mexican Fine Arts Center Museum (MFACM) (to name one) does not need the Smithsonian's credibility to keep its doors open, but the Smithsonian needs everything about the MFACM to create outreach and education programs, to sustain the arts, to build its Latino collections, etc.

This conference was a refreshing space in which certain authorities and privileges were made to give up space, to share access to voice, to share space on the virtual panel. But the technology that created some form of democracy, also provided for the avenue through which distance was maintained. You did not have to look me in the eye to ignore me. You did not have to face my body when listening, or fake listening. You did not have to hear or reply. Certainly, the public record on the Internet and in the future publication will join all of the panelists in a democratic space, or the possibility of democracy. But the online venue allowed for silence on certain issues—and Maurice's private pleas for me (and others) to post are part of the record of that silence.

I am suggesting that if we had been in the same room, the silence on certain issues would not have been possible. The naked denial of the last three topics would have been a social faux pas. The social conventions of a public conference would require us to reply to those with whom we disagree. And this "if we had been in the same room" is an unimaginable moment precisely because we rarely attend conferences or panels of those with whom we disagree, as Alexander Alberro has pointed out. But also, this "if" is also unimaginable because I and a few other panelists speak from a place that is not permitted within museum discourse.

Museums rarely invite their opponents to the table.

It has left me wondering about inclusion—as an argument—and what language/strategy requires listening, a response, and change. Demography is not enough to require listening, and it is not sufficient because demography is currently used to limit what presence we can have in public institutions. For some panelists, democracy is not a reason for inclusion—economics and demography?

I am more convinced than ever that the so-called public museum has much to learn from the so-called alternative museum. In the next 15 years, the major museums of New York City will be asking for help, trying to understand their new Mexican immigrant audiences. They won't know what to do when this population becomes the majority population in the city. They should look now to the community-based arts institutions and they should assist those institutions that wish to gain museum status. These relationships will make it possible for them to keep their doors open—and in this statement, I aim at the base economic necessity of museums, but utopian fantasies about democracy in the museum world are still alive for me, nourished by Maurice's clarity on how we might get there.

Simon Leung

I am writing this offline, in an airport—it's 2:33A.M. I missed my flight back to LA last night, so in total I will have spent 13 or so hours here before boarding the next flight as a "stand-by." Airports are cold, indeterminate places—always too crowded one moment and deserted the next; the architecture hums a constant low-level anxiety and melancholy. To pass your time in an airport you have to repress horror and fear, and wait and wait and wait. These are the illuminated signs of my environs: "Nothing to declare." "Something to declare." "Baggage claim." Signs at airport gates are words to live by—the wisdom of thresholds, eternally illuminated.

If I do have "something to declare" as a concluding statement, it will have to be declared without my having read what everyone has been posting. That makes me a bit anxious, perhaps because it makes me feel less than conscientious, for I would on the whole prefer to be in perpetual response to others in what I contribute here. But if I am consigned to writing as a stand-by, disconnected, and tenuously poised to take off (on a Deleuzean "line of flight," or so I've always aspired), perhaps I can utilize the heightened awareness of this threshold state I'm in to reflect on the liminality of museums.

I would like to address a few related issues that were in discussion as of Sunday morning. The first, as I recall, was a series of charts that described the possible futures of the museum as being utopian, dystopian, and "somewhere in between." Michel Foucault's theory of "heterotopia" is relevant here. Heterotopic space is certainly liminal, but it is not "somewhere in between" in a simple sense of Euclidean geometry. Rather, the heterotopic is a form of site that traces the spatialization of power, in particular the dynamic, structural relationship between center and periphery that comes as a result of shifts within the structures of power. One example is the cemetery—its centrality within society shifted as the moral, political influence of the church was altered through the gradual transformation of social, political, and economic life brought on by capitalism. The museum, I would argue, has always also been a heterotopic space. When I proposed in my first post that the corporate museum is "a theater of war," I was thinking of this heterotopic dynamic. Understood as such, the museum is in a state of continual reformation, and thus to answer your question Maurice, I have no "ideal art museum of the future." Psychically speaking, idealization is a defense—for me every aspect of the museum's status is contingent, much like art. That is a good thing. Regarding the "ideal art museum of the future," I am too Freudian (or too Didion, if you will pardon the grammatically inconsistent pun) to idealize idealization.

In terms of "What issues discussed in the conference have emerged as important to (me) or have altered (my) thinking?" I suppose I've answered in part in my posts already. But I would like to essay a brief reflection on what continues to interest me by extending the notion of museums as a formative site of the bourgeois subject. As I listen to the various voices, speaking eloquently about where they are in relationship to the function of the museum, I cannot help but wonder if the different "roles" that any one person may take on vis-à-vis the museum are constructing our sense of obligation to these roles—be that curator, director, historian, critic, artist, or intellectual. I have been paying attention to the bridging and diverging of identities: curator/art historian; artist/viewer; art professional/general public, etc.

At various stages of my life I've been an art factory worker (making Allan McCollum's *Individual Works* in a windowless loft in the '80s); gallery and museum preparator (painting and patching walls, hanging works, lighting—all the schlep work); assistant to rich abusive artist (who shall remain nameless); gallery guard (at Dia back when there were no galleries in Chelsea and you could read while guarding); offsite museum educator in N.Y.C. public high schools (6 1/2 years working through the New Museum of Contemporary Art traveling to over 15 high schools all over the city, where most of the students were non-white and came from working-class, immigrant, or poor families); museum education consultant (Jean-Michel Basquiat and Agnes Martin shows at the Whitney Museum of American Art); exhibition essay writer (did it for the money—I have lived most of my adult life under the poverty line); conference panelist/lecturer (didn't do it for the money necessarily, but the money certainly helped); guest curator (film program at Los Angeles County Museum of Art); and exhibiting artist (which I am happy to remain). I earn my living now as a college professor—for the third year in a row I'm teaching a 400-person lecture class on 20th-century art at a large public university.

When I do that, I am literally bringing the museum to young students who for the most part have little contact with "the art world" they perceive me to have come from and circulate in. Sometimes I give assignments to them where they have to go to a museum and look, write, think. What have I learned? I learn that most people (my students, or the "general public" as I think we are calling them here) don't feel that they have a right to contemporary art or modern art, that they were never taught to look at a complex object like art, that thinking about art is alien. I learn that most of them don't share the identifications everyone here does. But some of them do, and some of them learn to—and when that happens they get very excited when they see something they like. When the initial infatuation (fun factor) wears off and they get more critical, they start thinking about the museum, and through thinking comes the investiture of the feeling that they have a right to a culture from which they had felt alienated. I am not sure what that achieves, but I think the conscious negotiation of one's feeling of alienation is something the museum can still do pretty well. After all, so I always tell my students, your alienation is really the only thing you have that is irreducibly your own. Enjoy your alienation—you've earned it.

Jennifer González

As a nexus of architecture, people, and objects, museums inevitably perform the role of arbiters of value—aesthetic value, political value, social value. The conversation thus far has confirmed the fact that consensus on the proper function of museums is unlikely to be achieved, but the basic fact of their social importance remains unquestioned. Rather than conceiving of museums as gatekeepers, it might be more accurate to see the museum as the site of historical speech acts. It then becomes possible to recognize the history of museums as a series of enunciations that celebrate, ignore, or condemn particular artworks, scholarly rubrics, and forms.

These enunciations—displays of permanent collections, temporary exhibitions, and publications—inevitably change over time, but they also characterize what might be considered the extended monologue of a given institution and participate in a larger discourse between institutions. Dan Cameron hints at this possibility in his astute comments emphasizing the necessary variety and diversity of museum spaces, audiences, and collections.

When I suggested earlier that it was important to consider the question of whose myth the institution represents, I was not being merely polemical. Not only art museums but all museums—from the large-scale encyclopedic museum, to the small-scale, ethnically specific museum—sustain myths that naturalize the meanings of the objects they display. Display itself, as a technique of producing pleasures or epistemologies, has a rhetorical structure that is frequently based on the possibilities of mythmaking.

Since the 19th century, the logic of museum display has been largely progressivist and grounded in the literary paradigm of narrative—the art-historical narrative, the ethnographic narrative, the biographical narrative, and so on. (Scholar Steven Bann suggests that in previous centuries the reigning paradigms of display were metaphor or metonymy, for example.) Today most visitors come to museums looking for a good story that will confirm their already inscribed cultural assumptions. Is it possible that narrative, as a cultural form of representation, is partially to blame for this? Is it possible that the politics of display inherited from the 19th century will eventually change—that metaphor, metonym, and narrative will no longer be the primary, familiar, organizing trope of exhibitions in the future?

Mary Kelly's comments on what might be called the ethics of anticipation open up the possibilities of conceiving of museum exhibitions differently—beyond familiar pedagogical models. I agree that this is one of the more inspiring ideas presented this week precisely because it emphasizes the possibility of openness—openness to a situation that is not preordained, prepackaged, or transformed into a readily consumable story. I also agree that the museum has the potential to be a "machine for producing a love and respect for the disparate." It is precisely this kind of love and respect that shapes the ethics of many museums. If Agamben allows us to rethink [Immanuel] Kant by framing ethics as a kind of attention without prejudgement, purposefulness without a purpose, he also reminds us that this ethics of encounter is not limited to a historical time or geographical site.

Moreover, if ethics can be understood as a politics of encounter, then the museum, as what James Clifford would call a "contact zone," is always an ethical space. Art museums allow contact between people and things, but the form of that contact is highly regulated and historically charged. Beyond the subtle ethics referenced in Mary Kelly's comments, we might also ask, what are the political ethics of hierarchies of value in which all museums participate? Fred Wilson has commented that: "General art museums say they are multicultural museums. To my mind museums of this nature are about as multicultural as Great Britain in 1914. The 'empire' includes many cultures, but who decides what is important in that culture? Who speaks for that culture? Who chooses what is kept of that culture?"

I hope the museums of tomorrow will be more self-conscious about the myths that they produce, acknowledging the history and provenance of the objects they have on display in a way that makes a compelling argument to a diverse audience. Calling for this kind of transparency is not the same as calling for extensive wall text and pedagogical materials. Like Simon Leung, I agree that most people want art museums to continue to be a place of fantasy, a place where they might encounter the muses. It is not impossible to achieve historical transparency and a more progressive representation of the institution, the artist, and the art, while also allowing for an openness of encounter.

Alexander Alberro suggests that museums encourage their visitors to approach artwork with skeptical, critical, analytical thinking. This seems a healthy alternative to the mode of passive consumption that defines the visitor's somnambulist stroll through many current narrative-based displays. I would like to see the museums of tomorrow begin to transform their traditions of display through a self-conscious awareness not only of the social content of their representations, but also the rhetorical form of their argumentation. And since we are dreaming, I would also like to see an end to the way race discourse currently creates a hierarchy of values that perpetuates systems of unequal representation and forms of ignorance in art museums, art schools, art history, and art criticism generally. When this happens, familiar monologues in museums will become unfamiliar dialogues, allowing for new forms of enunciation to emerge.

Raina A. Lampkins-Fielder

When I entered this conversation, I came with the presumption that we were at a cultural crossroads and that we were going to step boldly forward together. I have a bit of a manifesto mentality perhaps and was looking for a discussion that would propel all of us who are invested in the future of museums toward some common direction of purpose—after, of course, getting through the obligatory dance with the devil (is that ClearChannel with horns?). I suspect that this was probably an unrealistic notion, but I enjoy the dream and never wish to get too cynical. I suppose we will be at this junction in the road for some time, so I guess we should pull up some chairs and be prepared to sit and chat for awhile. I'm game for the challenge and, as we've seen from many of the superb posts in this conference, it's well worth it!

This conference has certainly posed more questions than answers, which is both frustrating and heartening, but ultimately a good thing. Frustrating because, well, I'm an idealistic pragmatist and wanted theory to more fully support practice. Heartening because questions need to be asked and it is so rare that an assembly of thinkers of this sort are convened to weigh in on issues together. So, hats off to Maurice for bringing together a group of wonderfully thoughtful and passionate individuals and for facilitating a fascinating discussion.

As an educator I feel that there is nothing that I do that is unimportant. This doesn't mean that I don't mess up or have much to learn. But I owe a certain sincerity to all of those whom I serve—the artist, the public, the academy, the cultural worker, the institution, society. The fact that we, particularly in American museums, feel that we are under siege, spurs me to action to better the community in which I am also a member. And so, I aim to make this world a more palatable place in this short time that we have, through the programs that I create. Programs that encourage greater transparency between curatorial and art-historical practice, insist upon more rigorous scholarship and multisensory experiences for everyone from the novice to the expert, and bridge gaps between people and art museums. I, too, remind myself of the words of John Cotton Dana, which have profound resonance for me and constantly inform my practice.

When I think of the museum of the future—I'm reluctant to say "ideal"—I envision a place that allows me, as a visitor, to explore as broadly or as specifically as I may wish; one that does not underestimate my intelligence, but will lend me a hand if I desire guidance; a place invested in its community in whatever way it defines it; one that does not deny my presence; a place that grants me access and choice.

As a worker, I desire an institution that zealously embraces the spirit of revision and collaboration, both internally and externally; acknowledges the notion that definitions of "culture" and its expression are ever evolving; that is a forum for dialogues between artistic and aesthetic strategies, public needs and expectations, curatorial intentions, and cultural politics and trends; and that refuses to become the static repository of art, but rather a living entity that bristles with dynamism.

Joan Rosenbaum

The postings have been so impressive. The dialogue is stimulating to me—a person so embroiled in the very practical issues of day-to-day work running a museum. What is that? It's pure management: budgets, building, security, and personnel. It's also planning programs that fulfill the mission in a way that will bring in audiences in a city filled with museums and exhibitions. I rarely have the opportunity to think in a theoretical way that has been offered to me in this conference. While I frankly haven't had the time to engage in the way I would have preferred, I am grateful for the breadth of ideas that provide so much food for thought.

My own concluding remarks relate to my having been in the field for well over two decades—either working in museums or looking at them from the perspective of a funding agency. What would be the ideal museum? It would be one where contributions and audiences didn't dominate the life of a director so that experimentation and failure could be absorbed as part of the institutional life. It would be one where there might be funds for more fluidity in staffing, with an influx of new ideas from adjunct and consulting curators on an active rotating basis. It would mean a large endowment for a constant stream of contemporary projects that might take place on the Internet, in galleries, and in unexpected institutional locations. Ideally we would be open many more evening hours to accommodate working people, and we would have added large endowments to reduce the cost of admissions for those visitors. Added endowments would allow us to travel our exhibitions so they get wider exposure and aren't a financial burden to the potential borrowing museum in terms of insurance, shipping, and installation costs. I would have free brochures and audio guides for every exhibition, as well as related videos, accessible both in the museum and on its website. There would be a fund to exhibit and interpret, on a monthly basis, two interesting works from the collection in a kind of visual "dialogue" and on and on . . .

These don't sound so bold, I'm sure, to most of the readers, but it's what fuels dreams when money is an issue. But I'm also saying that I could go on and on because on the brighter side so, so much is possible in a museum. It is a venue where people by and large can be made to feel comfortable, exploring an enormous variety of art and thus an enormous variety of ideas. There are endless ways to make the connections between the museum and a vast audience of people of mixed cultures, class, and experience with art. But museum professionals are aware of this. They want and need to exist for a diverse public. Marketing is not anathema; corporate support and media partnerships are common; a sophisticated level of knowledge about the way children and adults learn is expected of museum educators; catalogues are published with commercial presses so they may be thought of as interesting, accessible books; films, music, and dance are done inside the museum; and neighbors are made to feel welcome with special festivals and free days. I could again go on and on. It's not theory; it's practice. I am exhausted by the challenges of fund-raising, audience development, and board relations, but while it's totally corny to say this, I am still thrilled by the idea of the museum, and its endless potential for providing solace, refuge, meditation, new ideas, and new ways to view the world. I'm sure my colleagues feel similarly. But duty to our jobs and commitment to the ideals of a museum are not enough. One needs to be able to swim around in ideas such as those posted in this conference to be reminded periodically of new ways to think about our work.

Thank you Maurice!

Concluding Statement

Maurice Berger

The question of the art museum's future is neither a simple nor an uncontroversial one, as the diversity of opinions and passionate disagreement that marked this discussion affirms. Indeed, the ideas that were circulated and debated have impelled me to rethink my own attitudes about organizing exhibitions and about the institutional imperatives of the museum.

From the outset, I held no expectation that we would solve the practical or theoretical question of the museum's future. Indeed, the category "art museum" suggests a broad, diverse, and often divergent range of institutional situations and imperatives. But our discourse—fragmented, passionate, spirited, intertextual, and eloquent—resulted in a continuum of important ideas, and yes, questions. I have learned much from each of you, much from the "metatext" that you have collectively created.

I thank Barbara Lynes and George King of the Georgia O'Keeffe Museum for their unwavering support of this conference. I would also like to single out the extraordinary work of the Georgia O'Keeffe Museum Research Center, an important resource for scholars of American art and the sponsor of this online event. I extend my gratitude to Molly McDow, Dave Rohr, and Alisa Smith of Panorama Point for their attention to every detail of the symposium site. Elizabeth Ernst and Jennifer Padilla of the O'Keeffe Museum followed through on the symposium's myriad demands, offering good ideas along the way.

Most of all, I would like to thank the 28 colleagues who joined me in an important dialogue that I believe will help stimulate further dialogue on the future and survival of the art museum.

Selected Bibliography

The following is a selected reading list of books and articles pertinent to this discussion.

Altick, Richard D. *The Shows of London.* Cambridge, MA; Harvard University Press, 1978.

Altshuler, Bruce. *The Avant-Garde in Exhibition: New Art in the 20th Century.* New York: Harry N. Abrams, 1994.

__________. *Collecting the New: Museums and Contemporary Art.* Princeton, NJ; Princeton University Press (forthcoming 2005).

Ames, Michael M. *Cannibal Tours and Glass Boxes: The Anthropology of Museums.* Vancouver: UBC Press, 1992.

__________. *Museums, the Public and Anthropology: A Study in the Anthropology of Anthropology.* Vancouver: UBC Press, 1986.

Anderson, Maxwell L. Intro. *The Wired Museum.* Washington, DC: American Association of Museums, 1997: 11–32.

__________. "Museums of the Future: The Impact of Technology on Museum Practices." *Daedalus: Journal of the American Academy of Arts and Sciences.* Cambridge, MA: The American Academy of Arts and Sciences (Summer 1999): 129–62.

__________. "Self-Censorship in Art Museums." In *The New Gatekeepers.* National Arts Journalism Program, Columbia University, 2004: 173–77.

Bennett, Tony. *The Birth of the Museum: History, Theory and Politics.* London: Routledge, 1995.

Berger, Maurice. "Critical Fictions: Race, 'Outsiders,' and the Construction of Art History." In Elsa Longhauser and Harold Szeemann, eds., *Self-Taught Artists of the Twentieth Century: An American Anthology.* Philadelphia, PA: Philadelphia Museum of Art; and New York: Museum of American Folk Art, 1998: 28–37.

__________. *Fred Wilson: Objects and Installations, 1979–2000.* Baltimore, MD: Center for Art and Visual Culture, 2001.

__________. *How Art Becomes History.* New York: Harper-Collins, 1992.

Binstock, Jonathan P., ed. *The 47th Corcoran Biennial: Fantasy Underfoot.* Washington, DC: Corcoran Gallery of Art, 2002.

Black, Barbara J. *On Exhibit: Victorians and Their Museums.* Charlottesville, VA: University of Virginia Press, 2000.

Boym, Svetlana. *The Future of Nostalgia.* New York: Basic Books, 2001.

Clifford, James. *The Predicament of Culture: Twentieth-Century Ethnography, Literature, and Art.* Cambridge, MA: Harvard University Press, 1988.

Cooke, Lynne, and Peter Wollen, eds. *Visual Display: Culture Beyond Appearances.* Seattle, WA: Bay Press, 1995.

Corrin, Lisa, ed. *Mining the Museum: An Installation by Fred Wilson.* Baltimore, MD: The Contemporary; and New York: The New Press, 1994.

Crane, Susan A., ed. *Museums and Memory.* Stanford, CA: Stanford University Press, 2000.

Crimp, Douglas. *On the Museum's Ruins.* Cambridge, MA: MIT Press, 1995.

Davalos, Karen Mary. *Exhibiting Mestizaje: Mexican (American) Museums in the Diaspora.* Albuquerque, NM: University of New Mexico Press, 2001.

__________. "In the Blink of an Eye: Chicana/o Art Collecting." In *East of the River: Chicano Art Collectors Anonymous.* Chon A. Noriega, ed. Santa Monica, CA: Santa Monica Museum of Art, 2000: 42–54.

__________. "Looking for Whiteness, Nation and Empire in All the Wrong Places: The Nelson A. Rockefeller Collection of Mexican Folk Art at the Mexican Museum." *Latino Studies Journal* (Fall 2000): 131–59.

De Salvo, Donna. *Past Imperfect: A Museum Looks at Itself.* Southampton, NY: Parrish Art Museum; and New York: The New Press, 1993.

Donato, Eugenio. "The Museum's Furnace: Notes Toward a Contextual Reading of Bouvard and Pécuchet." In *Textual Strategies: Perspective in Post-Structuralist Criticism.* Josué V.

Harari, ed. Ithaca, NY: Cornell University Press, 1979: 213–38.

Duncan, Carol. *Civilizing Rituals: Inside Public Art Museums.* London: Routledge, 1995.

__________. "John Cotton Dana's Progressive Museum." In *Self and History: A Tribute to Linda Nochlin.* Aruna D'Souza, ed. London: Thames and Hudson, 2001: 127–36.

__________. "Museums and Department Stores: Close Encounters." In *High-Pop: A Critical Reader.* James M. Collins, ed. London: Basil Blackwell, 2002.

Elsner, John, and Roger Cardinal, eds. *The Cultures of Collecting.* Cambridge, MA: Harvard University Press, 1994.

Fabian, Johannes. *Time and the Other: How Anthropology Makes Its Object.* New York: Columbia University Press, 1983.

Falk, John, and Lynn D. Dierking. *The Museum Experience.* Washington, DC: Whalesback Books, 1992.

Foster, Hal, ed. *The Anti-Aesthetic.* Seattle, WA: Bay Press, 1984.

Greenblatt, Stephen. *Representing the English Renaissance: A Representations Book.* Berkeley, CA; University of California Press, 1988.

Haraway, Donna. *Primate Visions: Gender, Race, and Nature in the World of Modern Science.* New York: Routledge, 1989.

Harris, Neil. "Museums, Merchandizing and Popular Taste: The Struggle for Influence." In *Material Culture and the Study of American Life.* I.M.G. Quimby, ed. New York: W.W. Norton, 1978.

Hewison, R. *The Heritage Industry.* London: Metheun, 1987.

Hooper-Greenhill, Eilean. *Museums and Their Visitors.* New York: Routledge, 1994.

Huyssen, Andreas. *Twilight Memories: Marking Time in a Culture of Amnesia.* New York: Routledge, 1995.

Karp, Ivan, and Christine Mullen Kreamer. *Museums and Communities: The Politics of Public Culture.* Washington, DC: Smithsonian Institution Press, 1992.

Karp, Ivan, and Steven D. Lavine, eds. *Exhibiting Cultures: The Poetics and Politics of Museum Display.* Washington, DC: Smithsonian Institution Press, 1992.

Keene, Suzanne. *Digital Collections: Museums and the Information Age.* Oxford: Butterworth Heineman, 1998.

Kelly, Mary. "Reviewing Modernist Criticism." In *Art After Modernism: Rethinking Representation.* Brian Wallis, ed. New York: New Museum of Contemporary Art; and David R. Godine Publisher, 1984.

Lerner, Adam. "The Museum and the Multiplex." In *The 47th Corcoran Biennial: Fantasy Underfoot.* Jonathan P. Binstock, ed. Washington, DC: Corcoran Gallery of Art, 2002.

Leung, Simon. "Notas sobre Warren Piece (in the '70s): Parte I / Notes on Warren Piece (in the '70s)." In *Negociações na zona de contacto / Negotiations in the Contact Zone*, Lisbon, Portugal: Assírio & Alvim, 2003:287–301: 303–15.

__________. "Site Specificity en Abyme." In *Surface Tension, Problematics of Site.* Los Angeles, CA: Errant Bodies Press, 2003: 161–74.

McClellan, Andrew. *Inventing the Louvre: Art, Politics, and the Origins of the Modern Museum in Eighteenth-Century Paris.* New York: Cambridge University Press, 1994.

Maleuvre, Didier. *Museum Memories: History, Technology, Art.* Stanford, CA: Stanford University Press, 1999.

Malraux, André. *The Voices of Silence.* Garden City, NY: Doubleday, 1953.

Nochlin, Linda. *Politics of Vision: Essays on Nineteenth-Century Art and Society.* New York: Harper & Row, 1989.

Pearce, Susan, ed. *Museums and the Appropriation of Culture.* Atlantic Highlands, NJ: The Athlone Press, 1994.

Pittman, Bonnie. *Presence of Mind: Museums and the Spirit of Learning.* Washington, DC: American Association of Museums, 1999.

Preziosi, Donald. *Rethinking Art History: Reflections on a Coy Science*. New Haven, CT: Yale University Press, 1988.
Rosenbaum, Joan. "The Jewish Museum and Its History." In *Masterworks of The Jewish Museum*. New York: The Jewish Museum; New Haven, CT: Yale University Press, 2004.
Rothstein, Edward. "America's Culture Gaps: The Tribulations of the Not-So-Living Art." *The New York Times* (18 February 1996): Section 4, 4.
__________. "Homo Sapiens in Museums?" *The New York Times* (12 May 2001): B 11.
__________. "The Black History Exhibit: Museums That Tell What to Think." *The New York Times* (20 April 1997): Section 4, 3.
Said, Edward. *Orientalism*. New York: Pantheon Books, 1978.
Sandler, Irving. *A Sweeper-Up After Artists: A Memoir*. New York: Thames & Hudson, 2003.
__________. "When MOMA Met the Avant-Garde." *Art News* 78 (October, 1979):114–25
__________. and Amy Newman, eds. *Defining Modern Art: Selected Writings of Alfred H. Barr, Jr.* New York: Harry N. Abrams, 1986.
Sherman, Daniel, and Iris Rogoff, eds. *Museum Culture: Histories, Discourses, Spectacles.* Minneapolis, MN: University of Minnesota Press, 1994.
Siegel, Jonah. *Desire and Excess: The Nineteenth-Century Culture of Art*. Princeton, NJ: Princeton University Press, 2000.
Simpson, Moira, ed. *Making Representations: Museums in the Post-Colonial Era*. New York: Routledge, 1996.
Stafford, Barbara. *Artful Science: Enlightenment Entertainment and the Eclipse of Visual Education*. Cambridge, MA: MIT Press, 1994.
Stocking, George. *Objects and Others: Essays on Museums and Material Culture*. Madison, WI: University of Wisconsin Press, 1985.
Terdiman, Richard. *Past Present: Modernity and the Memory Crisis*. Ithaca, NY: Cornell University Press, 1993.
Wallach, Alan. *Exhibiting Contradiction: Essays on the Art Museum in the United States.* Amherst, MA: University of Massachusetts Press, 1998.
__________. "La naissance du musée des beaux-arts américain." In *Les actes du colloque l'indépendance de l'art américain.* Paris: Musée du Louvre (forthcoming 2004–05.)
__________. "Norman Rockwell at the Guggenheim." In *Art and Its Publics: Museum Studies at the Millenium.* Andrew McClellan, ed. Oxford: Basil Blackwell, 2003: 97–116.
Weil, Stephen E. *Rethinking the Museum and Other Meditations.* Washington, DC: Smithsonian Institution Press, 1990.
Worden, Suzette. "Thinking Critically About Virtual Museums." In *Museums and the Web 97: Selected Papers.* David Bearman and Jennifer Trant, eds. Pittsburgh, PA: Archives and Museum Informatics, 1997: 93–109.
Yanni, Carla. *Nature's Museums: Victorian Science and the Architecture of Display.* London: Athlone Press, 1999.

Post-Colonial Art. New York: Routledge, 1996.
Stafford, Barbara. *Artful Science: Enlightenment Entertainment*

About the Participants

Maurice Berger, moderator, is a Fellow at the Vera List Center for Art and Politics, New School University, New York, and Curator of the Center for Art and Visual Culture, University of Maryland Baltimore County. His articles have appeared in many journals and newspapers, including *Artforum, Art in America, The New York Times, The Village Voice, October, Wired,* and *The Los Angeles Times.* He is the author of *White Lies: Race and the Myths of Whiteness* (Farrar, Straus & Giroux, 1999), *Labyrinths: Robert Morris, Minimalism, and the 1960s* (Harper & Row, 1989), *How Art Becomes History* (HarperCollins, 1992), *Constructing Masculinity* (Routledge, 1995), *The Crisis of Criticism* (The New Press, 1998), and *Postmodernism: A Virtual Discussion* (Georgia O'Keeffe Research Center/CAVC, 2003). He has served as curator as well as contributed essays to numerous exhibition catalogues for art institutions including the Whitney Museum of American Art, New York; the Solomon R. Guggenheim Museum, New York; the Philadelphia Museum of Art; Corcoran Gallery of Art, Washington, DC; Yale University Art Gallery, New Haven, Connecticut; Addison Gallery of American Art, Andover, Massachusetts; Santa Monica Museum, California; Grey Art Gallery, New York; the Studio Museum in Harlem, New York; the Museum of Contemporary Art, Chicago; and The Jewish Museum, New York.

Alexander Alberro, Associate Professor of Art History at the University of Florida, Gainesville, is the author of *Conceptual Art and the Politics of Publicity* (MIT Press, 2003). His essays have appeared in a wide array of art journals and exhibition catalogues. He has also edited and coedited a number of volumes, including *Two-Way Mirror Power: Dan Graham's Writings on Art* (The MIT Press, 1999), *Conceptual Art: A Critical Anthology* (MIT Press, 2000), and *Recording Conceptual Art* (University of California Press, 2001).

Bruce Altshuler is Director of the Program in Museum Studies, Graduate School of Arts and Science, New York University. From 1992 to 1998, he was Director of the Isamu Noguchi Garden Museum in Long Island City, New York. Altshuler is the author of *The Avant-Garde in Exhibition: New Art in the 20th Century* (Harry N. Abrams, 1994, and University of California Press, 1998), and *Isamu Noguchi* (Abbeville Press, 1994). As well as having contributed essays to numerous art exhibition catalogues, he has written extensively on modern and contemporary art.

Maxwell L. Anderson, Leadership Fellow at the Yale School of Management, New Haven, Connecticut, has directed three leading North American art museums, most recently the Whitney Museum of American Art. Past President of the Association on Art Museum Directors, he is the author of "Museums of the Future: The Impact of Technology on Museum Practices" (*Daedalus,* 1999).

George Baker will begin teaching modern and contemporary art history at the University of California, Los Angeles, in the fall of 2004. Currently on a Getty Research Institute fellowship, he is completing a book on Dada entitled *The Artwork Caught by the Tail.* He is also the author of *James Coleman: Drei Filmarbeiten* (Sprengel Museum, Hannover, 2002) and editor of an anthology of criticism of Coleman's work (MIT Press, 2003). A long-standing critic for *Artforum,* Baker is an editor as well of *October* Magazine and October Books.

Stefano Basilico is Curator of the University Art Collection at New School University, New York, and Adjunct Curator of Contemporary Art at the Milwaukee Art Museum, where he is currently organizing several exhibitions including *CUT: Film as Found Object,* which will debut at MOCA in Miami in November 2004, and, with Glenn Adamson, *Sleight of Hand: Virtuosity and Transformation in Art Today,* scheduled to open in Milwaukee in the winter of 2006. His art criticism and numerous artists' interviews have appeared in *Bomb Magazine*, *Time Out New York*, and *Documents* magazine.

Jonathan P. Binstock has been Curator of Contemporary Art, Washington, D.C., at the Corcoran Gallery of Art since January 2001. He has organized numerous exhibitions, including *Atomic Time: Pure Science and Seduction* (2003), featuring recent work by Jim Sanborn; *The 47th Corcoran Biennial: Fantasy Underfoot* (2002); *Primary Properties: Mary Judge, Joseph Dumbacher, John Dumbacher* (2001); *Jeremy Blake: Digital Projections* (2000); and *Andy Warhol: Social Observer* (2000). He is currently working on the *48th Corcoran Biennial: Closer to Home* (March 2005) and a retrospective of the art of Sam Gilliam (October 2005).

Dan Cameron has been Senior Curator at the New Museum of Contemporary Art, New York, since 1995. He has organized exhibitions of William Kentridge, Paul McCarthy, Cildo Meireles, Faith Ringgold, Doris Salcedo, Carolee Schneemann, David Wojnarowicz, and Martin Wong, among others. Most recently, he served as curator for the 8th Istanbul Biennial in 2003.

Karen Mary Davalos is Associate Professor of Chicana/o Studies at Loyola Marymount University in Los Angeles, co-Senior Editor of *Chicana/Latina Studies: The Journal of Mujeres Activas en Letras y Cambio Social* and coeditor of *The Chicano Studies Reader: An Anthology of Aztlan Scholarship*, 1970–2000 (with Chon Noriega, Eric Avila, Rafael Perez-Torres and Chela Sandoval, UCLA Chicano Studies Research Center Publications, 2001). She is the author of *Exhibiting Mestizaje: Mexican (American) Museums in the Diaspora* (University of New Mexico Press, 2001), and her essays have appeared in exhibition catalogues and journals, such as *Aztlan: A Journal of Chicano Studies*, *Latino Studies Journal*, and *Frontiers: A Journal of Women's Studies*.

Donna De Salvo is a writer and Senior Curator at the Tate Modern, London. Some of her past book and exhibition projects include: *Hand-Painted Pop: American Art in Transition 1955–62* (Rizzoli, 1992); *Past Imperfect: A Museum Looks at Itself* (The Parrish Art Museum and The New Press, 1993); *Face Value: American Portraits* (The Parrish Art Museum and Flammarion, 1995), *Ray Johnson: Correspondences* (Wexner Center for the Arts and Flammarion, 1999); *Giorgio Morandi* (Tate Gallery, 2001); *Century City: Art and Culture in the Modern Metropolis* (Tate Gallery, 2001); and *Andy Warhol* (Tate Gallery, 2002).

Carol Duncan is Professor of Art History at Ramapo College of New Jersey, where she has taught since 1972. She has written about various subjects including the representation of the family and patriarchal authority in 18th-century art; the appearance of state politics in 19th-century art; the depiction of nudes in early 19th-century art; and sexual politics in 20th-century art museums. She is author of *The Aesthetics of Power* (Cambridge University Press, 1993) and *Civilizing Rituals: Inside Public Art Museums* (Routledge, 1995).

Mark Alice Durant teaches at the University of Maryland Baltimore County and the Milton Avery Graduate School of the Arts at Bard College. His photographs, installations, and performances have been presented internationally at, among others, the Los Angeles County Museum of Art, the Museum of Contemporary Art in Chicago, and Artists Space in New York. In 1991, he co-founded the performance duo "Men of the World," who for ten years performed on the streets of cities that include Chicago, Toronto, Seattle, New York, Houston, and San Francisco. He has written extensively on the nexus of photography, performance, and cultural phenomena with essays appearing in such journals as *Art in America*, *New Art Examiner*, *Exposure*, *Afterimage*, and the *Boston Book Review*. His most recent publications include *Robert Heinecken: A*

Material History (Center for Creative Photography, 2003) and *Maya Deren and the Skin Between Us* (CameraWork, 2003). He was guest editor and essayist for the fall 2003 issue of the *CAA Art Journal* on the topic of photography and the paranormal.

Jennifer González is Assistant Professor in the History of Art and Visual Culture Department at the University of California, Santa Cruz. Her scholarly essays and reviews have appeared in various art magazines and journals, including *Bomb, Frieze, World Art, Diacritics, Art Journal,* and *Aztlan.* She has contributed chapters to *Prosthetic Territories* (Westview Press, 1995); *The Cyborg Handbook* (Routledge, 1995); *The Encyclopedia of Aesthetics* (Oxford, 1998); *With Other Eyes: Looking at Race and Gender in Visual Culture* (Minnesota, 1999); and *Race in Cyberspace* (Routledge, 2000). In 2002 she served as the Joanne Cassullo Teaching Fellow at the Whitney Museum of American Art Independent Study Program in New York.

Mary Kelly is Professor of Art and Critical Theory in the Department of Art at the University of California, Los Angeles. She is author of *Post-Partum Document* (Routledge & Kegan Paul, 1983) and *Imaging Desire* (MIT Press, 1996). Her project-based artwork is included in such collections as the Tate Modern, London; the Kunsthaus Zurich; the Art Gallery of Ontario, Canada; the Generali Foundation, Vienna; the National Gallery of Australia, Canberra; and the Whitney Museum of American Art, New York. Her work was recently documented in the monograph, *Mary Kelly* (Phaidon Press, 1997).

George G. King has been Director of the Georgia O'Keeffe Museum since 1998 and was Executive Director of the Katonah Museum of Art in Katonah, New York, for ten years beginning in 1988. He has also held positions at the Cooper-Hewitt National Design Museum, Smithsonian Institution, New York. He is a Trustee of the Association of Art Museum Directors (AAMD), the chair of the AAMD's Program Committee, and a member of its Professional Issues Committee. He is also a member of the Board of Directors of the Mountain-Plains Museum Association, as well as a member of the College Art Association and the New Mexico Association of Museums.

Barbara Kirshenblatt-Gimblett is University Professor and Professor of Performance Studies at the Tisch School of the Arts, New York University, where she chaired the Department of Performance Studies for more than a decade. She serves on the academic advisory committee for New York University's Master's Program in Museum Studies. She has received many awards and in 2003 was designated Distinguished Humanist by the Melton Center for Jewish Studies at Ohio State University. She serves on the editorial boards of *Museum and Society* (Leicester), *Journal of the History of Collections,* and most recently *Museum Anthropology.* Her books include *Destination Culture: Tourism, Museums, and Heritage* (University of California Press, 1998) and *Image Before My Eyes: A Photographic History of Jewish Life in Poland, 1864–1939,* with Lucjan Dobroszycki (Schocken, reissued 1995), which accompanied an exhibition at The Jewish Museum and provided the basis for a feature documentary film.

Miwon Kwon teaches in the Department of Art History at the University of California, Los Angeles and serves as a residency faculty member in the MFA in Visual Art Program at Vermont College. Her research and writings engage several disciplines including contemporary art, architecture, public art, and urban studies. She is a founding editor and publisher of *Documents,* and serves on the advisory board of *October.* She is also the author of *One Place after Another: Site-Specific Art and Locational Identity* (MIT Press, 2002).

Raina A. Lampkins-Fielder is Associate Director, Helena Rubinstein Chair of Education at the Whitney Museum of American Art in New York.

Previously, Lampkins-Fielder held positions at the Brooklyn Museum of Art, New York; The New Museum of Contemporary Art, New York; and the Andy Warhol Museum, Pittsburgh. She was curator for the *Everson Biennial* (Everson Museum of Art, 2002). Lampkins-Fielder also compiled a series of new British films entitled *Going Underground: British Independents and Beyond* (Brooklyn Museum of Art, 1999) as well as a series highlighting films about Africans abroad entitled *Black Beyond Borders: Mapping the African Diaspora* (BMA, 1999). She co-organized *alt.youth.media* for the New Museum of Contemporary Art, New York (1996) and was curator for two exhibitions there: *Keeping Track of the Joneses* (1998) and *Juegos Ilegales/Illegal Games* (1999).

Simon Leung lives in Los Angeles and New York and teaches in the Studio Art Department at the University of California, Irvine. His work has been presented at the Whitney Biennial (1993); the Venice Biennale (2003); the Museum of Modern Art, New York (1996, 2000); P.S.1 Contemporary Art Center (1993); NGBK [Neue Gesellschaft für Bildende Kunst], Berlin (1994); the Art Institute of Chicago (1997); the Museum of Contemporary Art, Los Angeles (2000); Generali Foundation, Vienna (1998); MIT List Visual Arts Center, Cambridge (2003); Kunsthalle Fredericianum, Kassel (2003); and the International Museum of Surfing, Huntington Beach, California (1998). His writing has been translated into German, French, and Portuguese. He has been coeditor of *Theory in Contemporary Art* since 1985, from which an anthology of essays was published by Blackwell in 2004.

Barbara Buhler Lynes is Curator, Georgia O'Keeffe Museum and The Emily Fisher Landau Director, Georgia O'Keeffe Museum Research Center in Santa Fe, New Mexico. She was on the faculty at various institutions, such as the Maryland Institute College of Art (1999–2001) and Dartmouth College (1980–86). Since 1999, she has been curator of many exhibitions at the Georgia O'Keeffe Museum, and her publications include books and exhibition catalogues, such as *Maria Chabot/Georgia O'Keeffe: Correspondence, 1941–1949* (University of New Mexico Press, 2003); *O'Keeffe's O'Keeffes: The Artist's Collection* (Thames & Hudson, 2001); *Georgia O'Keeffe and New Mexico: A Sense of Place* (Princeton University Press, 2004); and *Georgia O'Keeffe: Catalogue Raisonné* (Yale University Press, National Gallery of Art, and The Georgia O'Keeffe Foundation, 1999).

Olu Oguibe is Associate Professor of Art and Art History as well as African-American studies at the University of Connecticut, Storrs. He is also an artist, international curator, theorist, and editor. In 1994, he founded *Nka: Journal of Contemporary African Art* with New York writer and curator Okwui Enwezor. The following year, he published *Uzo Egonu: An African Artist in the West*, and in 1999, he coedited the first anthology of critical readings on contemporary African visual culture, *Reading the Contemporary: African Art from Theory to the Marketplace*. Oguibe has also served as curator or co-curator for numerous exhibitions. These include the *2nd Biennale of Ceramics in Contemporary Art* in Genoa and Albisola, Italy, in 2003; *Vidarte 2002: International Video and Media Art Festival* at the Palacio Postal, Mexico City, in 2002; *Century City* at the Tate Modern, London, in 2001; *Authentic/Ex-centric: Africa in and out of Africa* for the 49th Venice Biennale in 2001, *Five Continents and One City: 3rd International Salon of Painting* at the Museo de la Ciudad, Mexico City, in 2000; and the first inclusive exhibition of contemporary African artists, *Cross/ing. Time. Space. Movement.*, at the Contemporary Art Museum and the Museum of African American Art, Tampa Florida, in 1997. As an artist, Oguibe began to exhibit in Nigeria in the late 1980s, and to date his work has been shown in major museums and galleries around the world, including the Whitney Museum of American Art, New York; the New Museum of Contemporary Art, New York; the Whitechapel Art Gallery, London; the Migros Museum, Zurich; and the Bonnefantenmuseum, Maastricht; as well as in the Havana, Busan, and Johannesburg biennials. A former senior fellow of the Vera List Center for Art and Politics at the New School, New York, and the Rockefeller Research and Conference Center, Bellagio, Italy. Oguibe's most recent book, *The Culture Game,* was published by the University of Minnesota Press in 2003.

Joan Rosenbaum is Director of The Jewish Museum, where, for the last 22 years, she has been instrumental in creating the identity of the Museum by presenting exhibitions, education programs, and its diverse collection to audiences of all cultural backgrounds. She has been a frequent speaker and panelist on subjects related to art and Jewish culture and has contributed articles to The Jewish Museum's catalogues and other publications. Among her various honors, she has received an honorary doctorate from the Jewish Theological Seminary of America in 1993, and was decorated with the Order of the Chevalier for Arts and Letters from the Cultural Ministry of France in 1999.

David A. Ross has been a leader in the arts community for more than 30 years, serving nearly 20 years in the capacity of Director of the San Francisco Museum of Modern Art (1998–2001); the Whitney Museum of American Art, New York (1991–98); and the Institute of Contemporary Art, Boston (1985–92). Ross is currently Curatorial Director of UPX in Mexico City and, since 2002, has been Executive Director of the Beacon Cultural Project in upstate New York. He currently chairs the Board of Directors of the Miami-based Anaphiel Foundation and is a Trustee of The Studio Museum in Harlem. He also serves on the Board of Rhizome and the non-profit American Anti-Slavery Group. He is a member of the advisory board of the Committee Scientifico Fondazione CRT in Turin, Italy.

Edward Rothstein is Cultural Critic at Large for *The New York Times,* writing criticism on cultural politics, literature, music, intellectual life, the arts, and technology. He is the coauthor of *Visions of Utopia* (Oxford University Press, 2003) and the author of *Emblems of Mind: The Inner Life of Music and Mathematics* (Times Books, 1995; Avon Books, 1996), which was named one of the 25 best books of 1995 by both *Publisher's Weekly* and the New York Public Library. He has been the chief music critic (1991–1995), as well as a technology columnist, for *The New York Times*, and the music critic for *The New Republic* (1984–1991). His essays on science, politics, music, and the arts have been published in *The New York Review of Books, Commentary, The American Scholar, The New Republic,* and *The London Independent,* among other magazines and journals. He has won two ASCAP-Deems Taylor Awards for his music criticism, an Ingram Merrill Foundation Award, and was a Guggenheim Fellow in 1991.

Irving Sandler is Professor Emeritus of Art History at the State University of New York at Purchase and a former Acting Director of the Neuberger Museum of Art, Purchase, New York. He has written a four volume history of art edition that includes: *The Triumph of American Painting: A History of Abstract Expressionism* (Harper & Row, 1970); *The New York School: Painters and Sculptors of the 1950s* (Harper & Row, 1978); *American Art of the 1960s* (Harper & Row, 1988); and *Art of the Postmodern Era: From the Late 1960s to the Early 1990s* (Westview Press,

1996). He has also edited (with Amy Newman) *Defining Modern Art: Selected Writings of Alfred H. Barr, Jr.* (Harry N. Abrams, 1986). He has written monographs on Alex Katz, Al Held, Philip Pearlstein, and Mark di Suvero, and numerous catalogue introductions and essays as well as articles for *Art News, Artforum, Art in America, Art International, Arts Magazine*, and *The New York Times*. He was the art critic of the *New York Post* (1961–65) and is currently a contributing editor to *Art in America*.

Michele Wallace is Professor of English, Women's Studies, and Film Studies at the City College of New York and the CUNY Graduate Center. She is also author of *Black Macho and the Myth of the Superwoman* (Verso, 1980), *Invisibility Blues: From Pop to Theory* (Verso, 1990), and the forthcoming *Dark Designs and Visual Culture* (Duke University Press).

Alan Wallach has been Ralph H. Wark Professor of Art and Art History and Professor of American Studies at the College of William and Mary, Williamsburg, Virginia, since 1989. A critic and historian, he writes frequently about museums and also about American art of the 19th and 20th centuries. He was cocurator of the exhibition, *Thomas Cole: Landscape into History*—as well as author of the exhibition catalogue's principal essay—which was on view between 1994 and 1995 at the National Museum of American Art, Washington, D.C.; the Wadsworth Athaneum, Hartford, Connecticut; and the Brooklyn Museum of Art, New York. He is the author of a series of essays included in *Exhibiting Contradiction* (University of Massachusetts Press, 1998) and his writings have also appeared in leading periodicals and anthologies including *Art Bulletin, Artforum, Art History*, and *Harvard Design Magazine*. He served on the Board of Directors of the College Art Association from 1996 to 2000, and from 2000 to 2003 was a member of the Board of Managing Editors of *The American Quarterly*.

Sylvia Yount is the Margaret and Terry Stent Curator of American Art at the High Museum of Art, Atlanta. Previously she served as Chief Curator at the Pennsylvania Academy of the Fine Arts and in research and administrative positions at the Philadelphia Museum of Art and the Isabella Stewart Gardner Museum in Boston. Her exhibition projects at the Academy included *To Be Modern: American Encounters with Cézanne and Company* (1996), *Maxfield Parrish, 1870–1966* (1999), and a major reinstallation of the museum's historic collection, along with numerous contemporary art exhibitions. At the High Museum, her efforts have ranged from focus exhibitions of American sculpture, Ben Shahn, and Edward Hopper to a reinstallation of the museum's American Art collections. She is currently organizing a traveling retrospective of the work of the turn-of-the-century figure painter Cecilia Beaux.

Acknowledgments

The success of our 2003 online symposium and the publication of this book are the result of the help and generosity of many individuals and organizations. We are especially grateful to Maurice Berger, Senior Fellow, the Vera List Center for Art and Politics, New School University, New York. Those at the Georgia O'Keeffe Museum to whom we extend our gratitude include Elizabeth Ehrnst, former Research Center Coordinator; Heather Hole, Assistant Curator; Jenifer Jovais, former Exhibitions Coordinator; Linda Milanesi, former Director of Marketing; and Jennifer Padilla, former Assistant Director of Marketing. We are also grateful to others in Santa Fe who have helped us realize this project: Sarah S. King, Editor, and Molly McDow, Panorama Point. At The Center for Art and Visual Culture, University of Maryland Baltimore County, we wish to thank Franc Nunoo-Quarcoo, Professor of Visual Arts in Graphic Design; Antonia Gardner, Managing Editor; Mary Lou Kenny, Editor; and especially Maurice Berger, Curator.

David Yager, Executive Director,
Center for Art and Visual Culture.
Symmes Gardner, Director,
Center for Art and Visual Culture.

George G. King, Director,
Georgia O'Keeffe Museum
Barbara Buhler Lynes, Curator,
Georgia O'Keeffe Museum and
the Emily Fisher Landau Director,
Georgia O'Keeffe Museum Research Center

Center for Art and Visual Culture
University of Maryland Baltimore County

The Center for Art and Visual Culture at the University of Maryland Baltimore County, is a non-profit organization dedicated to the study of contemporary art and visual culture, critical theory, art and cultural history, criticism, and the relationship between society and the arts. The Center is committed to a rethinking of the relationship between arts institutions and the public, placing special emphasis on well-written, viewer-friendly catalogue and wall texts, rigorously documented and researched catalogues, the lucid application of critical and social theory to build connections between visual culture and the society at large, and creative exhibition and catalogue design. Disciplines represented include painting, sculpture, drawing, printmaking, photography, digital art, video, film, television, design, architecture, advertising, and installation and performance art. The Center sponsors art exhibitions, community outreach and public arts projects, and publications. Its exhibitions and accompanying catalogues—one-person and retrospective shows as well as thematic and experimental projects—give voice to artists, subjects, and curatorial approaches often ignored or under-represented in mainstream museums.

The Center for Art and Visual Culture serves as a forum for students, faculty, and the general public for the discussion of important aesthetic and social issues of the day. Through its traveling exhibitions and publication series, Issues in Cultural Theory, the Center is building a broad national and international audience. The Center places special emphasis on the role of education in the arts. Symposia, lectures series, conferences, film series, workshops, and visiting artist residencies create an ongoing dialogue about contemporary art and culture—from K–12 school-based initiatives to adult education and community outreach in Baltimore City. In 2000, the Center's Community Outreach/Public Art Initiative launched its inaugural project in Baltimore, the Joseph Beuys Tree Partnership.

Museums of Tomorrow: A Virtual Discussion
Issues in Cultural Theory 8
2004
Library of Congress Control Number 2004110544
ISSN 15211223
ISBN 1890761079

Published by the
Center for Art and Visual Culture
University of Maryland Baltimore County
Baltimore, Maryland 21250
www.umbc.edu/cavc

The Georgia O'Keeffe Museum Research Center
Santa Fe, New Mexico 87501
www.okeeffemuseum.org

Distributed by D.A.P.
Distributed Art Publishers
New York

Designed by Franc Nunoo-Quarcoo
and Karen Howard
Printed in China
Book composed in Monotype Walbaum Roman,
Italic and Expert, and Monotype Grotesque Bold